The Last Dance
but Not the Last
Song

The Last Dance but Not the Last Song

My Story

Renée Bondi
with Nancy Curtis

Fleming H. Revell
A Division of Baker Book House Co
Grand Rapids, Michigan 49516

© 2002 by Renée Bondi

Published by Fleming H. Revell
a division of Baker Book House Company
P.O. Box 6287, Grand Rapids, MI 49516-6287

Fourth printing, July 2002

Printed in the United States of America

Library of Congress Cataloging-in-Publication Data

Bondi, Renée.
The last dance but not the last song: my story / Renée Bondi with Nancy Curtis.
    p.   cm.
ISBN 0-8007-1808-9
1. Bondi, Renée. 2. Contemporary Christian musicians—United States—Biography. 3. Contemporary Christian musicians—Religious life. I. Curtis, Nancy, 1939– II. Title.
ML420.B685 A3 2002
277.3′0825′092—dc21   2001048932

For current information about all releases from Baker Book House, visit our web site:
http://www.bakerbooks.com

For current information about Renée Bondi and her ministries, visit her web site:
http://www.reneebondi.com

To Mike and Daniel

I love you with all my heart and all my soul.

Contents

Before You Begin . . .

I've gotten used to being on display. Whether it's the child studying my wheelchair, the senior citizen across the way smiling sympathetically, or the waiter eyeing me carefully as I use my bent spoon to eat pieces of a sandwich, I'm aware that people are watching. Some might watch out of pity, some out of admiration. I sense that all watch with unspoken questions.

It's part of the territory that comes with a disability.

It's what Renée Bondi faces everyday. But like Renée, I choose to think that people's unspoken questions are, for the most part, good-natured. That's because she and I, as followers of Jesus Christ, are constrained to think the best of others. We are called to be on display (as any Christian is). We are encouraged by God's Word to smile from the inside-out as the strength of the Lord shows up bountifully through our physical limitations. When people eye Renée, sitting in her wheelchair, smiling and singing, I believe they're thinking, *How great her God must be to inspire such faith and confidence.*

Somehow, I don't think Renée minds being on display. Her story inspires faith and confidence in people who observe her—especially people like me who become her friend. I remember the first time I saw Renée, I was struck by her warm smile and sunlit confidence in Christ as she sang and spoke from the platform. She possessed a genuine grace and a way of reaching out to others through her words and music. To be honest, I hardly noticed the fact that she was in a wheelchair (and I wondered if people looked at me the same way?!). Renée's happy-hearted disposition bolsters me greatly.

The woman whose autobiography you hold in your hands may be lacking literal use of legs and hands, but isn't it ironic that God should use a woman with quadriplegia to move the rest of us to step out to touch and embrace others?

This is what will strike you about *The Last Dance but Not the Last Song*. In a world that is splitting apart at the seams, we need to hear from courageous people who can extend the grace of God through their stories of hope and healing. My friend Renée does that . . . and more. You will discover a woman and her family who are very ordinary, yet so extraordinary. And like me, you will think, *If Renée can, by the grace of God, overcome her limitations, I can, too.*

Joni Eareckson Tada
Agoura Hills, California

Acknowledgments

When I was first approached to write this book, all I could envision was a huge, monumental task. As always, the Lord puts people in our lives at just the right time to help us with such projects.

Thank you, Nancy Curtis, for your perseverance, patience, and talent. Yes, I could tell story upon story, but you crafted it into a tangible book manuscript. I never could have done it without you.

Thank you to Lonnie Hull-DuPont, Chad Allen, and everyone at Fleming H. Revell for your patience, knowledge, and belief in this project.

I am grateful to those who took the time to read the initial manuscript—Jerry and Karen Franks, Tim and Debbie Robertson, and Michael Irion. Your enthusiasm gave me the courage to keep moving forward.

Special thanks to Ellen Rhoda, Sr. Assunta Highbaugh, Garrett Brown, and Msgr. Paul Martin for your valuable advice; Dr. Jacques Palmer and Randy Young for your medical counsel; Dwayne and Diane Ely for your photography; and Peggy, Claire, and Mai for arranging play dates for Daniel at just the right time.

I owe a great debt of gratitude to Deborah Benitez who wears many hats in our office and to my caregivers, Nancy

Sanchez and Debbie Robertson, for without them I would still be in bed!

Last but not least, I would like to thank my Lacouague and Bondi family for allowing themselves to be a bit vulnerable for the sake of ministry. And to you, my Lord, for your amazing attention to detail and unconditional love. May you alone be glorified.

1

Great
Was the Fall

When I rolled into the ballroom at the Hyatt Regency Hotel in Irvine, California, the irony was unmistakable. Almost eleven years ago, in this very room, I danced my last dance with Mike, then my fiancé. He had just given me my engagement ring, and I was undoubtedly the happiest woman on earth. I never suspected that in less than thirty-six hours, my life would be turned upside down, forever.

As I waited for my name to be announced, when I would go forward to accept the Walter Knott Service Award for Overcoming Disabilities, I couldn't help but think how different my life was from what I had designed, dreamed, and imagined that night. Sometimes our lives take turns we didn't plan and wouldn't have chosen. Mine definitely did. But, of this I am confident: God is real, and God is faithful. This is how I know.

Eleven years ago the occasion that brought me to the Hyatt Regency Hotel (then the Hilton) was the San Clemente High

School prom. I had a wonderful job teaching choir at San Clemente High, a large Orange County school where students could literally walk to the beach. Music had always occupied much of my energy, time, and heart. What could be better than merging my passion with my career? Still, my career was not without trials. My first year, there were only eighteen students in the entire vocal music program, which tells you where Bach, Brahms, and Mozart were on the priority list of all the surfer dudes at San Clemente High. But when we love something, when we cultivate it and fertilize it, it grows. Within two years the program had grown to 150 students and was still increasing.

Even more exciting than my profession was my love life. Mike's and my wedding day was scheduled for July, just two months away from the prom. I was ecstatic about our wedding and was in the middle of all the last-minute details. Most of all I was excited because Mike was not only the love of my life, he was also my best friend. Like any woman about to marry the man of her dreams, I couldn't have been happier about my life, and I had big plans and lofty aspirations for my future.

Saturday, May 15, 1988, was the big prom day. Mike was in town on business from Denver, where he had been living and working for five months as a staffing specialist for Martin Marietta, an aerospace company. We were asked to chaperone the prom, and I was as excited as the high school girls. I hadn't seen Mike in four weeks, so I was eagerly looking forward to this evening. He came by that morning for a visit, and then he went to see his family and to run "an errand." Meanwhile, I got a manicure and had my hair done (I had it put up in a French knot to see if I would want that "sophisticated" look for the wedding).

Mike took me for a romantic dinner that evening at the Velvet Turtle, one of our favorite restaurants. During the entrée he got a mischievous look on his face, like an excited child with a special secret. He reached in his pocket and produced a tiny little box, opened it, took out the contents, and handed it to me. "Well, here it is. I made the last payment and picked it up this afternoon," he said. My engagement ring!

A year before when Mike asked me to marry him, he gave me an exquisite teardrop sapphire necklace, and then we went to look at rings. Together, we chose the style—a unique one with the wedding band actually inside the engagement ring—and we even selected the diamond. When Mike presented the ring to me, I couldn't get over the fact that the same diamond that looked tiny lying on the black velvet in the jewelry store looked absolutely enormous in the setting! It was a rock! I was blown away. Mike slipped it on my finger, and it fit perfectly.

We were off to the Hilton for the prom. "Somehow" the news leaked out that I had my ring. Could it have been the way I was walking? You know, with my left hand preceding me into the room for all to see? And I guess I did ask my students once or twice, "Did you know Mike gave me my engagement ring tonight? Want to see?" "Did you happen to notice the sparkle coming from my left hand?" "Have you seen my ring?" "I'll bet you haven't seen my ring yet!" (In fact they had—several times.) Groups of excited girls gathered around to admire, to ooh and ah, while their dates waited, rolling their eyes in boredom.

When we weren't checking out the bathrooms and carrying out other chaperoning duties, Mike and I danced in each other's arms. Dancing was almost as important to me as singing. Mike, bless his heart, having absolutely no rhythm but knowing how much I loved to dance, had taken dance lessons the previous summer so that he could share my interest. The dance lessons paid off! We had so much fun that night. We did the swing and the jitterbug, and the band played our song, Glenn Miller's "In the Mood." It was a storybook, romantic evening. I felt like Cinderella dancing with my Prince Charming at the ball. We could not have imagined that we would never dance together again.

The next morning Mike and I had brunch with my family to celebrate Mother's Day. He left from the restaurant in his rental car to go to the airport for his return flight to Denver. I went to Nordstrom to pick up my bridesmaids' dresses and to shop for their gifts. Late that afternoon found me back at school where I conducted the orchestra in the spring musical, *Pajama Game*. This was a banner day because we played to a packed auditorium. Getting the surfers off the beach and into the theater on a sunny Sunday afternoon in southern California was near miracle status. The performance was wonderful, the audience enthusiastic, and the actors and musicians proud. I was doing what I loved.

I got home to the condominium I shared with Dorothy Henry and her twelve-year-old daughter, Jennifer, around 7:00 P.M. Living with them was just a temporary arrangement until the wedding. For five years I had roomed with my good friend Debbie Thomason, but in January she had gotten married. Assuming the newlyweds didn't want a third roommate for six months, I went to church and asked in several places, "Anybody here need a roommate?" Dorothy responded, and I moved in. I was so busy with my school work and my wedding plans that I was seldom home, so I really didn't know them very well.

That night I sat at the kitchen table, had a little dinner, wrote out some lesson plans, and got ready for bed at about 11:00. Before turning out the light, I admired my "rock" one last time. As I drifted off to sleep, my future felt as snug and secure as my cozy bed. I was safe and happy.

Suddenly, I woke up out of a deep sleep in midair. I had time to think only "Huh?" before WHAM! I landed on the top of my head, finishing the flip with my feet in the closet and my head against the dust ruffle.

Still half asleep, it didn't occur to me to wonder why I had dived off the foot of my bed or if I had really hurt myself. My only thought was simply to get back into bed. I rolled onto my left shoulder to get up, but as I did the right side of my neck went CRACK! The pain threw me to my back. I tried rolling onto my right shoulder to get up, but as I did the left side of my neck went CRACK! *Oh, man!* The excruciating pain threw me to my back yet again.

Now you've really done it, I thought. Since it was my neck, I assumed I had just aggravated an old whiplash injury that had bothered me since a car accident a few years earlier.

By now, I was wide-awake. I realized with some bewilderment and surprise that at twenty-nine years old, I needed help getting up. Because my bedroom was downstairs and Dorothy's upstairs, I knew I'd have to be loud to wake her up. So I took a deep breath and tried to yell "Dorothy!" but all that came out was a whisper! *Come on! You're a singer; you teach breathing!* I thought to myself. So I took a breath from way down deep and tried again, "Dorothy!" Still only a whisper. Now I was really scared. My bedroom door was shut, and I couldn't call out for help. Dorothy hardly knew me, so she wouldn't check on me the next morning. She didn't keep up with my morning routine. When she saw my door closed, she'd just assume I was sleeping in. I could easily lie there for hours, even all day or longer, and no one would find me.

About the same time I was falling out of bed, Dorothy woke up—DING!—wide-awake. She thought she'd heard a voice, so she got out of bed, walked to the top of the stairs, and thought, *Renée wouldn't be on the phone at 2:00 a.m.* Within one minute of my fall I heard Dorothy's voice. "Renée? Renée!" I heard her footsteps on the stairs, then her hand on the doorknob. Without even knocking or stopping to wonder why she was entering my bedroom unannounced in the middle of the night, Dorothy opened the door, and I breathed a sigh of relief. Seeing me flat on my back, she asked, "Why are you lying on the floor?"

I said, still in a whisper, "I don't know, but it's my neck. It's killing me. I don't know what I did, but I did something big. I can't get up. Call the paramedics."

Dorothy stared at me on the floor, then picked up the phone and called 911. When she hung up, she said, "Okay, they're on their way. I've got to go out to meet them."

"No!" The pain was excruciating, and I couldn't bear being left alone. "Don't leave me!" I pleaded.

"I have to," Dorothy responded. "They'll never find us." My logical side knew that. We lived in one of those really expansive condo complexes; our unit was way in the back and not particularly well marked, so she was right. The paramedics would never find us, at least not easily or quickly. But I was scared. "Please don't leave me!" I insisted again.

"I'll get Jen," she offered. She stepped to the door and stuck her head out to call for her daughter. It was at that time that the strangest sensation came over my body. The only way to describe it would be as a wave, maybe a wave of silence. All of a sudden, starting at my neck, I felt this WHOOOOOOOSH as a wave slowly rippled from my neck all the way down to my toes. *What on earth was that?* I thought. *I can't be paralyzed! All I did was go to bed!* Although the thought did cross my mind, I didn't think for one minute that it could actually be true. Like the light of a firefly, the idea was there and gone. Looking back, however, I now firmly believe that the undulating wave was the onset of paralysis, because I never moved again.

Jenni came in, somewhat disoriented after being awakened from a sound sleep. Her hair was disheveled, her nightgown was hanging off her shoulder, and her eyes were barely open. She definitely was not with the program. I whispered, "Jenni, Jenni, come pray with me, come pray with me."

She stared at me on the floor with that typical southern California surfer girl look that insinuated, "Uh . . . What's goin' on? Uh . . . What do I do now?" But she sat down next to me, took my hand (noticing that it was completely limp), and started praying, "OurFather whoartinheaven hallowedbethyname thykingdomcome thywillbedone . . . onearthasitisinheaven . . . giveusthisday . . . ourdailybread . . ."

As she was going through her prayer, I was saying my own. "Let's go, Lord, I'm ready. I'm your instrument. I'm your tool.

I'm your tool. I'm your instrument. I'm your instrument. I'm your tool. Use me!" It was weird that I was praying these words. Although I had accepted Christ into my heart years earlier and had an active prayer life, "instrument" and "tool" were not words I commonly used when praying. And besides, it would have made much more sense for me to pray that this injury would not be serious, that the pain in my neck would go away, and that I could just return to bed. Looking back, I think the Holy Spirit was praying through me, that the words were almost or even actually prophetic.

I heard the fire engines arriving. Such a familiar sound. All my life my father had been fire chief of our hometown station, and now my brother Danny was also, so the roar of the fire engine was a sound I had been raised hearing. Dorothy met the paramedics and, being a medical assistant (which I take as no coincidence), she told them, "She's complaining of pain in her neck, her voice has been reduced to a whisper, and she's as white as a ghost." In disbelief she added, "I don't know how she did it, but I think she's broken her neck."

I heard the paramedics coming into the condo, and I could almost sense the heaviness of the equipment I knew so well—the drug box, the scope, the oxygen, the radio—as they came toward my room. It was all familiar, but it was also very strange, knowing that they were coming for me.

When the paramedics entered the room, one went straight to my feet and tickled them to see if there was any response. There was none. The first question EMTs ask an injured person when they come on the scene is not "What happened?" or "Where does it hurt?" They ask the victim her name to see if she's cognizant and if they can trust the information that is given when they do ask about injuries. So they asked me my name, and I said, with rising panic, "Renée Lacouague. Yes, Danny is my brother. Please call him!"

Stunned silence. Because my brother was the fire chief of Station 7 in San Juan Capistrano where I lived, they knew him well. So all of a sudden this was a very personal situation. The victim was almost family.

The paramedics were efficient and gentle. They tried very hard not to move me as they put the brace on my neck. At the time I thought they did this to prevent further pain, which by then was completely out of control—sharp, biting, shooting pain that I had never experienced before.

They lifted me onto the stretcher, covered me with a blanket, and rolled me out into the night toward the waiting ambulance. On the way to the hospital, I looked at the meters and hoses above my head, listened to the hum of the tires on the freeway, and wondered if it was a good sign that they didn't turn the siren on. It seemed that the familiar fifteen-minute drive up the freeway was taking an awfully long time. I just wanted to get to the hospital so that the doctors could see what was wrong, fix it, and take away the pain.

In the emergency room, myriad faces and voices blurred around my bed. Because of the brace on my neck, I could look only straight up. I couldn't see who they were or what they were doing.

Then I saw the face of my only brother, Danny. He is six years older than I (I'm the baby of the family). When I was in junior high, he was in college five hours away, so I really didn't know him very well. As his face came into my field of vision, his big blue eyes reflected his concern, yet there was so much peace. I had never been so glad to see him.

"What happened?" he asked, gently shaking his head in disbelief.

"I don't know. I just went to bed. That's all I know. I just went to bed," I whispered.

His friends, who had brought me in, had already warned him: "It's bad. It's really bad. It looks like she broke her neck, and there's no movement." Given their information and his training and experience, Danny knew my condition, but he couldn't imagine how it happened.

I felt somewhat relaxed now that Danny was there. I knew he'd take over. That awful feeling of being alone in my pain, helpless among strangers, began to subside. A few minutes later my sister Denise arrived, and once she and Danny were both there together, I relaxed even more. Denise is a nurse, not only by profession but also by nature. She is the consummate caregiver. "What happened?" she asked when she came in.

"I don't know. I just went to bed and went to sleep. The next thing I knew, I woke up in midair, diving off the foot of my bed. It's so weird. I don't know."

She went right into her nurse mode. "Don't worry. We're going to take care of this, sis," she reassured me. With Danny and Denise's medical backgrounds, I knew they would monitor my care.

However, the fact that they both came to the hospital in the middle of the night did suggest to me that maybe I had done something serious. I knew why Danny was there, but why did he call Denise? I still had no idea I had broken my neck; I didn't even know I was paralyzed. I learned back at the condo that trying to move caused intense, wracking pain and that I was wise to lie still, so I didn't even try to move. But I assumed I could move if I wanted to. After all, all I did was fall out of a normal-sized bed. Who gets seriously hurt doing that?

But as they stood by my bed, Danny and Denise knew what I did not. I was in critical condition, and injuries like mine were potentially fatal. If a person breaks his or her neck and survives, there are frequently complications like blood clots, kidney problems, and respiratory issues that can be, and often are, deadly. The question for my brother and sister wasn't simply whether I would walk. They wondered if I would live.

The first hours at the hospital are hazy. I was in such pain that nothing is clear. But I do remember a doctor with a thick French accent asking, "Renée, I need to put your head in traction. Do you mind if I clip a bit of your hair?"

"I don't care if you cut my head off! Just take this pain away!" I retorted, half kidding, but half in earnest. I heard the whir of the clippers as he shaved my neck from ear to ear underneath my long hair. *Hmmmmm. This must be serious.* Then I faded off.

The next thing I knew it was morning, and I was waking up in the intensive care unit. When I opened my eyes, Father Paul Martin was praying over me. My first thought was, *Oh no! He's administering last rites!* I looked up at him incredulously and asked, "Am I *that* bad?"

He smiled reassuringly. "Well, when you do it, you do it up big, don't you, sweetheart?" he said. I was really glad to see him. He wasn't just a pastor at our parish; he had played a major role in my life. He was like a grandfather to me. Denise had called him, and he rushed over before an early morning service, so he could stay only a few minutes. At a time when I was confused and bewildered, his presence brought peace and comfort.

Of course, I was completely oblivious to what was happening out in the ICU waiting room. Danny and Denise had decided during the night not to call Mom and Dad or my oldest sister Michelle until morning. As daylight approached, Danny left to go tell them in person what had happened.

When Dr. Jacques Palmer, the neurosurgeon, came in to report to the family, Denise was alone to hear the news. "It's a tragedy," Dr. Palmer said gravely as he showed Denise the X ray of my neck. Even if she hadn't been a nurse, she would have seen the damage. The spinal column was snapped in two and so grossly misaligned that Denise gasped in disbelief. Her worst fear was confirmed. Her sister had broken her neck!

Dr. Palmer continued, "These first few days are critical in determining the extent of neurological recovery, if any. In a few days, after her condition has stabilized, I'll do surgery to fuse the broken cervical vertebrae. Unfortunately, that's about all we can do for her. The surgery will stabilize the neck, but it won't help her neurological condition; the damage to the spinal cord has been done and most likely is irreparable."

Soon another doctor came in, looked at the X rays, and confirmed Dr. Palmer's diagnosis. As he left the room he turned to Denise and added, "I'd rather be dead than live like this." He left, leaving Denise alone to sort out what she had just been told. When Danny came back with Mom, Dad, and Michelle, Denise had to give them the report and explain the prognosis by herself.

Later that morning, Dr. Palmer came in and talked with me alone to explain my prognosis. When he spoke, I recognized his thick French accent from the night before. "You broke your neck at the fourth and fifth vertebra. This has left you quadriplegic," he said evenly.

"What's quadriplegic?" I asked.

"Your entire body from just beneath your neck is completely paralyzed. Based on the nerve damage, you most likely will never walk or even move your legs or feet again. In all probability, you will have no feeling below your upper chest and no use of your arms or hands."

At least he didn't tell me I'd never sing again. That would come later.

2

When
I Was a Child

I was born Renée Louise Lacouague (pronounced *la kwog*) on June 21, 1958, the fourth of four children. When I joined the family, Danny was 6; Michelle, 4; and Denise, 2.

Mom and Dad brought me home to the 261-acre family ranch in San Juan Capistrano, California, then a small town with the refreshing wholesome atmosphere of orange groves, agriculture, and openness. It was the kind of rural town you'd expect to find in Texas or the Midwest. Friendliness was a way of life and everybody knew everybody's name. This is surprising to those who know today's southern California, with its bustling beach cities, yuppies, and SUVs.

The *family* ranch. That's an interesting story in itself. Surprisingly enough, it begins in the tiny village of Ainhoa, in picturesque southern France, in what is known as the Basque Country, nestled in the Pyrenees Mountains just fifteen miles from the Bay of Biscay. In 1924 Marie Sansinena, my mother, was born there.

When World War II raged, the Germans invaded France and, unfortunately, five German officers forced the Sansinenas out of three rooms of their home. The officers occupied these rooms for four seemingly endless years. As one might imagine, it was a terrifying time for a sixteen-year-old girl. The occupation did not end until the Allied forces invaded France, forcing the Germans to retreat. When they left, they took everything they could with them, including the family's car and bicycles.

Many years before, in 1910, Pierre Lacouague left the same small Basque village and, looking for a better life, boarded a ship headed for America. After docking in New York and taking a train cross-country, he worked as a farmhand for the Echenique Ranch in San Juan Capistrano, California.

While working there, Pierre met Bonifacia Mujica, who also had emigrated from the Basque Country. After earning enough money, Pierre purchased 261 acres from the Echenique Ranch in 1920, and he and Bonifacia were married. They planted walnut orchards and orange groves, and the land became the Lacouague Ranch. Pierre and Bonifacia had two daughters and one son named Jean-Pierre Lacouague, my father.

As a young man, Jean-Pierre, also known as John, left the family ranch in 1942 and enlisted in the U.S. Army to support the war effort against Germany. As part of the northern Europe campaign, he was stationed in England, France, Belgium, Holland, and Germany. He fought at the Battle of the Bulge and further east toward the Elbe River near Berlin.

Stationed in Belgium after the allied victory in Europe, Jean-Pierre had the opportunity to follow the advice of his father and visit the birthplace of his ancestors in Ainhoa. Twice Jean-Pierre borrowed a jeep and made his way to the Basque village. On one of these visits he stopped by the Sansinena home because the Sansinenas were friends of his father. Jean-Pierre met all of the Sansinena family with the exception of Marie, who was his age but happened to be away that day. He made the comment that he missed meeting the one he should have met. Later Jean-Pierre returned to the Lacouague Ranch in California.

In 1946 Terry Oyharzabal, a young woman from San Juan Capistrano who knew one of my mother's uncles, visited Ainhoa. Mom and Terry became friends, and it was at Terry's encouragement that Mom made the decision to come to California. Young and foolish (Mom's own description of herself), she boarded a TWA airplane, when transcontinental flight was still in its infancy, and began her long journey to a new life in America.

I am amazed when I think of Mom all alone in New York City. She had never even been outside the isolated little area where she was raised, and now suddenly, at twenty-three years old, here she was in New York City—huge and impersonal. And she spoke not a word of English. Her flight to Los Angeles had been cancelled, so she had to spend the night in New York City. Somehow she found her way to a Basque hotel. The next day was Sunday and Mom, not one to be stopped by small obstacles like vastness, unfamiliarity with her surroundings, and language barriers, went looking for and found a church. Upon returning to the hotel she learned there was a flight leaving for California; unfortunately, the flight went to San Francisco. She took it and then had to book another flight to Los Angeles.

When Mom finally arrived at the Burbank Airport (then the only airport in L.A.), it was nighttime, so some of her first sights in America were lights and billboards. Never had she seen so many lights—quite a contrast to the occupied village that had been darkened for camouflage during the war. To Mom, the beautiful bright lights represented freedom.

On a Friday night a month after she arrived, Mom and Terry went to a basketball game at the local high school—the center of activities in family-oriented San Juan Capistrano. During the evening Terry pointed out Jean-Pierre—tall, rugged, dark-haired, and blue-eyed—and introduced them to one another. At long last Marie and Jean-Pierre had met. God's providence was obviously at work, and had been for many years. Mom knew who he was, that he had visited her home in Ainhoa, and it was quite a treat to carry on a conversation in Basque, four thousand miles (an ocean and a continent) from her native Basque country. Mom and Dad were married in Serra Chapel at the San Juan Capistrano Mission in 1951.

Mom and Dad are the kind of people who seem rare in America today. Mother's experiences—being raised in Europe, mastering three languages as a young child, enduring the occupation of Nazi soldiers in her home, courageously coming to America when she was but a young woman—all created a certain kind of personality. Mom is a survivor. She learned how to do what had to be done.

On the ranch, when I was growing up, meals were at 6:00 A.M., 12:00 noon, and 6:00 P.M. without exception. By 6:00 in the morning our house was bustling with activity. As a child, I woke up to the aroma of bacon and coffee, the sound of eggs sizzling in the skillet, and the movement of Dad and the ranch hands coming in to enjoy the full-tilt breakfast Mom prepared each and every morning. At lunchtime they were back for another hot meal, and then in the evening Mom prepared a delicious dinner for the family. Mom wasn't one to play with us kids or to create our fun for us. Rather, she took care of our needs. Although the women at church liked and respected my mom, she rarely spent time with her friends, seldom called another lady on the phone to invite her to lunch. It was more important to her to take care of her family. Period.

Although my dad's official name is Jean-Pierre, his American name, John, seems to fit him better. I can sum him up with two terms: World War II veteran and farmer. The connotations of those two terms paint a picture that captures him exactly. He was hard working, talented with his hands, resourceful, patriotic, tenacious, unyielding in his discipline, yet never too harsh. The line between right and wrong was never fuzzy with my dad. He was a tremendous provider, although not of the latest bells and whistles. Unlike his father, my dad has a great sense of humor; he is very quick and very funny.

Mom and Dad enrolled all four of us children in parochial schools. My parents were not interested in providing us with cars, motorcycles, or TVs for our rooms; rather they invested in our education, which would bring high yield in equipping us for adulthood. All four of us attended the parish elementary school at San Juan Capistrano Mission Catholic Church, called the Mission by locals because it is one of twenty-one missions founded in the 1700s to 1800s to bring Christ to California.

For high school, they chose an all-boys school about an hour north in the L.A. area for Danny. After making sure we three girls had piano and ballet lessons, Mom chose San Luis Rey Academy in Oceanside for us because it was a strong academic school and provided opportunities in the fine arts. We could substitute our ballet lessons for P.E., take private voice lessons, and participate in the musical productions that the school put on each spring.

Dad always expected our best and taught us to expect the same from ourselves. I vividly remember coming home one day when I was in fifth grade, excited to share big news. I exclaimed, "Dad! Dad! Look! I got a 98 percent! I got the highest grade in the class on the math test!"

He said, "Well, good for you! So, which one did you get wrong? Why the 98? Why not 100?"

"Well, I don't know." It hadn't occurred to me to check what I'd missed; I was too busy enjoying what I got right.

So together we looked and examined what I had done wrong, whereupon he said matter-of-factly, "Okay, next time, get the 100 percent. You can do it." This wasn't a traumatic experience for me. Psychologists might say, "Oh, he was too hard on you. You did the best you could, and he burst your bubble." He didn't burst my bubble. He admonished in a way that prompted me to examine my error and fix it, to strive for my best. We had a deal on grades: if we got an A, he gave us 10¢; B, 5¢; C, nothing. For a D, we paid *him* 5¢ and for an F,

10¢. We never got the D's or F's or even many C's. We just didn't. (The one exception was when I got a D in high school chemistry. I hated chemistry.) I certainly wasn't the sharpest kid in the class; it was simply a matter of expectations at home.

The church and its activities were an important part of our lives. We were there every Sunday without question, and because we attended the church school, we were there every school day as well. In addition, there were sports, festivals, picnics, and other events that our family enthusiastically attended. Being at the Mission was almost as normal as being at home.

I was the roly-poly, good-natured, giggly kid whom the teachers liked because I always had a smile on my face. I started piano lessons when I was in second grade and took ballet from an early age, but ballet was not my gift; it was my sisters' gift. Both of them were great dancers; I was too pudgy and chunky. A guy at the grocery store called me Lumpy one day and, wouldn't you know it, the name stuck. I was definitely heavier than most other girls, but it never bothered me. I don't remember crying or wishing I could be skinny. Instead, I laughed a lot. I always had friends. Sure, in junior high there were a couple of girls who were stuck on themselves and had to have the perfect outfit and perfect makeup. They were skinny, and always boy crazy, but my friends and I simply weren't that way.

The first time I really felt the Holy Spirit was in the fourth grade. Mrs. McKray would tell us we had to say our prayers, and I loved my prayer time. I can still picture the yellow graph paper with the chart on it. At that age I loved to check things off. Everything in order. Everything in its place. When I got home from school, I'd get a snack (or maybe two—after all, there was a reason my nickname was Lumpy!) and then go out and play for a while. Later, I'd go inside to do my praying, checking off each prayer as I prayed it. One day I was in my bedroom, sitting on the end of my bed in prayer, and I had this overwhelming sense of God's presence, an overwhelming sense of peace. I didn't know exactly what it was at the time, but I remember saying, "God, you are holy. You are good," and being real still.

From then on my prayers were filled with fresh, new meaning; I prayed with my heart as well as my mouth. Everything became more real—at least, as real as it can be in fourth grade. It was my first personal touch from God, my first awareness of the Lord drawing me to himself.

The concept of "family fun" wasn't part of the routine in the Lacouague household. I think keeping the ranch going, with its orange groves, cattle, and hay fields, consumed almost all of the adults' time. However, every summer we loaded into our gray Ford station wagon and headed for, of all places, Ely, Nevada—the site of a huge, annual Basque picnic. Despite its location, the picnic was a weeklong paradise for us kids and almost as much fun for the grown-ups, with Basque folk dancing, great food like barbecued lamb, beautiful singing, lively games, and nonstop activities. The kids played while the adults reminisced, renewed friendships, talked of the old country, and entertained themselves with belly-up-to-the-bar singing.

After the picnic our family continued the fun another week by camping with several other families, but I didn't know until years later my parents hated camping. They went for the fellowship and to give us kids a vacation. When I was about twelve, however, Mom began escaping this "family fun" by using these two weeks for a trip to her homeland. Perhaps one reason she did this was because of Dad's unyielding stand against owning an air-conditioned car. His idea of air-conditioning was rolling down the windows!

Because of their unified example, because they daily modeled integrity, honesty, ingenuity, hard work, and morality, my parents instilled in the four of us the values of productivity and success. They imparted a reverence for God as well. We knew the difference between right and wrong, between slothfulness and industry, between perseverance and giving up. And there was never any doubt about which side of those diametrical issues we were expected to come down on, just as there was never any doubt about whether there would be consequences if we came down on the other! The greatest inheritance our parents will leave us four kids will not be money or land or antiques; it will be the legacy of Christian integrity, hard work, and perseverance.

Our closest neighbor, Gordon Sunde, had something we didn't have—horses. Denise and Michelle would walk through the orange groves to Mr. Sunde's house almost every afternoon to spend carefree hours riding his horses. But frankly I was a little afraid of the beasts, so I never cared to go. Gradually, however, the desire to be out of the house and with my sisters pulled me along with them. My sisters, typically feeling older and braver and more skillful, jumped at the chance to create their own amusement at the expense of my fear.

When I was about eleven, Mr. Sunde had a two-year-old mare named Tar Baby who was very high strung, very skittish, and not fully broken. The components were perfect: a hyper horse; a chicken hearted, clueless little girl; and two older sisters who wanted to play the joke. With my sisters looking on in great anticipation, I blindly climbed onto Tar's bare back, but much to their surprise and undoubtedly to their disappointment, Tar just settled right down, and off we rode. I guess it was one of those kindred-spirit type things. Tar and I were immediately soul mates, and she became a *very* important part of my life.

My passion for riding led to an interest in barrel racing. I set up a makeshift course where I trained Tar to bolt from post to post, to pivot around the barrels, and to race to the finish. We had no trainer and we took no lessons; we just loved each other and let our instincts guide us. Soon we began to compete in the local gymkhanas, at first in the twelve-years-old-and-under division. Mr. Sunde was kind enough to let me take Tar on Saturdays, ride across town to the arena, compete, and bring her home in the afternoon.

Predictably, I wanted Tar to be officially mine. But Dad didn't like horses. Part of his job in the army was to care for the horses—to keep them fed and watered, to brush their coats, to clean their stalls. To Dad, a horse meant work and was definitely not on his list of preferred uses for his hard-earned money! But Dad's good parenting worked against him here. After all, it was from him that I learned the importance of tenacity, so I persisted in my desire to own that mare.

Mr. Sunde knew that Tar should be mine, but he also knew my dad. One day he rode up on her, and from the front yard he called out, "John! Come out here! Let's talk about this horse!"

Dad came to the porch and called back, "I don't want to buy a horse—not that horse, not any horse!" Then the two friends sat down to visit while enjoying a cold drink on a warm afternoon. Finally, Mr. Sunde broached the subject again. "Well, John, what do you think about $250 for the horse?"

Dad shot back. "I wouldn't give you a dime more than $175."

"SOLD!" Mr. Sunde announced.

I don't know who was more surprised—me or Dad—but it was definitely one of the happiest days of my life.

Having Tar did what all parents want ownership of a pet to do for their children: it taught me responsibility. Loving and riding her were no problem, but now, at twelve years old, I had to take care of her physical needs—feeding, brushing, cleaning, and many other duties. All of these activities took me out of the house and away from *My Three Sons* on TV, furnished a circle of wholesome friends with whom I rode, and provided an interest whereby I had fun and also gained a sense of success and accomplishment.

When I began showing in the thirteen-to-seventeen-year-old division, we started winning. Every Saturday, it seemed, I would come home with a blue ribbon or a trophy. Pretty soon Mom and Dad began to notice and take interest. They started showing up at gymkhanas to watch me ride. Even then I knew that my neat-as-a-pin, cleanliness-is-next-to-godliness mother was setting aside her discomfort with dirt to be at the arena watching me ride.

When I moved off to boarding school, San Luis Rey Academy, caring for Tar Baby became increasingly more difficult, but she was still a priority. Mom drove me to school every Monday morning, and on Fridays I'd ride the train home and spend the weekend training and showing Tar. Soon we moved up to the next level of competition, the regional shows in L.A., and continued to bring home trophies.

Unlike many who attend boarding school, I loved it! One big perk was that I didn't have to care what I looked like. I could roll out of bed ten minutes before class, brush my teeth and hair, splash some water on my face, throw on my uniform (I didn't have to decide what to wear!), walk downstairs, and be in class on time.

One of my favorite places at school was the beautiful, small chapel downstairs below our dorm rooms. There was a balcony upstairs where I would kneel and look down on the chapel. The quietness and beauty of the chapel made it seem like holy ground, and kneeling automatically put me in a place of devotion. Captivated, I'd stare at Jesus on the cross and study the nails in his hands and feet, thinking about the incredible pain he must have endured. I wondered why anyone would do this for me. Then my thoughts would turn to the resurrection and what it meant. Jesus actually conquered death and opened the gates of heaven. Wow. Here I began to build my personal relationship with Jesus and the Father.

On the other hand, I did have a mischievous side. Michelle and Denise had great stories about raiding the kitchen in the middle of the night—stories of heisting big drums of ice cream and taking them upstairs to feed everybody. Then they'd have to flush down the toilet what they couldn't eat to destroy the evidence.

So, when I was a sophomore, I decided that the time had come for me to embark on my rite of passage and carry on the Lacouague tradition. I enlisted Stacey and Heather, my roommates, and at 1:00 A.M. we headed downstairs. Unfortunately, to get to the kitchen we had to pass through a long corridor—right by the doors to the nuns' quarters. Nervous beyond belief, we crept down the hallway and breathed a collective sigh of relief when we made it to the kitchen door. Next problem: getting in. On our hands and knees, we tucked our fingers under the door, trying to swing it toward us to open it when—oops!—a light came on at the other end of the hallway!

We scrambled for the adjacent dining room and took refuge under a table. As the footsteps approached, more lights came on until after what seemed like an eternity we saw the hem of a robe and fuzzy slippers standing at the dining-room door. As our hearts pounded in our ears, the fuzzy slippers deliberately moved toward our hiding place and slowly circled our table—twice. Then they stopped. Frozen with fear, we waited. All of a sudden—YIKES!—we saw the face and eyes of Sister Brenda, one of the younger nuns who was highly respected for her intelligence and wisdom, staring at us under the table. Obviously she was not at all amused.

"Hi," I offered.

"Get out from under the table, girls." Embarrassed and terrified, we left our foxhole and stood like soldiers in front of Sister Brenda. "What are you doing down here?"

"We came to get something to eat." It sounded as lame as it was.

"I'll get you something to eat," she stated. "What do you want?"

I knew not to mess with it—not to tell her that our ravenous appetites had somehow mysteriously disappeared. I knew just to answer the question. "Ice cream," I said.

Heather found her voice. "Potato chips."

And Stacey, our aspiring ballerina, placed her order too. "An apple." We all, including Sister Brenda, looked at Stacey in disbelief. Nobody, but nobody, would risk expulsion for an apple! We all laughed, and Sister Brenda got our food from the kitchen. After her "this is serious" lecture, Sister Brenda sent us back to bed. Having experienced the reality of "your sins will find you out," my life of crime ceased at San Luis Rey Academy for Girls.

As I moved into my junior year, music became increasingly more important to me. I took voice lessons and was cast in the lead role in the school musical, just like my sisters before me. As a result, Mr. Lampson, a fellow cast member's father and the music director of Oceanside High, invited me to join his advanced choir during my senior year.

By then I had saved enough money from my part-time job to buy my own car—a ten-year-old, brown '65 Mustang. Now I had transportation, a little independence, and my parents' trust to commute to school—no more nights at the Academy for me! Oceanside's choir met before my school started, which worked out perfectly, so I accepted Mr. Lampson's invitation. Besides, involvement meant that I'd get to go with them to Mexico City to sing in a big choir festival the following summer. My general motto was "If it involves travel or singing, count me in!"

Every morning during my senior year I left home early, sang for an hour with Oceanside's choir, and then went to the Academy for the rest of the day. For sure, I was an outsider at Oceanside, which was most apparent in my school uniform, complete with a blue plaid skirt and white knee socks! I didn't mind, though. After all, I was there to sing, not necessarily to make friends. But I was all too aware that "Academy girls" were the natural enemies of the Oceanside coeds because—you guessed it—high school boys sometimes overlooked girls at their own school to date Academy girls. Not that I was anything gorgeous or special to look at—because I wasn't. But that didn't change anything. I knew the score and was sensitive to anything that might damage a working, though precarious, relationship with the other girls.

We never know when something will happen that could completely change the course of our lives. Neither did I know as I entered choir on one otherwise uneventful morning that

Mr. Lampson would make an announcement that would eventually launch my life into a different orbit. "You know that every year I am invited to select two students to audition for The Young Americans," Mr. Lampson said. "This year I'd like to give one card to Theresa Blackford," (Theresa was this amazing soprano who already looked and sounded like an opera singer), "and the other to Renée Lacouague."

Ohmygosh. This is not a good thing! I thought. The whole choir will hate me for the rest of the year! From the back row I frantically tried to get Mr. Lampson's attention to let him know that he should definitely not be giving this to me. Later, in his office, Mr. Lampson tried to reassure me, "Now, Renée," he said. "I really think you should be doing this. Your voice is good. You have a legitimate shot at it."

"You've just set me up for the kill!" I argued. "Already I'm in Oceanside's top choir when I don't even go to this school, and now you single me out for this? If you want me to have any friends at all, you'll take it back. Why don't you give the card to Mona?" She was a really cute alto and a great performer. Mr. Lampson saw my logic and the passion behind my plea, so he gave the card to Mona. He insisted on giving me a letter of recommendation, however, so I could still audition.

The next day he informed the choir of the change in plans, and I was off the hook. Besides fearing the disparagement of my peers, I knew there wasn't a chance I'd make it into a group like Young Americans. Get real! This was a *national* singing group. I didn't even plan to go to the audition. However, Mr. Lampson was very organized, and he saw to it that on the appointed day Theresa, Mona, and I were heading to Chapman College for the audition.

The ride there was memorable, but the ride back was unforgettable. Mona had a little VW bug, and we all rode up laughing and giggling, not taking much seriously, especially not this audition. We were just three girls on a lark having fun. It never occurred to us to consider what the ride home would be like if, say, two of us made it and the other didn't.

Fortunately, our lack of foresight had no consequences, for on the way home, that little bug was bursting with three screaming girls, raging with surprise and anticipation, because we had all made the initial cut and were being called back to the final audition.

The next Wednesday night, off we went again. We were three high school girls in a blue bug headed for Patriotic Hall, which is not in the best part of L.A. This time reality settled in; we talked on the way how chances were slim to nonexistent that all three of us would make it. Somebody in the car was going to return home pretty bummed while one or two of the others would be elated. Of the three of us, I knew that I was the weakest, so I told them in all sincerity, "Don't worry. I won't be crying that hard because I just don't expect myself to make it. So when you make it and I don't, don't worry. I'll be thrilled for you." And I meant it.

When auditions began, each contestant had to stand, give his or her name, and sing something a cappella. Theresa sang some gorgeous opera aria and she was amazing. I, all decked out in tangerine pants; a white, polyester blouse; and a matching tangerine cardigan, stood up and sang, "Romance! . . . A very pretty song. I love you! Romance!" It was a light aria that sounded as dorky as I looked, but that's what Sister Mary Catherine said to sing, so I sang it.

After sight-reading, rhythm testing, and a tonal memory evaluation, they put us on our feet to do some dancing. Remember, dancing wasn't my thing. It was Michelle's and Denise's talent, not mine. But this was a simple movement, a basic Charleston, yet here were all these little pom-pom queens, gorgeous and skinny. I noticed Mona; she was a cute little thing going for it. Just rocking! And there was Theresa, large, but keeping up just the same. And here I was, a size 13/14 at age seventeen. I wasn't a tank, but I wasn't itty-bitty either. *I'm really going to make this,* I thought. *Yeah, right.*

At the end they called all two hundred of us back to the auditorium to announce the new Young Americans. We were seated in a big semicircle a couple of rows deep. They started calling names, and I confess I was getting pumped. Part of me thought maybe I did have a shot, but the other side was responding, *No way. Don't even go there.* The reader called, "Theresa Blackford," and I started screaming because I was so excited for her. Several names later I heard, "Renée . . . La?. . .La? . . ." There was another Renée whose last name began with L, so at first I assumed he was calling her. The longer he repeated "La," however, and being used to people stumbling over the pronunciation of Lacouague, I finally called out, "LACOUAGUE?"

"YES!"

I started screaming at the top of my lungs, and everybody started laughing. Theresa and I made eye contact—a silent "Can you even believe this?"—and then I caught Mona's eyes and held up crossed fingers. Amazingly, it was a clean sweep! That little VW bug must have been bouncing as it carried us back down I-5 that night. We were delirious!

At first we went to rehearsals twice a week—Wednesday nights and Saturday mornings. At the Academy and at Oceanside, I was an A singer. In YA, I was a C, maybe even a C-. And I knew it. Others would open their mouths to sing, and I would open mine to gape. When the guys would sing, I'd melt. Amazing! I remember telling Mom, "You should hear those guys sing. I don't know what I'm doing there. I'm way out of my league!"

Whenever there was an upcoming show, everybody had to audition, and the director would pick fifteen guys and fifteen girls out of the one hundred. I did *one* show the first two years I was in the group. Unfortunately, Mona and Theresa stayed in YA for only a year and dropped out, but I wasn't about to quit. I went every Saturday morning, and I learned a lot just from watching the others. I was totally enamored.

That first summer, the year I graduated high school, YA was split into three groups. My group was to spend several weeks in summer musical theater in Michigan and put together three musicals. However, I had also qualified for state finals in barrel racing, which was a huge thing. Capistrano Valley was very small; everybody knew everybody, and the horse world was very supportive of me. Unfortunately, the timing was horrible; the barrel-racing finals were scheduled for the same time as the summer musical theater in Michigan. I had to choose. I knew there was no career for me in riding horses, and I think I was already moving toward a teaching career. Although my rodeo friends were astounded, I chose musical theater, skipping the state finals, and I never regretted my decision.

The decision to make Young Americans my priority led to the inevitable. I needed to sell Tar Baby. Although I loved her with all my heart, I knew that that era of my life was over, that I was moving in another direction. I also knew that I would not be available to ride and care for her. It was time.

I stood in the ranch yard and watched the new owner load Tar into the trailer. As the truck started to inch down the driveway, I felt like part of me was being wrenched away. My beloved Tar Baby was leaving, and with her all the joy and exhilaration I'd experienced on her back. I felt the sting of finality and the grief of separation as I watched my childhood companion disappear out of my life. Big, hot tears spilled out of my eyes and rolled down my cheeks. I found a little comfort in thinking, *I will do this again. This is not forever. When I have a family, I'll raise my children on horses. Someday I'll put my son or daughter in front of me in the saddle and teach them to ride.* It was, of course, a dream I'd never get to enjoy. To this day, it is still one of my greatest disappointments.

3

On the
Road

When I returned from Michigan, I enrolled in Saddleback
Community College and returned to the Mission church. One
Sunday morning after church I grabbed Father Martin and
asked, "Where are all the people my age?"

"I don't know. Do you?"

"Well, I hope you don't mind me saying this, but the music
is pretty boring. It doesn't have much to offer. Maybe you
could jazz it up a bit with a guitar—make it more contemporary so it would appeal to young people. I'd be willing to
help."

"I'd love you to help. Let's do it."

Two weeks later we started holding contemporary services in the gym, leaving the more traditional one in the Serra
Chapel. I led music for two services on Sunday morning and
one at night. I loved experimenting to see which music
worked, and my favorite role was getting the congregation
on their feet and participating. Father Martin had given me
a venue where I learned how to use my music as a ministry.

The experience sparked my love for leading worship and bringing Catholics into a more personal relationship with the Lord.

During my sophomore year Young Americans was recording an album, *A Salute to Richard Rodgers*—a tribute to the Broadway composer. When we auditioned for the album, the director wisely chose "Bali High" from *South Pacific,* which has a very tricky melody. The director taught it to us, then we sang it back to him individually so he could hear the precision, clarity, and timbre of our voices.

Because we were auditioning for an album and not a performance, we were selected solely on the basis of our vocal technique and control, which were my strengths. Therefore, I was chosen—finally! Not only was I on the album, which boosted my confidence, but perhaps more importantly I got to know the director and he came to know me personally. Suddenly I wasn't just one voice in a sea of one hundred; I was one of thirty voices, one of fifteen girls, and one of five second sopranos. The director became aware of my distinct talents and unique personality.

That album was my proverbial breakthrough. From that time on, I was chosen for virtually every show, including the Richard Rodgers national tour. Finally, all my work and tenacity paid off! The next fall, instead of registering for college classes, I boarded a bus with fourteen other girls and fifteen guys plus band members and crew. Before the tour officially began, we went back to Michigan to organize our show. When we arrived on our summer campus, I was surprised to discover that the show was not yet written. Instead, the writers would get to know us during that first week and would then write the show around our strengths and personalities.

One of our writers was Jim May, a wonderful pianist and arranger for Great America Amusement Park in Chicago. The first time I met him, Milton Anderson, the YA founder and director, asked me to sing, "In My Own Little Corner" from *Cinderella.* Jim can make a piano talk, so it was fun singing with the special extras he spontaneously threw in. Never would I have guessed that Jim would become a very important person in my life and a treasured friend.

They encouraged me to sing with my eyes to express the song, and I enjoyed following their direction. Recognizing the actress side of me (the ham, if you will) they created a Cinderella spin-off—a combination of the pre-ball maiden and a Carol Burnett charwoman—around my voice and personality. My other featured parts were Maria in *The Sound of Music* and Aunt Eller in *Oklahoma*.

One of the last orders of business before we departed for the tour was choosing our seat assignments. I raised my hand and announced, "I get car sick. Unless you want this bus smelling like barf, I need the front seat." Predictably, no one objected. My seatmate was Bob Kevoian, who is now one of the most famous rock 'n' roll DJs in the country. He is the Bob of the award-winning "Bob and Tom Show" out of Indianapolis.

Our bus seats became our apartments; we lived there for nine months. We put down carpet remnants on the floor, hung plants, and taped pictures of home on the windows. On the first leg of the tour, we traveled the Pacific Northwest, and after Christmas break we toured the rest of the United States doing one-nighters, with maybe one night off every three weeks or so.

Being on a different stage each night posed logistical challenges. Each time we stopped to do a show the truck had to be emptied, costumes put in place, microphones set up, sets readied. There is an incredible amount of plain grunt work that goes into putting on a show, and we did it all ourselves. Just as each of us had our part on stage, each of us also had an operational role—no exceptions. The peculiarities of each auditorium and stage required a lot of problem solving. We learned quickly that our responsibility was first and foremost to "make it work!"

Everybody seemed to have an overdeveloped sense of humor, so there was never a dull moment. There was the afternoon in Kansas when Mark, a fellow YA, and I walked to K-Mart to buy toothpaste, and he kicked into one of his animated character voices that made me laugh so hard I sat down on the side of the highway and literally wet my pants. I totally lost control. I was more than a little embarrassed to walk into K-mart, make my purchase, walk back down the highway and into the auditorium in my green fatigues with the telltale dark circle on the seat of my pants.

Another story that still gets passed around involves the Cinderella-charwoman character I played. I had done the show hundreds of times and my timing was down to an art, so as usual I went to pick up my mop and bucket just seconds before going on. But it wasn't there! Panicked, I started running around backstage and yelling in my stage whisper, "Where's my mop and bucket? Where's my mop and bucket?" Just then a custodian walked out of the restroom carrying (guess what?) my props, so I snatched them out of his hands and hit the stage just as my music cue started.

I started mopping only to discover the mop was wet! That would never do because the dancers who would be coming later couldn't dance on a wet floor. The "make it work" mentality kicked in, and I used the mop to make elaborate circles in the air, stopped to sing, and then plopped the mop into the bucket, bent over, and started swishing it up and down. I was into the water up to my elbows when I realized, *this thing stinks!* And as I was singing and smiling and swishing, I noticed the entire cast cracking up in the wings! Not knowing what the joke was, I kept singing and smiling.

Finally, Prince Charming entered on cue. Normally he would pick me up, twirl me around, and we'd start the big waltz number. Instead of the expected embrace, he kept backing away! I was trying to get him to put his arm around me when he motioned, "I'm not touching you!" Then he whispered, "Somebody threw up in the bathroom, and the janitor used *your* mop and bucket to clean it up!"

In addition to the laughter, there were sweet, serious times too. When you're thrown in with a small group of people and live and work together as closely as we did, you get to know each other really well. Herb Chapman, the brother of singer Steven Curtis Chapman, intrigued me. He had a strong walk with the Lord and read his Bible a lot on the bus. Being unfamiliar with anything but the most well-known parts of Scripture, I was curious. Once I got on the bus, and as usual Herb was reading, so I plopped down next to him and asked, "Herbie, what are you reading?"

He looked at me incredulously. "You don't know what this is?"

"Oh, I know it's the Bible, but what are you reading, really?"

"I'm reading in John 10 where Jesus says his sheep know his voice and follow him." *This guy knows something I don't,* I thought. I sat with him for a long time, reading over his shoulder. This was the first time I saw the Bible as a personal avenue to Jesus. Herbie openly desired to know his God, and by watching him day after day, week after week, I learned that the Bible was personal—not just a book to be interpreted by whoever is in the pulpit.

Julie Turner was another devout Christian who lived her faith before us every day. I believed in God, but that belief didn't necessarily govern the way I made decisions for my life. Julie was different. She would come to me every once in a while and say something like, "You know, the Lord told me to give you this book, Renée." And I remember thinking, *Really? What does his voice sound like? Is it a high voice? A low voice? Does he have an accent? Maybe he sounds like Charlton Heston. Or James Earl Jones.* I had never heard the voice of God and didn't know that anyone except Abraham and Moses had. But Julie said she heard him. Did she? Could I? Hmmm. I was drawn to Herb and Julie because I knew Christ was in them.

Although YA is not a Christian organization, we did sing in a Baptist church once in Texas. At the end of the service, we sang a powerful arrangement of "Precious Lord, Take My Hand," and the pastor did an altar call, asking for those who didn't know Jesus to come forward and be saved. While watching others move toward the altar, I kept feeling a tug that wouldn't go away. Being a performer, I wanted to make sure the tug was real and not for show. I thought, *God has always been that foundation in my family, but I think I need to respond for me personally.* So I got up and by walking to the altar I publicly made a profession of faith in Jesus Christ as my personal Savior and Lord.

Looking back, I can remember when I sensed God's hand on my life—as a fourth grader while praying, in the chapel at the Academy, in the Baptist church. God drew me closer as I was ready to receive him. After the altar call my personal faith began to grow, and I was drawn to those whose faith I shared.

I struggle to explain what our final performance was like. After nine months on the road, we were tired of the bus, tired of setting up and tearing down, tired of loading and unloading. But we were not tired of performing. We had experienced the power of music and had come to a new understanding of what music can do. Some songs make people laugh and forget about their worries, other songs wrap themselves around hearts and move people to tears. There was something about watching the audiences respond that made me realize music can truly move the soul. And we were not tired of each other. We were like family. Nevertheless, we knew that an era in our lives had passed, and we would never be together the same way again.

Returning from the tour, I went from traveling throughout America—playing the part of Maria von Trapp every night, enjoying the music and applause—to being a waitress at Harry's Family Restaurant. Reality check! Fortunately, I loved my job. I had worked there weekends and summers since I was fourteen. I was among friends and enjoyed seeing the regular customers. "Good morning, Al. How's your daughter?" "Hey, Bill. How's business at the gas station?" "Good to see you, Myron. How 'bout a cup of coffee before you jump on the tractor?"

But the travel bug had bitten.

Mom and Dad had a tradition of giving us kids a trip to Europe to meet Mom's family when each of us graduated from high school. But the year I graduated, I wasn't ready to go. "Why would I go to Europe before I've seen America?" I asked my mother. Two years later God had me performing in almost every state.

Now that I'd done the U.S. tour, I was ready to see Europe. Michelle and Denise had loved their trips abroad and were eager to go again. So the plan was for all three of us to go backpacking through Europe on $5 a day. We called it "appreciating local color." Truth was, my sisters were paying for their trips, so we went cheap!

I assumed before we left that I knew my sisters pretty well; I was surprised to discover I didn't. Although Denise and I were only two years apart in age, our birthdays fell so that Denise was a junior, Michelle was a senior, and I was in eighth grade. So while my sisters had palled around in high school and shared many of the same friends, I was the pipsqueak kid sister who was too young to tag along.

We flew into Frankfurt and went to Berlin and Amsterdam, and the wonder of the old country began to unfold. But while I was being awed by the beauty and history of Europe, I was also realizing that my sisters are very different. Michelle is a timekeeper. It's all about the schedule. Got to be here at this time, got exactly thirty minutes to enjoy it, then we move on to the next stop on our well-planned agenda. No room, no time, no reason for flexibility or unexpected delights. Denise, on the other hand, couldn't have cared less about Michelle's itinerary. "Ooooooh, let's stop and have a latté. Ooooooh, isn't this pastoral setting spectacular; let's stop and gaze a while. Let's linger to appreciate this statue and read all about the sculptor and the conditions pertaining to the creation of this masterpiece." All the while, Michelle was chomping at the bit to get back on schedule. By the time we reached a campsite just outside Amsterdam, maybe a week into our tour, I knew trouble was brewing in River City.

I went by myself to a little store in the campground and looked for something yummy to buy. The pickings were pretty slim; the best I could do was a big, stale peanut-butter cookie. I brought it back to the campsite and called a powwow of the Lacouague sisters. When we were all seated cross-legged in our tent, I ceremoniously broke the cookie.

"This is our peace pipe," I explained, "and we all have to eat it. We have a long way to go, and we've got to get along on this trip! We need to be more in the middle. Otherwise we're never going to survive. I don't know squat about where we are. I don't know how to get anywhere we want to go, or anything about traveling in Europe. You guys know everything; I know nothing. So I'm totally content to go anywhere you want. But you two need to work together. Michelle, you need to lighten up and, Denise, you need to speed it up!" They laughed, said they understood, and from then on we had a great trip.

We went down through Belgium to France and caught the train from Paris to Bayonne, the big city near Ainhoa where my aunt and my cousin Christian would pick us up. As our train neared Bayonne I told my sisters I felt nervous. They were baffled, but I'd never met these people. I was the only one they didn't know. They spoke no English. My French was horrible while Michelle and Denise spoke French fluently. I've heard it said, "If you speak three languages, you're trilingual. If you speak two languages, you're bilingual. If you speak one language, you're American." Sadly that was me. What if I didn't measure up?

As the train slowed to a stop, we picked up our backpacks and headed for the door. Through the window I saw a woman who looked identical to my mother. Identical! There was no denying she was my mother's sister.

We drove through the mountains until, near the end of our journey, we looked down into a valley at the sleepy village of Ainhoa. It was one of the most beautiful sights I had ever seen. We crossed over creeks on one-lane stone bridges. We paused for sheepherders and their flocks to cross the road.

We saw ox-drawn plows furrowing the countryside. The sky was a brilliant blue, and the hillsides were a lush, deep green I'd never seen before. As we drove into Ainhoa, it looked just like I had imagined. The main street of town was lined with old, white stucco houses with wooden shutters and red-tile roofs.

I was eager to meet my grandmother; I'd had so many relatives, including my sisters, tell me how much I looked like her and acted like her. I didn't have to wait long. *Amatchi*, which means grandmother in Basque, was waiting in the doorway of the family home, built in the 1500s. But when I saw her, I was a little taken aback. She was as wide as she was tall! I did a quick aside to my sisters, hissing, "Thank you very much," before warmly greeting her. However, she was a great lesson in not being judgmental about appearances. She was funny, animated, and a great storyteller. She was delightful! I adored her and to this day, I feel honored to be likened to her. Furthermore, I owe her a debt of gratitude because it was from her that I inherited my love and talent for singing.

One night while we were lingering at the dinner table, as the French are accustomed to do, I asked my grandmother (through Christian, who translated for me), "Amatchi, I understand you like to sing to the Lord. Can I hear something?"

Her brow furrowed and she muttered something like, "Oh, bah," as if to say, "You don't want to hear me sing." But others at the table chimed in, eager to hear a song. Her expression lit up as she lifted her head and began to sing, *"Dios mio, Dios mio, hacercate a mi."* (My God, my God, come close to me.) It was the sweetest sound I'd ever heard coming out of any woman's mouth, much less an elderly woman. Her tone was angelic, with absolutely perfect pitch. It gave me chills to hear the beauty of her voice and the devotion with which she sang.

We stayed in Ainhoa for a couple of weeks. Then we left with Christian on an overnight train to Frankfurt where we met up with our boyfriends who had just flown in. Michelle and I were dating brothers, Dave and Jerry Klein, whom we met at church when I was leading music there. They had always wanted to go to Europe, and Jerry was fascinated that I had family in France.

For the next month the six of us toured Austria and Germany. If there's a God's country, it's Austria. You know the old adage about seeing something so beautiful it takes your breath away? Well, that's not just a saying. It really happens. And it happened to me again and again as we gazed upon the Alps. Because I was a major Julie Andrews fan, we took the *Sound of Music* tour in Salzburg where the movie was filmed. And of course I *had* to go running up the mountain singing, "The hills are alive with the sound of music!" twirling around with my hands in the air, just like Maria von Trapp.

I remember thinking, *Lord, it's pretty amazing that you could design and create all this.* I wasn't particularly spiritual at the time, but I was aware enough to say, "Wow, God!" I wasn't praying every day, and we certainly weren't doing Bible studies on this camping trip. But I don't see how anyone, regardless of one's belief system, could look at the Alps and not recognize there is a Creator. We concluded the trip by spending the final week in Ainhoa to drop off Christian and to introduce Jerry and David to the family.

I praise God for those eight weeks. I received a crash course in European geography, gained an appreciation for European culture, and acquired a sense of who I am based on where and whom I came from. Meeting my European family explained a lot about my parents and their priorities.

But most of all, I gained a deep and unshakable appreciation for my sisters. Michelle was put together, neat, organized, systematic, enterprising, and motivated. Denise was aesthetic, tranquil, observant, circumspect, free-spirited, and individualistic. Each was totally different from the other but equally special. Before the trip, we loved each other, of course. We had to; we were sisters! But traveling together and being together nonstop for two months, we got to know each other as adults. We developed a bond—the adhesive that would keep us together through turbulent times. We couldn't have known then how much we would later need and rely on each other.

4

Flying
High

After taking a year off school to tour the United States with
the Young Americans and after spending the autumn on our
European trek, it was definitely time to resume my college
studies. That spring I entered Cal State University Fullerton
as a junior, majoring in music education. Michelle and I
shared a house in El Toro that my parents had helped her
purchase. She and Dave Klein were history. Now she was
dating a guy named Doug, her future husband, while working as a dental hygienist, and I was working part-time at Tibbie's Music Hall, a dinner theater where alumni of Young
Americans performed. Ten of us—five guys and five girls—
waited tables and then, after dinner, performed a musical
show. It was a great job; I couldn't believe I was getting paid
to do this! We were all good friends, and we laughed all the
time on and off stage.

About that time a guy I knew from YA started a singing
telegram business, and he asked me if I wanted another part-
time job. "Sure!" I quickly responded. "Sounds like fun, and

I can always use the money." I developed a Dolly Parton character—complete with a tight-fitting red pantsuit, enormous bosoms, blonde wig, gobs of makeup, and—don't ask me why—tap shoes. I showed up at all kinds of parties to surprise the "lucky" guest of honor. I went to homes, parks, hotel ballrooms; I even made my appearance at the entrance to an upscale restaurant, much to the horror of the maitre d'. "Is Mr. Benjamin Johnson here?" I'd sing out as loud as I could with my Tennessee twang. All eyes were immediately on me, waiting to see who the poor guy named Benjamin Johnson would be. Of course, his family and friends were only too eager to identify him. I'd race to him and, in my best Tennessee accent, I'd drawl out, "Well, honey, if you're not the cutest thing I ever saw! I'd like to take you back to Pigeon Forge with me! But I'll bet someone as cute as you is already took." Then I'd put my arms around him and run my fingers through his hair while singing a couple of Dolly's songs, ending with "Happy Birthday." Back then I thought it was a hilarious job; now I can't believe I did it.

One Saturday night the secretary booked two appearances back to back but way across town from each other. Still in costume, I was literally racing from the first location to the next when I saw red lights in my rearview mirror and heard a siren.

I don't have time for this! I found a wide shoulder and pulled over, and before the policeman could open his door, I jumped out of my car and ran back to the patrol car with my taps clattering on the pavement, leaned down, and talked through his open window.

I was dressed as Dolly Parton, so I stayed in character. "Hey, there officer, sir. I'm sorry, but I'm in a real hurry because I'm already late to deliver my next singing telegram. So, if you're going to give me a ticket, could you please hurry it up because I really have to get going!"

The policeman howled. "Well, in all my years of being a patrolman, this is a first. Where are you going?"

"Just down to Charlie Brown's Restaurant in Marina del Rey."

"Well, get back in your car, Miss Parton, and I'll give you an escort."

"Wow! Thank you, sweetie!" I said, pinching his cheek. I ran back to my car and scooted into the seat. He turned his siren on, and I followed close behind him as we raced through the streets of L.A. Ten minutes later I was running across the parking lot toward the restaurant, waving "thank you" to the policeman as I went by. Not only did I get an escort, but I didn't get a speeding ticket!

Late one Sunday afternoon I was returning from an engagement, and when I got about a mile from our house, my car died. I got out and raised the hood—like I expected to be able to identify a problem. Yeah, right. In desperation I walked to the house and called Danny. "The car just died," I said. "Any idea what might be wrong?"

He tried his best to be patient with his kid sister who was interrupting his Sunday afternoon. He gave me a list of things to check, and I walked the mile back to the car and went through the list. Finding nothing wrong, I walked back home and called again.

"It's not the battery because the lights and radio work. I don't want to leave my car on the street, I need it tomorrow, and nobody's open on Sunday. I know it's a long drive and I *really* hate to ask, but could you just come up here and see about it, *please?* I don't know what else to do."

"All right. It'll be about fifteen minutes before I can leave, so I'll be there in about an hour, and I'll see what I can do." I walked back to the car and waited for my brother who, sure enough, pulled up forty-five minutes later. "Having a little trouble?" he wisecracked as he gave me a playful bump on his way to my car. He opened the hood, examined the hoses, inspected the battery, checked the oil. Everything seemed fine. With me standing anxiously by, he then slid into the driver's seat and turned the key. "Oh, I should have known," he moaned. "You're out of gas!"

The next summer, after finishing my junior year of college, the dean of choral music at CSUF invited me and a few other choir members to Eugene for the two-week Oregon Bach Festival. Helmuth Rilling, a famous conductor, came every year from Stuttgart, Germany, to give seminars to conductors, and the students applied his instruction by conducting our choir, the Festival Choir.

Accompanied by members of the Los Angeles Chamber Orchestra, this was lofty, high-quality music. Roger Wagner, conductor of the L.A. Masters Chorale, a prestigious choral institution, came and auditioned members of the Festival Choir, and, much to my surprise, he invited me to be a member of his group for the remainder of the summer! This was a major coup, especially at the young age of twenty-one!

But there was a conflict. My job at Tibbie's required six nights a week, leaving only Monday evening to be with Jerry, who was still my boyfriend. The Chorale sang on Mondays. I told Jerry I wasn't going to sacrifice our one evening together, but he wouldn't hear of it. "What? Are you kidding? This is an incredible opportunity! Don't worry about us. I'll drive you to and from your shows, and we'll visit on your breaks. We'll make it work."

Still not wanting to tie up every night, I posed an alternative plan to the director at Tibbie's, and we found another YA alumna with my look, sound, and personality type to fill in for me two nights a week so that I could be off. I trained Jan and as part of her preparation she'd come to the shows and watch me, so she could learn her part and moves. Jerry also came to watch and be with me, so he and Jan sat together and as they got acquainted, they became good friends, such good friends that Jerry told me he was going to San Diego with Jan's family the next weekend to show them around. Although this was typical of Jerry's thoughtfulness, the whole setup didn't sound quite right to me. "Do I have anything to worry about?" I asked him.

He assured me, "Oh, no, Renée. No way." But late Sunday night, the doorbell rang, and when I opened the door, there stood Jerry. I took one look at him, and I knew why he was there by the expression on his face. He didn't have to say a word. Seeing my look of horror and dismay, he softly said, "I'm sorry, Renée. I'm just so sorry." Jerry and I had been together for four years, and I thought he was the man I'd spend the rest of my life with. Deeply wounded, I felt betrayed by a good friend, Jan, and I was disappointed with Jerry's weakness. The next several months were a total disaster; I was heartbroken.

By my senior recital over a year later, I was finally able to move on and was dating another terrific guy named Craig. In making my recital guest list, I remembered what a huge part of my college success Jerry had been. I knew that part of why I was graduating and doing my senior recital was because of Jerry's support for four years. So I sent him an invitation with a note: "It would be silly not to invite you to my senior recital when you were such a huge part of my college years." He came, and I was glad to see him. He met Craig, and everything was very comfortable. His relationship with Jan had not lasted, and I think seeing me again and watching me reap the benefit of my years of hard work, now conducting my recital choir, reminded him of what we once had. Soon he called and suggested that maybe we could try again. Jerry was a terrific man, a sweetheart of a guy, but I knew we couldn't go back.

Ironically, my first teaching job was in the same place I started my education—the parochial grade school at the Mission Church where my brother, sisters, and I spent our elementary years and, interestingly, where my father also attended as a child.

The timing was perfect. At the same time I moved out to begin teaching, Michelle was ready for her next "roommate"—Doug. They were married at our church in October, 1982. It was a special time.

Teaching general elementary music was not my first love. My training was in secondary school, so I wanted to teach choral music in the public high school. But the three big high schools in our area were locked up; their choral directors had been there for years, and there would be no openings until someone retired. I wanted to live in that general area, so I took the church school job and waited for something else to open up.

Being a teacher in a school where I had been a student was a lot of fun, but being inexperienced and having not been around little kids very much, I had a lot to learn. On my first day with the first graders I was writing words to a song on the board, but when I turned and saw their puzzled little faces, I realized they couldn't read! I also learned that they liked to participate. One day I was teaching them about rhythm; for review I asked them to name something with a beat. Every hand in the classroom went up.

Jennifer: "My hands! Clap clap, clap clap, clap clap!"

Brian: "My heart! Boom boom, boom boom, boom boom!"

Nicholas: "A drum! Tap tap, tap tap, tap tap!"

Vincent: "A clock! Tick tock, tick tock, tick tock!"

Julia (clueless): "I live on a hill." I thought to myself, "And what does living on a hill have to do with rhythm?"

Thank goodness, the choral director position at San Clemente High came open, and I jumped at the chance to interview. Unfortunately, I wasn't a very good interviewee. I was nervous and talked nonstop. Also, I looked very young, which was a plus in the elementary school but not in the high school. For some reason principals seem to prefer teachers who look older than their students! My competition was one of the pianists for the 1984 Olympics, which were in L.A. that summer, and he got the job. I stayed on at the Mission.

Around that time we were planning Denise's wedding to Joseph Loyatho who, interestingly, was also Basque, born and raised in Hasparren, about twenty kilometers from Ainhoa. Dominic, an old friend of hers from elementary school, called and invited her to the opening festivities of the new Basque Cultural Center in San Francisco. In true Basque style, there was lots of dancing and loud music, and Dominic and Denise were having a great time on the dance floor. Exhausted and hot, Denise stopped and said she needed something to drink.

Dominic offered, "Okay, I'll go to the bar and get you a screwdriver!"

Denise protested, "No, I just want a glass of water."

"You can't be Basque and drink just water. I'll get you a screwdriver."

"I just want a glass of water!" By now she was exasperated.

Dominic continued to argue, so finally Denise said, "Never mind, I'll get it myself." She headed for the bar, which was lined with six or seven rows of men gathered around to sing. Yelling over them, she asked the bartender, "Can I get a glass of water?"

In Basque he yelled back, "You can't be Basque and drink water. How about a real drink?"

She reiterated, "Just *water*, please."

Still the bartender protested, "If you're Basque, let me fix you something with a kick in it."

Just then, the guy she was yelling over ripped into the bartender in Basque. *"Zertako ez diozu baso bat ur emaiten? Ori da nahi duena!"* (Will you give the nice lady what she wants, which is a glass of water!)

The bartender grumbled back something like "Keep your shirt on," handed him a glass of water, and he gave it to Denise. The nice man who stood up for Denise was Joseph, and they were married in January of 1985 in Serra Chapel at the San Juan Capistrano Mission.

The next summer my friend Linda Hammontree and I went to Europe with the choir representing the U.S. at the First International Symposium on Choral Music in Vienna, Austria. After performing at the symposium and hearing fabulous choirs from around the world, Linda and I toured for a few days, then she returned to the U.S. while I headed for Ainhoa to sing at Christian's wedding.

Knowing I'd be in Europe and would have some time between the symposium and the wedding, I contacted my friend, Johannes Muses, before I left California. I met Johannes the preceding summer at the Oregon Bach Festival; he was one of Helmuth's German conducting students who came as his assistant. Because Johannes was from Europe and I'd traveled through his country, I enjoyed talking to him, and we struck up a friendship. Anyway, I wrote Johannes and let him know that since I was going to be on his continent, I thought I might drop by Stuttgart to say hello.

He quickly responded. "Oh, you must come, and when you're here, you can sing with the Gächinger Konterei at the European Music Festival in Stuttgart." The Gächinger is one of the most well-known choirs in Germany, so I was thrilled at the prospect.

Just two nights before I left home, Johannes called. "I'm so sorry, Renée, but I've been called to Argentina to direct a choir whose conductor has been taken ill. I'm afraid I won't be here when you come. But come ahead anyway. It's all arranged for you to sing with the Gächinger."

That wasn't the news I wanted to hear. Now I'd be all alone in Stuttgart and wouldn't know anyone in the choir. I could sing in German, but I had no conversational German skills at all. I admit a little hesitancy did creep in. *Should I be doing this? Is it a good idea for me to be all alone in a strange country?* But I'd learned a lot from my sisters when we traveled through Europe; surely I was smart enough to figure out how to exchange currency, find hostels, and take the right trains. I also figured that if my mom could leave France and come all the way to America to live, surely I could find my way around for a few weeks. How hard could it be?

When I got off the train in Stuttgart, I was exhausted and hungry, so I walked up to a vendor in the station and took an egg out of the carton. *A hardboiled egg,* I thought. *Yum. A little protein—this is good.* I paid the vendor, walked outside, sat down on the sidewalk, and pulled out my map to get my bearings. While concentrating on the map, I absentmindedly hit the egg against my belt buckle to crack the shell. Whack, whack, whack! *Oh, no!* The egg suddenly disintegrated in my hand. I looked down just in time to see the raw, broken yoke sliding south. My khaki shorts now had a lovely yellow streak right down the front. In that moment, one thing became crystal clear: making assumptions was a bad idea, especially in a foreign country!

I hailed a taxi, which dropped me off in front of a large building marked "Bachakademie." I walked up the stairs, rang the doorbell, and a large German frau opened the door. "My name is Renée Lacouague, and I'm here as a friend of Johannes Muses," I said, with all the dignity I could muster despite the egg down the front of my shorts.

"No," the frau said in her broken English. "No, no Renée Lacouague, but come in." I followed her to the counter where she repeated, "No Renée Lacouague. Johannes is gone. I have no record of Renée Lacouague."

While we were talking, a nice man who had been standing on the other side of the room came forward. "Hello. I'm Wilhelm Gerherdt," he said in broken English. "You're here for Johannes?"

"Yes, I am. I know he's been called to Argentina, but he said he had left instructions that I was to sing with the Gächinger."

"If Johannes said you'll be singing with the Gächinger, then you'll be singing with the Gächinger. Our first rehearsal is tomorrow at 6:00 in the evening at the Stiftskirche." He gave me the address along with instructions to show up the next afternoon.

I thanked him, walked out the door and down the steps, and started down the street. By this time, it was starting to get dark. *Okay, that's set. Now what do I do? I guess I need to find a place to stay.* I stopped and opened my *Let's Go Europe on $5 a Day* to find a hostel, and just then Wilhelm came out to go home for the day. "Renée, where are you staying tonight?" he called out.

"Well, I actually don't know yet. I was just about to look in my book to find a place."

"Would you like to come stay with my family and me tonight?"

I quickly dashed my eyes to the ring on his left hand. "Wow. That's a nice offer. But don't you think you should check with your wife to see if it's okay?"

"Oh, no. It'll be fine. Come on." We drove to his lovely home and although I felt rather awkward walking in unannounced, his wife was gracious. He and his family were very hospitable, and I felt like I was getting an inside look at what a German family was really like.

The next day Wilhelm gave me a ride to the rehearsal. I got my music, my pencil, and situated myself among the altos. I smiled at the lady next to me and tried to introduce myself. "Hi. I'm Renée, and I'm from America."

"Yah!" she thundered at me, smiling and demonstrating her lack of dental care. I think she was nice, but she kind of intimidated me.

Helmuth came in and, as is his habit, he got right to work. We were singing the *Bach Mass in B-Minor*, which fortunately I had sung with him before in Oregon. We opened with the downbeat of the Kyrie, and the German alto fraus who surrounded me hit it with full force, sounding stronger than most bass sections in America. I'm sure I did an involuntary double take. Noticing the hair on their legs, I laughed. *There must be hair on their chests, too!*

I was doing just fine until about page 10. The further into the piece we forged, the more lost I became. Helmuth would instruct in German, "Go back to page 73, top score, third measure, fourth beat." I could only count to ten in German, so I had no idea what he was saying. It's hard to look professional while peeking over the shoulder of a lady next to you just to see what page you're on.

It was a thrill to be singing Bach in Germany, where the composer was born and raised. I stayed about two weeks, singing in concerts on the weekends, and then it was time to push on to Ainhoa.

I took the overnight train to Bayonne. Knowing enough to be cautious, I selected a compartment with people who looked innocent—two older couples who were already asleep. I put my backpack overhead, settled into my seat, reclined, and closed my eyes. Suddenly, I felt someone looking at me. I opened my eyes and there, peering into the window from the aisle, were two guys about my age. Their eyes were fixed directly on me. I closed my eyes for a few minutes and looked again. They were still there and still staring straight at me. Closed my eyes. Looked again. They were gone. Sigh of relief.

I started to doze off, but again I felt their gaze. It was creepy. I opened my eyes and sure enough they were back, staring straight at me. This time, with an obvious attitude of annoyance, I stared back, hoping they'd get the message that I was aware of them and considered their presence an intrusion. I closed my eyes yet again, but this time I heard the door open, and one of the guys came in and took the seat right next to me.

Immediately, I jumped up and walked out. I had my money and passport in my fanny pack around my waist, so I just left my backpack and got out. Fortunately, the second guy was not in the aisle, so I went straight to the conductor. "There are two guys lurking around my compartment and staring at me. It doesn't feel right; they're making me very uncomfortable. Would you keep an eye on my car?"

"No problem. I'll be happy to do that," the conductor replied.

When I returned to my seat, they were gone, but a little while later they returned, and just then the conductor came and told them to leave. I got up, thanked him, and he said, "You were smart to let me know. I'll continue to watch."

Returning to my seat again, I thought, *I've been protected. The Holy Spirit within me was repelled by the spirit in them, making me feel uncomfortable and at risk, alerted to possible danger. I've put myself in some situations, traveling alone, where I really could have been hurt. God has been watching out for me. Thank you, Lord.*

Thanks to God's protection and a fatherly conductor, I arrived safely in Bayonne and enjoyed singing at Christian's wedding. It was fun to be with my family in Ainhoa again.

The summer was over and I planned to do graduate work at USC, so I boarded a flight to California. After nine hours in the air, I got into L.A. about midnight. The next morning I was still asleep, trying to shake off the effects of jetlag, when the phone rang. It was Austin Buffum, the Coordinator of Music for the Capistrano Unified School District. "Renée, we've been trying to reach you. While you were in Europe, the guy we hired last year for San Clemente High gave his notice, and we want you to interview for the job. School is starting today. Can you come down this morning?"

Awakened out of a deep sleep and fighting through the cobwebs in my mind to comprehend what I was hearing, I hesitated. "Oh, Austin, I'm jetlagged, I'm a mess, and I know I didn't interview that well last time."

"Just get down here."

I quickly showered, put my hair in a bun, and donned the most matronly dress in my closet. This time I was too tired to babble or be perky, which must have been an improvement because they asked me to start the next day.

The next morning came, and I was in the classroom without the benefit of a new-teacher orientation. I knew very little about the public school system and was thrust into the hot seat. What's more, my assignment was split. Periods one and two I taught choir at Shorecliffs Junior High, then I jumped in the car and scooted over to the high school for the remainder of the day.

I had a total of eighteen students in the two high school choirs. Kids being kids, a couple of my students had gone to the guidance counselor and had their choir assignment switched, saying that my predecessor had placed them in Madrigals, the top choir. The minute they opened their mouths, I knew I had a problem; their voices were mediocre at best, and their attitudes stunk. I got permission from the skeptical but supportive principal to reaudition.

I opened the audition to the entire school, and I also launched a major recruiting campaign. I went out to the football team and singled out the best-looking guys I could find. "Matt, Carlos, Nathan, Mike. I checked, and I know you need a fine arts credit. Come, be in my choir." Then I went to the swim team. "You, you, you, and you. Have you taken care of your fine arts credit? No? You're now in the choir." I didn't care if they could sing or not. I needed bodies.

Next I called the local Presbyterian church. The youth choir director was Bob Perry, one of my student-teaching supervisors, and I knew he had a fabulous program with an excellent praise team. "Bob, give me the names and phone numbers of your nicest, most popular guy and girl who can sing." He gave me two juniors, Cameron Brown and Suzy Deluca. I called them at home and told them Bob Perry had raved about their talent. "The school choirs are kind of flat right now, but we're rebuilding. I sure could use your leadership and talent." I tried not to beg.

I held the audition, put the top nine singers in Madrigals, the rest in Concert Choir, and we were off and running. I did have some angry kids, however. I got some crank phone calls and some nasty letters from students, but it was worth it because I had a fresh start, kids properly placed, and the choir had already grown from eighteen to thirty-five. Cameron and Suzy were largely responsible for the success of the choirs that year. Suzy was in Madrigals and led the group with her personality and talent. Cameron was a key component to Concert Choir. He wasn't that strong of a singer, but he was popular, so the other kids followed his example. Because he loved choir, they loved choir too!

I loved what I was doing. The kids fascinated me because they were from all backgrounds. Some were rich kids who had everything tied with a bow and handed to them; some kids had little. Some were from broken homes, others from loving homes. Some sailed through their classes and were top athletes with futures that looked secure; others I prayed would not drop out. The students were diverse, and one of the good things about choir was its level ground. Everybody, regardless of background, had a part to sing.

It was my mission to encourage the kids to be the best they could be. When they sang well, I'd say, "Did you hear yourselves? Did you hear what you just did? That was awesome!" And if they were just going through the motions, I'd remind them, "You're better than this. Why are you settling for mediocre when you can be sensational? Let's sing it this time like we're being recorded!"

My first day at Shorecliffs Junior High, where I taught the first two periods, a tall, good-looking boy walked in with his head down and his arms hanging at his side. His body language told me immediately that he was a kid who needed to be noticed. "Hi, I'm Miss Lacouague. What's your name?"

"Scott Wyatt," he mumbled. "You know, brother of Holly Wyatt."

"Who's Holly Wyatt?"

"You don't know who Holly Wyatt is?"

"No, I'm new here. I don't know any of you guys."

"Valedictorian of San Clemente High. Rhodes Scholar. Scholarship to USC. Beautiful. Brilliant."

Without reacting to who his sister was, I responded, "So, who are you?" I wanted him to know right away that his identify was not in his sister and that he had nothing to live up to in this class. The next spring he landed the lead in the junior high musical and did very well with it. His mother and sister came, sat in the front row, and were very proud of him.

I tried to get to know each of my students. Some days I would ask a student to have lunch with me, sometimes I would single a kid out and visit with him for just a minute as he came into or left class. "How's it going? How's school? How's home? I appreciate how hard you're working in here." I tried to notice if someone needed a little encouragement, and then I offered it. And I always tried to keep a sense of humor.

My second year of teaching the high school program grew to about ninety students, the numbers being boosted in part by my junior high kids who signed up for choir when they came to high school. Plus, word had leaked out that we had a lot of fun, went to choir competitions in L.A. and at Magic Mountain Amusement Park, and learned cool music.

Anyone who has chaperoned a group of kids knows the overwhelming sense of responsibility that goes with being in charge of other people's children. Parents entrusted their children to me, and I took seriously my responsibility to return their kids safely to them. That year I took the choirs to L.A. I had good chaperones, so at about 11:00 P.M. I slipped into my flannel nightgown and was headed for bed when someone knocked on the door. "Miss Lacouague, Miss Lacouague, it's me—Scott Wyatt!"

I opened the door just a crack and talked through the chain. "Scott, I'm in my nightgown. What do you need?"

"It's Dan and Nina!" Then he whispered. "They're in bed together!"

"Scott, no way."

"Yeah, Miss Lacouague. I didn't know they were in there, so I unlocked the door to my room and walked in. Dan started yelling for me to get out. Maybe I shouldn't be telling you this, but I thought you ought to know."

Well, I didn't really think anything was going on—I mean, who would be that dumb? But then, Dan and Nina were an item, and Scott did look disturbed. What if he was right and I ignored it all? That wouldn't look good when it came to the principal's attention Monday morning. And I certainly didn't want my students returning from their choir trips pregnant. Not good PR. So, nightgown and all, I followed Scott down the hallway to his room. Sure enough, there they were. I saw lots of skin and started yelling.

"Dan! Nina!" They froze. "Get out of that bed! Right *now!* Both of you! I can't believe you two! How could you pull a stunt like this? And to think I trusted you!" I was furious.

All of a sudden kids howling with laughter came spilling out of the woodwork—out of the bathroom, from under the bed, from behind doors, from inside the closet. I stood frozen. Kids in hysterics were doubled over, holding their sides, falling on the bed and on the floor. Dan and Nina uncovered and crawled out of the bed, showing me that Dan had on street shorts and Nina a strapless swimsuit top and jeans.

I dropped to the floor and joined the laughter. "You guys are gooood. You got me 100 percent. Never have I been so royally had."

At the same time I was teaching choir at Shorecliffs and San Clemente, I held a part-time job as music director of our church. One Sunday morning after church a gal approached me and said, "Hi! I'm Rosie Dunnigan. I like the kind of music you do, and I would love to come sing with you this summer if you want an extra singer. I know it's kind of scary; you don't know me and you need to make sure the quality is good, but maybe it'll help you to know that I lead music at the Newman Center at UCLA."

The Newman Center is the Catholic Student Center on campus, so that information gave her credibility. "Why don't you come a half hour early next week and bring your guitar. We'll put some stuff together, try it out at church, and see what happens." That was the beginning of a long friendship. Rosie and her fiancé, Greg, were to be married the following April. As our friendship grew, Rosie started inviting me to meet Greg's friend Mike Bondi. "He's just perfect for you," she'd say.

I'd respond, "No, I'm dating Craig. He's a great guy who's very good to me and I like him a lot. I'm not sure if we're quite right for life, but we're certainly okay for now." Craig and I did break up eventually. When we did, Rosie started her campaign again, but I wasn't eager to get reattached. Rosie finally resorted to lying. She'd say, "Renée, I've told Mike Bondi all about you, and he's just dying to meet you."

At the same time, unbeknownst to me, Greg was telling Mike, "There's this friend of Rosie's named Renée who leads music at our church. Rosie's told Renée all about you, and she really wants us to introduce you to her." Mike was no more interested in meeting me than I was in meeting him!

Finally, just to shut them up, I offered, "Why don't you bring him to church next Sunday night, and we'll all go to dinner afterwards."

On the appointed night Rosie and I were leading the opening song when I saw Greg walk in with Mike. "Is that him?" I asked with my eyes while singing.

She nodded yes, still singing and strumming her guitar.

"Not bad!" I replied nonverbally. We had this full-blown conversation without saying a word. We had a great time during dinner. Greg and Rosie were right; Mike and I had a lot in common and compatible senses of humor. Neither of us was really interested in dating right then, so we didn't even exchange phone numbers. We had a great time, but that was it until several months later.

Rosie and Greg's wedding was in April of 1985. Mike was there and because I didn't know many of the guests, we ended up sitting together at the reception. We danced a lot, so I knew from the start that Mike was a *horrible* dancer. He had no sense of rhythm whatsoever, but he was out there doing it, dancing for all he was worth, and I liked and admired that. He was obviously secure with himself.

The next week he called. "My company is having Family Night at Disneyland next week. My whole family is going. Would you like to join us?" It was to be our first date, the beginning of an incredible courtship.

Mike was always really good about supporting my students and me; he didn't mind getting dragged to all my music stuff—the concerts, musicals, competitions, even rehearsals, and he often helped me chaperone field trips. His family was sports-minded, so we did a lot of outdoorsy stuff like volleyball, skiing, and walking on the beach. We especially enjoyed going backpacking, and camping, and going to church together.

From the beginning I was impressed with the way Mike handled himself. First, he blended well with my family. My parents liked him, and he quickly developed a rapport with Michelle and Denise and their husbands, Doug and Joseph.

The Lacouague family was an old family, very well known in Capistrano. He was a stranger in my territory, the town where I had grown up. Everybody knew me and nobody knew him, so he had to meet a lot of people; he met each new situation with poise and grace.

Mike didn't fit my preconceived checklist of what I wanted in a man, not at all. I had always gone for the tall, 6'4", shy musician type. Mike was 5'8", couldn't sing his way out of a bucket, and had no sense of rhythm. He was handsome and had a good body, but he didn't have "the look" that made me do double takes. But as I threw my checklist away and got to know him, I realized what a quality man he was.

We dated for weeks before Mike tried to kiss me. He was wise enough to understand we needed to get to know and like each other as people before moving to passion. I firmly believe this is one of the reasons why our relationship has lasted and withstood my paralysis. We were best friends first.

Another positive was that he came from a stable family. He loved and respected his parents and was very close to his brother and sister. Plus, he was a college graduate and had a good job. I didn't consciously make a list entitled Favorable Mate Traits and evaluate Mike to see how he scored. However, I was aware that in choosing my lifetime mate, I had to consider more than just how he made me feel when we were alone. How would he fit into my whole life, and how would I fit into his? I needed to consider family gatherings, common ideals, mutual faith, parenting skills, security, social graces, and character. No doubt about it—Mike was definitely husband material!

On my birthday in 1987, Mike took me out for an elegant dinner. After dessert, he pulled out a handsome wooden, heart-shaped box (I still have it!) and gave it to me to open. Inside, there was a beautiful sapphire necklace. "I didn't buy a ring because I thought we'd like to pick the ring out together." Then he smiled and said, "Renée, will you marry me?" My mind was racing. *Ohmygosh! This is it! This is really it! It's really happening! This is it!* I said "yes" right away.

The three years I spent at San Clemente High were some of the best of my life. I was proud of my accomplishments. The program had grown from eighteen students to a hundred and fifty, and being in choir had become much more "cool." Students liked to hang out in the choir room, and we were singing some challenging music. I loved that being a music teacher entailed teaching music history also, and a lot of music from antiquity focused on God, the patriarchs, and the church. Bottom line: I could talk about God and get away with it!

Mike and I were getting married that summer, and because he had taken a job in Denver, I would not be returning to San Clemente High in the fall; this was my last year there. If I planned to become Mrs. Mike Bondi, then of course I would have to join him in the Mile High City. The decision to leave my students was agonizing but inescapable—so much so, in fact, that for a long time I had not mustered the courage or figured out a way to tell them. I decided to procrastinate and not tell them until closer to the end of the school year.

Before the "fat lady sang," I wanted to accomplish one more thing with my choir—to see them stretch musically as far as they could. As a final tribute to my students, I enrolled the Madrigals in the Orange County Music Festival, which would take place in March. This was no ordinary festival. It was to be held in a huge performing arts center with most of the top choirs in southern California participating. Dr. Howard Swan, known as the grandfather of choral music and considered to be the ultimate judge for choral competition, would be rating the participants. Although my students didn't know it, this would be our last hoorah, the grand finale, the culmination of our three years of training and practice.

My students gasped when I first told them the piece I had chosen for the competition.

"Brahms!"

"But it's so *heavy!*"

"And it's *German!*"

"Do you really think we can pull this off?"

"C'mon, Miss Lacouague, give us a break!"

I smiled inwardly. I deliberately chose a piece by Brahms because the music was passionate and complex. It was a melodic love song that flowed and swelled, moving from peaceful to intense. It would push our choir to its limits. "Gang, I know you can do this," I reassured them. "I know this isn't the song you would have chosen, but if you'll trust me, we can make beautiful music."

The big day arrived, and the huge auditorium was packed. Dressed in tuxedos and formal dresses, we walked onstage. We had known that achieving our goal of a "Superior" rating from Dr. Swan could only be accomplished if everyone worked together, so we had put in months of long, hard, disciplined hours of practice. We translated the lyrics so we'd know what we were singing, laughed at each other's German, and sang difficult measures repeatedly until we had them down cold. Finally, we did make beautiful music together, and now it was time to show our stuff.

As they settled into their places on stage, their eyes turned to me, waiting expectantly. I smiled at them confidently, gave them a thumbs-up, and mouthed, "You can do this! Let's go for it!" I lifted my arms, and the accompaniment began.

Together, they hit the first chord. Their harmonics were perfectly balanced. Their German was rich and authentic. The sopranos floated over the high notes, the boys' voices were full and robust. By the end, we were in a trance. We forgot about the audience, the judge, and were caught up in the making of great music. I brought the piece to a close, and the audience was silent for a full five seconds. Then they broke into thunderous applause. It was a *Mr. Holland's Opus* moment.

While the Madrigals accepted their applause, I gave them another thumbs-up and exclaimed in a whisper only they could hear, "Yes! Yes!" It was undoubtedly our best performance ever. We had *nailed* it! The kids knew it, and I knew it. Now we had to wait to see if the judge agreed.

Offstage there was a flurry of excitement mixed with relief. We did some premature celebrating before they headed for the bus, and I awaited the results. When I stepped onto the bus, I didn't have to ask for silence.

As I opened the envelope, I felt like a presenter at the Academy Awards. My stomach fluttered as I opened the rating sheet and read aloud what it said.

"Now *this* is Brahms!" Dr. Swan had written, and the rating was a Superior. The students roared in celebration. It was the last time I took a choir to be judged, and the memory could not be any sweeter.

I was flying high. I was marrying the most wonderful man I'd ever met and was having a ball with wedding plans; my music program was a huge success; I was blessed to have had the opportunity to travel and see the world; I had friends and family to love. My life was full, and I saw nothing but blue skies up ahead.

But in just two short months, I wouldn't be flying high at all. I'd be flat on my back. It was a crisis of faith such as I had never imagined. I wouldn't get to choose the song. Could I still trust God to make beautiful music of my life?

5

Flat on My Back

After Dr. Palmer delivered the revolting news, he said, "I'll let your family come in now." He left, and I was alone for a few minutes, trying to process what he had just said, but the prognosis was just too overwhelming for me to comprehend it fully. I simply didn't believe him. Dr. Palmer obviously didn't know what he was talking about, or maybe he was exaggerating to prepare me for the worst. How could I be out dancing with Mike two nights ago and now be paralyzed? It didn't make sense. Things like that just don't happen, especially not from falling out of bed!

Mom and Dad came in first. Now that we all knew the score, they looked even worse than before. I saw the depth of sadness and seriousness on their faces. They were incapable of trying to cheer me up or of trying to reassure me that everything was going to be okay. They came over, touched me, and Mom asked, "How are you feeling?" It was awkward. No one knew what to say. When Danny, Denise, and Michelle came in, their faces showed the same look.

There was not a smile anywhere—not from the doctor, not from the nurses, not from my family. *Okay*, I thought. *I guess I won't be getting out of here tonight. I suppose I'm going to be here for a while.* I think God sometimes places a hedge of protection around us, allows our minds to be slow to catch up to reality so that the shock of a tragic situation doesn't blindside and overwhelm us. In addition, I was so drugged I was in and out of consciousness.

Meanwhile, Mike had gone to his office that morning in Denver on what seemed like a normal day. He was in a meeting downstairs when his secretary came in, pale and somber.

"There's a phone call from your dad."

"Tell him I'll call him back."

"No, you need to talk to him now," she insisted. Confused, Mike excused himself and followed her back upstairs and picked up the extension.

"Hey, Dad. What's up? I'm in a meeting."

"Mike, there's been an accident. It's Renée. They don't know how it happened, but she has broken her neck."

That's all he could get out. Unable to continue, he handed the phone to Sandra, Mike's mother, who continued the explanation. "She's in the ICU, and it's serious, Mike. They don't know if she's going to make it."

Mike broke down in sobs. He explained what little he knew to the others in the office. They had all met me when I went to Denver with Mike on a house-hunting trip after he had been offered the job, so I was not just a name. Already, without being asked, the secretary was on the phone, booking Mike a flight. He ran home, threw some clean clothes in a suitcase, and within two hours he was on his way back to California.

Understandably, he was in a state of shock and confusion— totally traumatized by the blow and unanswered questions. How could she be in critical condition and paralyzed when we were dancing the day before yesterday? How could she have broken her neck? As he stared out the window of the airplane, he kept remembering the only other person he'd known who had a broken neck—a friend in junior high school. She had died within twenty-four hours of her accident. He was expecting that I'd be dead by the time he reached the hospital. The two-and-a-half-hour flight from Stapleton International to John Wayne Airport seemed like days, and when he landed, his mom, dad, brother Steve, and best friend, Alex, were waiting to rush him to Mission Medical Center.

When Mike came into the ICU, he walked over to me and put his cheek against mine. "Hi, honey. I'm here." I looked up, and there he was, smiling broadly. His was definitely the happiest face I'd seen all day; he put a glow on the whole room.

I returned his smile weakly and whispered, "Well, I guess now we'll get all the really good parking places!" He laughed out loud! Later he told me that right then he knew we'd be okay. Even though my body was broken, my personality wasn't. I was still the Renée he loved. As long as we had our sense of humor and our trust in God's faithfulness, we'd make it.

As glad as I was to see him, still again came the gnawing question. *He just left yesterday to go back to Denver. Why is he back so soon? Why would he spend the money to come back here when he just left yesterday? He probably thinks this is more serious than it really is. He didn't need to come. It wasn't necessary.*

I drifted in and out of consciousness that first day or two. Once when I was in the twilight zone I heard one of the nurses say in a disapproving voice, "Oh, she's got Dr. Palmer? Poor thing."

I opened my eyes and asked in my whisper, "What do you mean, 'Poor thing'? Is Dr. Palmer bad?"

They were startled that I overheard them. "No, he's the best neurosurgeon in the hospital. It's just that his bedside manner is often abrupt, and he's a bit tough on us. But he's an outstanding doctor, so don't worry. You're in excellent hands."

Well-wishers started streaming into the hospital—friends, students, colleagues, YA alumni, church parishioners. Of course, no one but immediate family members could come into my ICU room, and even their visits were limited to once every two hours for ten minutes. Because there were so many visitors, Michelle set up a Dear Renée book, placing it on a music stand in the ICU waiting room so people could write a note to me. I still have the book.

When I started to be conscious of my surroundings, I realized that even though I was in the ICU, I was in a private room with a window. My neck was in Gardner-Wells tongs traction. This was to minimize any further damage to the spinal cord. Furthermore, I was not lying on a normal bed but on a canvas rack called a Stryker frame, feared and hated by every person who's ever been subjected to it.

The Stryker serves two purposes—to keep the patient in cervical traction and to enable the patient to be rotated to prevent harmful pressure sores. When I was lying on my back, there was no problem; it was just like lying on a cot. However, every two hours the nurses would carefully flip me over so that I was suspended face down, looking at the floor, with my body weight resting on straps that were affixed to the frame. Of course, I couldn't feel the straps on my body so when they turned me, I had the sensation that I was being dumped out onto the tile floor, and there was nothing I could do to protect myself or stop it.

Every time they rolled me over, I freaked. I knew with my intellect there was no way I could fall out, but nevertheless it unleashed every alarm in my emotional composition. I would tell the nurses, "I know you're wonderful medical professionals and you know exactly what you're doing, but I have to be honest and tell you that I just don't trust you." I was so traumatized every time I had to be turned that, during the day, I demanded that a family member be present to help. At night, I demanded that one of two hospital staff I knew from church—Robert, an RN, or Oscar, a critical-care tech—be present to help. Even with the reassurance of family and friends, being turned was sheer torment.

Knowing how traumatized I was, one day my dad crawled under the Stryker, lay on his back under me so that I could see him, and pulled a tablet and a pencil out of his pocket. "I'm going to draw a picture of how you are strapped to this cot," he explained. "I know you can't feel it, but there are straps here, here, and here, and others that crisscross there, there, and there. You see, Renée, there's no way you can fall out of this thing." That reassured me somewhat. I just needed to hear it from my dad. I was still very fearful, but the utter terror subsided a bit. Regardless of my fear, I still felt like a pig on a rotisserie.

Others crawled under the frame to talk to me when I was bottoms-up—Mike, my sisters, Danny. Letters, notes, and cards were placed under me on the floor so I could read them. All of this helped break the monotony of looking at the tile and helped divert my mind from my condition.

Early on Dr. Palmer stopped Mike in the hallway. "Mike," he said, "I've been wanting to talk to you. I know you must be confused about what to do about Renée. It's good that you're here with her during these first days, but it's going to be much harder as time goes on. Things are different now; life is different. Your life with Renée is not going to be like you thought. Her life is going to be hard and it's going to be very, very difficult for you."

Mike considered Dr. Palmer's words. *What is he trying to tell me? Does he think I'm going to leave Renée? I planned to spend the rest of my life with this woman! Why would I leave now when she needs me more than ever? Does he really think I'm going to walk out at the most traumatic time of her life?* Dr. Palmer's reality check just didn't make sense to Mike at all. How could his life be turned upside down overnight? *Surely a miracle will happen*, Mike thought.

On Wednesday, just two days after I went to the hospital, in walked Jim Krembas and Jim Walsh, my principal and vice principal. Knowing the rules, I was quite surprised to see them in the ICU. "Hi, guys!" I whispered weakly. "How'd you get past the nurses?"

"We did some persuasive talking! The doctor authorized our visit so we could give you *this*." Smiling broadly, they held up a plaque so I could read the inscription.

TEACHER OF THE YEAR
1987–1988
SAN CLEMENTE HIGH SCHOOL
RENÉE LACOUAGUE

I started to tear up. With belabored speech I gasped, "Oh, you didn't have to do that, really."

"No, we didn't just 'do that,'" they assured me. "This award was decided two weeks ago. That's why we had to come now, so that you'd know for sure that this honor was yours before the accident, not given out of sympathy. You earned it, and you deserve it. Congratulations!"

Eager to see my reaction, Michelle had slipped into the room, and I could see her in the background. Tears of joy were dripping down her cheeks. She knew how desperately I needed some good news, and she was thrilled that I had this award to cheer me up and divert my attention.

I cried some more as I tried to express my appreciation. Exhausted, I thanked them as best I could for bringing me the plaque, making them promise to proclaim my gratitude to everyone at school.

The next day Dr. Palmer did the surgery that would stabilize my neck and reinforce my spine so that it would hold the weight of my head. The night before the operation, my church held a prayer service to pray for me. Everybody in my family went, except Danny, who stayed back to keep me company.

Fortunately, we had entertainment for the evening. Unbeknownst to me (practically everything was "unbeknownst to me" at that point!), Jeff Davis and Joe Moros, the assistant principal and an English teacher from San Clemente, took a video camera on campus and asked teachers, secretaries, and students if there was anything they wanted to share with Miss Lacouague. Some teared up and couldn't speak, but others did things to make me laugh. They brought the video to the hospital and it provided the evening's entertainment for Danny and me. It was fun to see my kids and to be entertained by their crazy antics. They were hilarious! And it felt really good to laugh.

After the service Mike returned to my room and brought the report. "Renée, the church was full." The church holds eight hundred. Some thoughtful person made a video for me, and weeks later when I watched it, I felt like Tom Sawyer in the balcony watching my own funeral! I was surprised and pleased to see dozens of my students in attendance, including some I suspected had never been in a church before. Their presence astonished me, especially when I considered that the service was at night, which meant they didn't come just to get out of class!

The surgery was a five-hour procedure. Working through a six-inch incision beginning at the nape of my neck and running downward, Dr. Palmer removed the shattered bone fragments from my spine and bolted metal splints into place. He then took a portion of healthy bone he had extracted from my hip and placed it around the splints. The foreign bone would then fuse itself to the original spine, creating a rigid column that would hold up my head.

After surgery I was returned to the ICU and the Stryker until the next day. Dr. Palmer came in with Randy, the orthotist, who was carrying a chrome device that looked like it was from outer space. He explained that the apparatus was called a halo and that it was used to put a broken neck into traction and to hold the spinal cord perfectly in place while the vertebrae healed.

He prepared me for what they were about to do. "First we're going to give you a local anesthetic to numb the area, then we're going to screw in four supports through the skin so that they'll come to rest against your skull, two in your forehead, and two on the back of your head. We'll attach the halo ring to your skull with the screws. Then we'll have to pick you up and slip the hard-shell vest over your chest and across your back. After we have secured the vest we will then attach the halo ring to the vest with four steel bars." Any time somebody wanted to move me, I panicked. Movement meant pain.

Trying to be lighthearted in a scary situation, I quipped, "Then bring in your two strongest, most handsome orderlies." Randy walked out and about fifteen minutes later returned with two hunks. "They'll do," I said, laughing.

First came the injections of lidocaine. When they swabbed my head with alcohol, I knew what was coming. I could hear Dr. Palmer's thick, French accent behind me as he directed the others. I dealt with it in the same way I dealt with most scary situations. I started singing at the top of my lungs, which of course was only a whisper. "The hills are alive . . . with the sound of music. . . ."

They stopped and laughed. "Well, we're not sure if we've ever had a patient sing to us before, but keep going! Sounds great!"

Injections completed, Randy gently explained, "Now we're going to attach the screws."

I continued to sing. "With songs they have sung for a thousand years . . ."

They either had to interrupt me or talk over me to tell me what they were going to do next. "Now we'll start assembling the apparatus and, as we screw it together, you're going to hear a clicking noise and maybe feel some vibration. It's not anything we're doing directly to you, so don't worry. It may sound weird, but it's not going to hurt."

I wasn't sure I believed or trusted them, so I sang some more. "The hills fill my heart with the sound of music. My heart wants to sing every song it hears." I was quiet for a moment. "Dr. Palmer," I said, "my voice is so pitifully weak. Will it ever get any better?"

"Your intercostal muscles are paralyzed. Most people with your level of injury have difficulty speaking in a normal voice. I don't expect that you will be able to sing again."

"Thank you *very much*," I said sarcastically.

"I just want you to be prepared to face the reality of your situation."

The halo contraption had two front bars and two back bars that came down and attached to a circular brace that went around my rib cage. I felt like a robot. The good news was that when they finished attaching the halo, they moved me off the Stryker to a regular bed. But the halo brought its own set of problems. When I was lying down, which was 99 percent of the time, my head could not rest on the pillow. Instead, it was suspended in air between the bars. It made sleeping really difficult because I couldn't get into that snuggly position on my pillow. All I could feel was my shoulders and head, and even they were suspended so that nothing touched them.

Nights were the worst. The days were filled with visitors, doctors, and nurses coming in to check on me—all kinds of activity. But at night, everybody went home and I was alone. So completely alone. The contraption on my head kept me from getting comfortable, so I couldn't sleep. I was exhausted and knew I needed rest, but as soon as I started to drift off—DING! I was awake. Perhaps my subconscious was kicking in. *You know what happened the last time you went to sleep!*

Surprisingly perhaps, I didn't lie there and wonder what life was going to be like now or who would take care of me or how I'd support myself—none of those logical questions. Rather, I just prayed. "Lord, help me get through this night." They gave me medication to help me sleep, but it didn't work. Sleeplessness became a real problem.

Many knew about my insomnia and tried to help. My friend Debbie brought me a snuggly, fuchsia teddy bear and tried tucking it between the halo and my cheek so I'd feel its coziness. Robert and Oscar, whom I wanted whenever I had to be turned on the Stryker, worked the graveyard shift. They'd come by often to keep me company, especially during their breaks. Many times Robert stroked my hair, just like I was a baby, trying to comfort me into drifting off. Sometimes it worked, sometimes it didn't, but I will forever remember his kindness.

Evidently it got back to my students that I had trouble sleeping because late one night I heard a familiar voice outside my window. "Miss Lacouague? Miss Lacouague?"

"Cameron? Is that you?" I asked in disbelief.

"Yeah, it's me."

I had to laugh! "What are you doing out there? It's late!"

"I heard a couple of good jokes at school today that I thought you might like, so I came by to tell them to you."

"Cameron, you're crazy, but go ahead. I could use a good joke." Soon we were laughing and chatting, Cameron sitting outside the window and me laying flat on my back in the hospital room. He came many nights to keep me company. Sometimes he brought the newspaper and read me articles he thought I'd be interested in, and he'd fill me in on the events in school that day.

One afternoon Scott Wyatt and some of his buddies came bursting into the room. Scott called out, almost too loudly, "Hi, Miss Lacouague. How are you?" and then he whispered, "I brought you something to see." While his buddies guarded the door, Scott pulled his new golden retriever puppy out of his athletic bag and made an elaborate introduction. "Miss Lacouague, this is Joey. Joey, say hello to Miss Lacouague."

I busted up at seeing the wiggly contraband in my hospital room. Scott held him close to me so that he licked my face, and I wished I could wipe away the wet doggie kisses! We all laughed. My students had an inexhaustible supply of ways to lift my spirits. I never knew who or what was coming through the door next!

People were incredibly good to me while I was in the hospital. Gifts from friends, relatives, colleagues, students, and parents made my room look like a boutique. One day when a group of students gathered around my bed, laughing and telling stories, a hospital volunteer stuck his head into my room. "I've come to see who the special person in this room is," he said. "I've never seen such streams of people going and coming from one hospital room, and flowers just keep arriving. All the nurses and orderlies know your room number by heart because they're asked about it so many times a day. Your room is absolutely beautiful."

I was completely prone for nearly two weeks, so now it was time for my first trick—sitting up—and my next device of torture was the cardiac chair. Dr. Palmer warned it would be a slow process. "Be patient, Renée," he stated. "Initially you may get very light-headed and nauseous."

A nurse and a physical therapist transferred me to the cardiac chair, positioning me flat on my back. I was such a Raggedy Ann doll that in the blink of an eye I could flop off the chair, so they had to strap me on—chest, waist, and legs. I hated to be moved because any jostling started the pain all over again.

Then the "fun" would start. They would crank up my back to forty-five degrees, and we'd wait to see if my blood pressure would adjust to the new position. If that worked, they'd lower my feet and legs to forty-five degrees and again sit and wait. When my head was elevated and my feet were lowered, the blood tended to pool in my legs because my body was not strong enough to pump it back up. When that happened, I would either throw up or pass out, so at the first hint of discomfort, they'd take me back to the prone position, wait, and start all over again. If I withstood the change of position, we'd move forward and crank my back up and my legs down another step. Realizing how difficult it was just to sit up—something anyone else does automatically without even thinking about it—was very discouraging.

For a treat, Michelle took me for a roll down the hallway in the cardiac chair one day. It was the first time I'd been out of my room. "Where do you want to go?" she asked, as if there were hundreds of exciting places to go in the hospital.

"The chapel," I replied. So off we went, with Michelle pushing from behind. Sitting up even a little was still very much a strain, but I was okay at first. Then as my body became more and more fatigued, big, black spots appeared before my eyes, and I started feeling dizzy and sick.

"Michelle! Michelle!" I still couldn't talk above a whisper, and obviously I couldn't wave my arms or do anything else to get her attention. "Michelle! Michelle!" Finally she heard me and came around to face me. "I'm going. I'm go—"

She grabbed a nurse and together they quickly lowered my head and raised my feet, right there in the hallway as people were passing by. Everybody needs an audience when they're fainting, right? When they got my head down and my feet up, I started coming back. Dr. Palmer's words danced mockingly in my ears. "It's a slow process."

They also put me in the cardiac chair to give me baths. I hated my nakedness. I felt so exposed, almost violated. I had to come to grips with the reality that modesty was now a luxury I couldn't afford. The shower was my first link to thinking about what life was going to be like outside the hospital. Was it always going to take *all morning* to shower, to fix my hair, to go to the bathroom? Would someone always have to dress me? Would I ever have any privacy again?

One morning when I was going through these mental gymnastics, Vicki, Danny's wife, walked in. Vicki is quiet, sweet, and sensitive to her surroundings. "How are you feeling today, honey?"

"Oh . . . okay." Tears came quickly. "Vicki, I'm scared. Will you pray for me?"

"Right now?"

"Yeah," I said sighing. "Just pray that I can sing again."

"Don't you want me to pray that you can walk again or use your hands and arms?"

"Oh sure, that too. I'm scared I won't be able to do anything again."

Vicki started to pray. It was obvious she wasn't just saying words; she was talking to someone, and that someone was

God. "Oh, Lord. We come before you heavy-hearted but knowing you are all-powerful. . . ." As Vicki prayed, I felt a release of my worry and fear. There's something about prayer that can turn even the coldest hospital room into a place of peace. As she continued, I relaxed more and more.

Meanwhile, Mike, Denise, and Bev, my ICU nurse who was sweet enough to take a personal interest in me, started touring local rehab facilities to find the very best one. How amazing that Bev would spend her days off with them. They decided on Long Beach Memorial Spinal Cord Injury Unit, where I'd be an inpatient for months of physical therapy.

Late in the afternoon on Thursday, four days before I was scheduled to be transferred, I was dozing, and I woke up with the feeling that someone was looking at me. I shifted my eyes to the right, and there was Dr. Palmer, leaning against the window in his green scrubs, arms crossed, staring at me. Startled, I blurted out, "Hi!"

He quietly said hello and kept staring. There was something different about his demeanor. His gaze made me uncomfortable, so I shifted my eyes away, then back, then away, then back to check, and he continued to stare. I couldn't figure out why he kept watching me; I certainly wasn't doing anything that interesting! "I feel like you want to say something," I said to break the silence.

Quietly and deliberately he replied, "I just wish I could do more."

I grinned. "I wish you could too, but I know you can only do so much." Ironically, I felt the need to reassure him. He was obviously deeply troubled by his medical limitations.

"I've come to say good-bye," he said. Suddenly I felt empty inside.

"Why? I'm not moving to Long Beach until Monday."

"I have to fly up to San Francisco first thing in the morning to attend a seminar. When I get back, you'll be gone."

"Well . . . this is scary."

"Long Beach is one of the finest rehab hospitals in the country. You'll get excellent care and you'll be very well taken care of."

"I'm going to miss you a whole lot. When I figure out how to write again, yours will be the first note I write to let you know how I'm doing."

He walked over to the bed and put his hand on my shoulder. "You are obviously one very special lady. You are loved tremendously. I just wish I could do more for you and for everybody who loves you so much." It was pretty special to hear this from the doctor known for no bedside manner!

"When Mike and I get married, I'll send you an invitation. I'll even save you a seat in the front row."

"You do that," he said with half a smile. Then Dr. Palmer turned and walked out the door.

I was utterly and totally helpless. He had been my lifeline, my security. I had relied on him completely to fix my body. His hands were the only ones capable of reaching down to pull me up, and he had just walked out of my life. Who was going to be that hope for me now? Without him, I was defenseless, unprotected, and abandoned.

6

Picking Up the Pieces

Denise rode with me in the ambulance from Mission Medical Center to Long Beach Memorial. It was scary to be leaving the security of known caregivers and to be going someplace new. I trusted the staff at Mission. I knew intellectually that the staff at Long Beach would be capable of taking care of me, but I was terrified. I felt like I was on a skydiving mission and someone was trying to push me out of the airplane.

It was a beautiful day in June. As we made the forty-five-minute trip up the freeway to Long Beach Memorial, I enjoyed the sunshine and blue skies. The freeway was moderately congested, and I was reminded that life had gone on while I was in the hospital. It was comforting to have Denise with me.

When we arrived, the orderly wheeled me around the corner, and nurses started asking the usual check-in questions. Some they asked and answered themselves, looking at my chart. "Age? 29. Address? 30395 Avenida del Toro. Weight? 125 pounds."

"Oh, 125 pounds," I whispered from the stretcher. "That's good! That means I'm finally down to what I put on my driver's license." The nurses laughed.

My family moved my boutique and reproduced it in my new room, a full day's work of carrying, hanging, and positioning all my flowers, pillows, stuffed animals, and posters. When they were done, the room looked as cheery and friendly as a hospital room can, which was a good thing since it would be my home for the next five months.

The nurses smiled a lot, and I began to relax. I was glad to be where I could get to work. I knew physical therapy was my conduit to walking, feeding myself, dressing myself, writing my name, combing my hair, brushing my teeth, going to the bathroom alone, and all the other daily tasks we take for granted. I was certain I could do anything if I worked hard enough and that this paralysis, while serious, was just a temporary inconvenience.

The regimen began. A typical day started with breakfast at 8:00, followed by being dressed and in my wheelchair by 9:00—a *major* feat—and rolling down the hallway to the physical therapy gym. Therese Vernon was my physical therapist, and God gave her to me—no doubt about it. She was hilarious. Considering the shape I was in, I really needed someone to make me laugh, and she did! But she also made me work.

She would pull my wheelchair alongside the mat, a ten-by-ten-foot padded square that sat about two feet off the floor, and transfer me to it. In one exercise, Therese would place my feet squarely on the floor and then hold me up in a seated position. Next, she would put my arms behind me and prop me up like a picture frame so that I would learn to balance while sitting up. It was weird to sit on my bottom when it felt numb and to use my arms as supports when they felt like they were very asleep.

I also had to learn to find the center of gravity for my head. Heads are heavy, and if my head were off to one side, I'd topple over. If I started to fall, I'd just tumble right on over because I had no muscles to bring myself upright again. Of course, Therese was always right there to catch me. The only place on my torso where I had movement was my shoulders, so I did shoulder shrugs—thousands and thousands of them—always with Therese applying resistance.

In another exercise, rehab staff would place my wheelchair inside a frame, lean me over, and tuck a sling under my fanny. Then, like a pulley, they would crank and slowly lift me into a standing position. There were two problems. The first was that I was like a rag doll; I had no control, so they'd have to hold onto me so I didn't flop over. The second was that I wasn't used to standing, so about half way up, as my blood would pool in my legs, I'd start to get lightheaded, and they'd have to drop me back down, wait, and start all over again. Sometimes it took as much as forty-five minutes to get me up, and when they did, there was a tray about chest high where they'd put my elbows and I could prop up somewhat. It felt odd to be standing; I felt so weak, limp, and floppy. One day Mike happened to walk into PT just at that time. "Hi, Honey. Oh, you're standing!" he exclaimed happily.

I started singing, weakly, "Don't cry for me Argentina. The truth is I never left you. . . ." from the end of *Evita* when Eva Peron is really sick. It made him laugh, and it became a standard joke between us.

Next came occupational therapy. A contraption came up over my head and had strings that came down and attached to troughs on both sides. They placed my arms in the troughs, trying to train my shoulder muscles to direct my arms. I would do my shoulder shrugs to get my arms to move, but my appendages flailed wildly and completely out of control. Then I'd laugh and sing in a whisper, "I got no strings to tie me down" from *Pinocchio*. I guess music helped me lighten up and laugh instead of cry.

While I was in this contraption, the occupational therapist would attach a writing brace to my wrist, insert a pen, and place a piece of paper in front of me. "Now, Renée, just see if you can mark anything—a line, a scribble, just get the pen on the paper." It was one of my first reality checks. I had no control, not even a hint of a muscle that would allow me to aim the pen or create pressure enough to make a mark. Tears inadvertently spilled out of my eyes. "I can't even write; I can't even sign my name!" But after a few minutes of reality, I'd shake it off and tell my therapist, "Okay, let's keep going. Let's just keep going."

Another day my OT inserted a cookie in my writing brace and instructed me to eat it. As I was struggling to get it to my mouth, all of a sudden something clicked in my mind, and I stopped. This scene was familiar. Was it *déjà vu*? Had I dreamed something like this? As I pondered my unexpected reaction, I had a flashback. I remembered one afternoon when I was about thirteen; I was home alone watching the After School Movie. On this particular day, the movie was *The Other Side of the Mountain,* the true story of Jill Kinmont, an Olympic skier who broke her neck in a skiing accident. At the hospital sitting in her wheelchair, Jill struggled to get some potato chips from the bowl in her lap to her mouth. The feat accomplished, she proudly looked to her fiancé, waiting for his approval, but he looked at her in horror and said, "I thought you were going to show me that you could walk."

"I'm never going to walk," she reluctantly admitted to herself and to him, and when he left that day, he never returned. In my flashback, I remembered myself on the couch, sobbing at the sadness and hopelessness of the situation. I felt so utterly sorry for the woman whose promising future had been shattered. It seemed so unfair. *Oh, no,* I realized, *I'm just like Jill Kinmont!* The impact of this realization hit me like a brick shattering a windshield. Who would have thought as I watched that movie that I'd be in the same position now? I sat stunned.

Hospital life continued, and therapy was repetitious and monotonous. I had no movement below my upper chest, so there were very few things I could do. What little I could do I did over and over again—like two hundred shoulder shrugs at a time, and then the PT would say, "Okay, now let's do twenty-five more."

Many times I heard the French accent of Dr. Palmer saying, *You're never going to walk again, you're never going to sing again, you're never going to use your hands again.* So I'd think, *Why do this? It's not going to make any difference. If it's not going to change anything and give me the big stuff, then why do it?* But then I'd snap myself up short and think, *No! I can't let negativity take over. If the PT says the next twenty-five will help, then I'm going to do them!* I still thought I'd walk again, and walking again meant having my whole body back.

I still could not fathom how I could fall out of bed and end up like this, forever! Maybe if I had been hit by an eighteen wheeler, I wouldn't have expected to walk again. But to be paralyzed from falling out of a normal bed onto a carpeted floor? That just didn't seem logical. Still, I was in denial.

After lunch came recreational therapy, which I thought was a total waste of time. I knew why we were doing it—to learn ways to enjoy ourselves—but I would have preferred to do eight hours of PT and OT because I saw these as my highways to wholeness, to walking again. But I was a model patient; I did what I was told, assuming they were the experts and knew best. By using special equipment, a therapist taught us how to play cards and games.

The nurses always placed me beside a thirteen-year-old named David. Evidently they thought we might be good for each other. David was also a quad. He and his twin brother Daniel were junior lifeguards at Seal Beach. Dave dove in and hit his head on a sandbar, breaking his neck at the same place as mine. My teacher instincts kicked in, and my heart went out to him. He was quiet and withdrawn, and I made it my project to draw him out. "So, Dave. Did you ever think playing cards could be this complicated?" "Tell me about your friends." "What kind of music do you listen to?" He reminded me so much of one of my students.

In addition to therapy, we patients had counseling sessions together, and we got to know each other's story. Julie had turned down a marriage proposal from a boyfriend. Later that day he came to her house and shot her and then himself. He lived through it and has since been released from prison, but she was left paraplegic, sentenced to life in a wheelchair. The good news is that she is now a District Attorney in Long Beach.

Eldon was a character. When Mike, Denise, and Bev, my ICU nurse, visited Long Beach on a scouting expedition to locate the best rehab center, Eldon had Christmas lights on his halo. He made quite an impression. He broke his neck in a motorcycle accident. Although he had a serious, sensitive side, we could always count on him to keep things light for us.

Carl was an Asian man using an alias. After several weeks, he finally shared his story. He and his wife emigrated from Japan and started a nursery business in Riverside. Possessing an excellent work ethic and having their priorities in the right place, Carl and his wife used their money to fund their kids' education. When Carl was fifty and his kids had graduated from college, he decided to splurge for the first time in his life and buy the Corvette of his dreams. After he drove it for a year, his practical side kicked back in, and he decided to sell it. He ran an ad in the paper, and a young woman who identified herself as a college student called and made an appointment for her and her dad to come see it at 5:00 P.M. When the doorbell rang at the designated time and Carl opened the door, he was greeted by two gunmen who shoved him and his wife into the bedroom, tied them to the bedposts, put the mattress on top of them, and began shooting. His wife was killed, and Carl was left quadriplegic. All over a stupid car! I sobbed when I heard his story. "Oh, Carl, if I had my arms, I would hug you. I am so sorry!"

Mr. Ho was an older gentleman who had Guillain-Barré syndrome, a very painful, debilitating condition that attacks the nervous system without warning. I saw Mr. Ho sitting in his wheelchair at the piano, obviously suffering. "You're in a lot of pain, aren't you?" He broke down and cried. He had been a classical concert pianist, so the pain was not only physical but emotional. We cried together. The good news was that Guillain-Barré reaches a point and then reverses itself, so Mr. Ho eventually recovered completely.

One of the saddest cases was Dr. Richardson, a professor at the University of Southern California who had been a quadriplegic since his teens. Even though he was a quadriplegic, his break was low enough on the spine that he was able to drive. One day when he was on the lift getting into his van, the lift broke. He toppled off and sustained a brain injury, leaving this brilliant man, who had conquered insurmountable obstacles, with the intellectual capacity of a three-year-old.

The hospital was a scary place. The stroke victims' unit was right next to our spinal cord unit. Everywhere you looked, there were braces, hardware, wheelchairs, and broken bodies. I think most visitors had a hard time; anyone with any sense of compassion would. For most, looking past the wheelchair and seeing a real person who recently enjoyed a normal life is a learned ability. A few of my friends stayed away because they just couldn't handle it. Others came but looked neither right nor left so that they wouldn't have to see. Some eventually came to know and care about the other patients.

We did therapy five days a week and had weekends off. I hated the weekends because, as far as I was concerned, we were wasting time. In fact, I was scared of weekends because it felt like they robbed me of progress. I wanted to work seven days a week, because each day I worked meant I was a day closer to walking, to returning to normal life. The good news was that I had lots of visitors on the weekends.

One of God's greatest miracles through this whole thing was his provision for Mike's job. Mike had been working for Martin Marietta for just a few months before the accident. At the time the defense industry was in a bit of a recession, and his company was offering early retirement and laying off employees who had been there for years. Two days after my accident, Mike's boss, Don Petermann, flew to L.A. to cover a business trip that was supposed to have been Mike's responsibility. While in California, Don not only came to the hospital to see us, but he also said to Mike, "Don't worry about your job. We're going to take care of you." And they did.

The second part of this miracle is that while Martin Marietta was in a cut-back mode, the company actually created a job for Mike in California. Furthermore, Martin Marietta had only two west-coast locations; one was in northern California in Sunnyvale and the other was in Long Beach! His new office was just minutes from the hospital. God obviously orchestrated the whole thing. It was one of the first times I realized God is actively involved in the practical aspects of our lives.

Mike was by my side every day. He came to the hospital before work and fed me breakfast, came back to check on me at lunch, and then was back for the evening as soon as he got off work. He learned how to care for me and was partners with me in everything I did. When I was down, he lifted my spirits. If I wanted something, he got it. If I needed to vent, he understood. I wasn't always pleasant to be around, and I sure wasn't pretty to look at either.

God knew that Mike and I needed to be by each other's side if we were going to make it through this ordeal together. If he had told me on the phone from Denver that he still loved me, I wouldn't have trusted that. It's too easy to say things on the phone when you're not there to see the realities. Mike not only told me he loved me, he showed me he loved me— every single day. I could see his love for me in his eyes. He wasn't faking it. He wasn't guilt-ridden. He truly loved me, and I came to trust his love because his actions matched his words.

Mom came to the hospital every day; she just needed to be close. She watered the flowers and rearranged the bouquets, opened my mail, displayed the cards, scratched my nose. She was there and available for whatever I needed or wanted.

Michelle and Denise both had infants, but they took turns coming each afternoon and were usually the last to leave at night. I didn't mind when other visitors left, but it was hard when Michelle and Denise would go. As hard as I'd try not to, I'd tear up. Through their own tears they would try to smile as they waved good-bye from the door, but they told me later that they'd get down the hall, around the corner, and then break down. "Just rip my heart out and throw it on the floor!" Michelle cried out one night. This tragedy was incredibly hard on my entire family—not just me.

One day I was being taken from therapy back to my room and I saw a mirror. "Stop!" I said to the orderly. "Can you turn me so I can look at myself?" It was the first time I'd seen myself since the accident. I still had the halo on. I looked into the mirror and made faces. *Those are my eyes. That's my nose. I've lost weight; I like it—looks good. Oh, but my hair. I hate the way they've combed it back with no bangs. So this is what my visitors see when they come; they have to look through all this hardware.* I smiled at myself in the mirror and analyzed myself. *Okay, it's still me.* "Okay, I'm ready. Let's go," I said to the orderly. Sometimes it's good to stop and take stock—to consider not what has changed but what has remained stable. Whenever life seems to be falling in around us, it's reassuring to know that never is everything lost.

Visitors kept pouring in. Father Martin came every single Wednesday night—his only day off—for the entire five months that I was there. He'd stay from about 6:30 to 10:00. We'd talk about everything spiritual—Old Testament patriarchs and prophets, the miracles of Christ, the parables, spiritual warfare, the end times, healing, suffering. Sometimes our discussions would spring from questions Mike and I had, and sometimes our discussions would take us in unplanned directions. Often we'd hit on the obvious questions. I'd ask questions like, "Why did this happen? Why did God allow me to break my neck? Did he deliberately put me in this wheelchair? Why?"

Father Martin would shake his head. "I don't know, Renée. This one has me backed against the wall. I don't understand it, either. There are some things we're never going to understand this side of heaven. We just have to trust that God loves us and believe that he works all things together for our good. He's not going to waste your pain." That was probably the most honest and satisfying answer he could have offered. Both Mike and I loved our time with Father Martin. His consistency and care represented God's faithfulness to us.

My good friend Jim May, the wonderful pianist and arranger from Young Americans, came nearly every Monday on his day off. After tour, our paths had crossed a few times, and then one afternoon in 1980, eight years before the accident, we saw each other at a YA rehearsal. When I started to leave, he asked where I was going.

"To sing at church."

"How about if I go with you and play the piano?"

"But you're Jewish! Do you really want to play the piano at my church?"

"Sure. It'll be fun."

"That would be terrific!" So he went with me, and after that he came now and then to play at my church. Also, Jim became integrally involved in the groundwork for an album I was thinking about recording for church.

Over the years we had become good friends, so after the accident I was always really glad to see him. On one of his first visits, he walked in and sang out, "Hi, hon. How are you feeling today?" I just looked at him and raised an eyebrow.

"That just about sums it up!" We laughed. I usually tried not to complain, but every once in a while it just felt good, and Jim was a friend who would put up with it! "I saw a piano in the dining room. Let's get out of here."

We chatted and laughed as he rolled me down the hall, and then he sat down at the piano. He played so beautifully it was like warm oil covering my body. How I had missed it! Then he suggested, "Let's sing!" After all, that's what we did together; we sang!

"Jim, I really can't sing."

"Aw, come on. Let's give it a try." So he started off, "He will raise you up on eagle's wings, bear you on the breath of dawn . . . ," a song we had planned to put on the album.

I joined in as best I could, but the strain of sitting for so long and then singing was too much, and I started to feel faint. With the back of my head, I hit the trigger that lowered the backrest of my chair, reclined, and tried again. I was still woozy, so I reclined so that I was lying down completely. Jim continued to play while I got into position.

"Okay? One more time!" he said, smiling.

With some of the strain off, I attempted to sing again, but my voice was faint and breathy. I had no lung capacity or power, so I had to breathe every few notes. My pitch was good, but my voice had absolutely no force. Jim stopped playing and looked at me in dismay. Big tears welled up in his eyes. He left the piano bench, put his arm over me, buried his head beside my face in the pillow, and we both wept. He had not realized until then that I had not only lost the ability to move, I had also lost my voice. Maybe more than anyone else, Jim understood and shared my grief.

A couple of times Jennifer and Greg Lapp, friends from college, came all the way from Bakersfield, about 140 miles. Jennifer had a knack for finding thoughtful things to do. For example, she'd stop by the Hallmark store, buy cards, and then with pen in hand she'd say to me, "Okay, I'm sure there are people you want to write notes to." She held cards up to my eyes. "Pick the ones you like and tell me who you want to write to. Dictate what you want to say, and I'll do the writing and mail them on my way home. Or maybe you want to write a note to Mike and hide it somewhere in this room where he'll find it." So she'd write as long as I had messages. What a sweet idea!

I heard a story once about a family who received one of those dreaded phone calls; a grandparent had died in another state. As they were scurrying around, trying to get ready to fly out, a little old man from church carrying a box under his arm knocked on their back door. "I heard your sad news, and I wanted to help. If you'll gather up all your shoes, bring them to me, and find me a corner out of your way, I'll polish them for you." Gratefully, the family members responded, and soon the little man was kneeling on the kitchen floor with a pile of scuffed shoes in front of him. Later, the mom went into the kitchen and found that the little man had slipped out, leaving a row of gleaming shoes on the table. The family had received many phone calls from well-meaning friends who had offered, "Let me know if I can do anything." But this little man didn't wait. He had taken the next step by coming up with a practical way to help. It's tragic that we sometimes pass up opportunities to be helpful because we fear our gesture will be perceived to be insignificant, when in reality it would have been a gem. Jennifer's cards as well as the thoughtful actions of countless others were gems to me.

My high school friend Liz worked nearby and volunteered to come over to feed me my meals. She'd enter my room with a big smile, looking a little windblown because she'd ridden over on her moped. Sometimes she'd pick up my guitar and we'd sing "Hear, O Lord" and other songs from high school, which broke the monotony of the day. Mike and my family knew they could always depend on her.

Many people I didn't even know very well came, some regularly. Rick Delanty, the art teacher from school, stopped by one night. "If you could get out of here for the day," he said, knowing I wasn't allowed to leave, "where would you go?"

"Oh, to church! I would love to sit in the quietness with no one around, to pray at the altar, to feel God's presence there." Of course, I certainly didn't think God was only at church; nevertheless, there's a special awe that one feels in a sanctuary. How I missed church!

A few days later, Rick returned and unveiled a beautiful pen and ink sketch of our sanctuary, already framed. There were the arches, the altar, the pews, the cross. "Since you can't get to church right now, I thought I'd bring the church to you," he said. It was incredible, and I had it hung where

I could always see it. I was amazed at how creative people were in using their gifts and talents to make my life easier or happier.

The hospital chaplain came in almost every morning to bring me communion. One day she said, "Renée, let's pray."

Having difficulty coping with the day's challenges, I replied, "Oh, I can't even pray."

With her experience, she could instantly see I was at the end of my rope, truly depressed. "Okay," she said slowly. "Let's reduce this to the simplest denominator. Breathe in. Say, 'Jesus.' Breathe out. Say 'mercy.'"

As she guided me, I complied. "Breathe in. 'Jesus.' Breathe out. 'Mercy.' 'Jesus.' 'Mercy.'" It kept my mind from going to worse places and reminded me of God's presence. Sometimes when our hearts and minds are full and our bodies are exhausted, we need to reduce our prayer to the simplest of conversation with God. He hears and understands even that. Even now, I pray this prayer when I'm having an exceptionally tough day.

Insomnia was a continuing problem, so the doctor prescribed halcion as a sedative. One morning at 4:00 A.M., I had a full-blown anxiety attack—acute claustrophobia. I thought if I didn't get out of that hospital, I'd suffocate. I hit the call button with my head. "Get me out of here! Get me outside! I've got to have fresh air! Somebody get me *out of here!*" The nurses came running and tried to calm me down, but I was in a frenzy of hysteria, and nothing they said made any difference. Finally, they rolled me down the hall and outside where I could see the sky, breathe the fresh, crisp air, and feel the breeze on my face. That was all I needed. No more halcion for me!

Sleepless nights would have been a perfect time to talk to God, but I couldn't. I was too far down to be capable of reaching up. I never doubted that God was there, but I had no success in talking to him for very long. I'd wake up in the early morning hours, and I'd start praying, but my mind would do flip-flops. "Lord, I don't know what is going on, but this is big. Lord, this is really big. I don't understand why I'm here in this hospital instead of out teaching my kids, leading worship at church, getting ready to marry Mike." *Mike. How can he stay with me? I'm not the woman he was going to marry. I can't be a normal wife. I doubt that I can even give him children.* "Father, can you just heal me? You've got the power; You've got the miracles, Lord. Heal me, Lord. I need to walk again! I can't spend the rest of my life in that chair!" *Mom and Dad. Ugh. They looked awful when they came in last night—so tired and sad. This is very hard on them.* "Lord, if it's not Your will to heal me, then please take the pain away. Please just take the pain away, Lord." *My students. My kids. Who's going to teach them? What's going to happen to the program I worked so hard to build?* "I'm really sorry, Lord. I'm trying to be with you here."

It is no exaggeration, and it's not something I'm proud of, but in those early morning hours, I could not pray for more than ten seconds before my mind would go somewhere—to the dripping of the IV, the voices of the nurses at their stations, the footsteps coming down the hallway. One night in the wee morning hours when I was trying to pray, into my head popped words from a song I'd sung many times as the music director at church.

Be not afraid. I go before you always.
Come, follow me, and I will give you rest.

I thought, *Hmmmmmmm.*

If you pass through raging waters in the sea,
you shall not drown.
If you walk amid the burning flames,
you shall not be harmed.
If you stand before the power of hell
and death is at your side,
know that I am with you through it all.

Really?

Blessed are your poor
for the kingdom shall be theirs.
Blessed are you that weep and mourn, for one day
you shall laugh.

Right. I'm really going to laugh this way. I can't even move!

Be not afraid. I go before you always.
Come, follow me, and I will give you rest.

And then, a couple of nights later, in the early morning hours when it was just me and the Lord—everybody else was gone—the words to this song, which I had also sung hundreds of times, came into my head.

You who dwell in the shelter of the Lord,
who abide in his shadow for life,
say to the Lord: "My refuge,
my rock in whom I trust!"

And he will raise you up on eagle's wings,
bear you on the breath of dawn,
make you to shine like the sun,
and hold you in the palm of his hand.

I wasn't just remembering words to some songs; what I was hearing didn't come from my memory. The music came from my soul! It was as though the words bypassed my mind and were being played like a recording to my heart. God was talking to me! *Be not afraid, Renée. I go before you always, Renée. Come follow me, and I will give you rest. I will make you shine like the sun! I will be with you through it all! I will hold you in the palm of my hand! I will raise you up on eagle's wings!" Not some little wussy bird! Not some San Juan Capistrano swallow! On eagle's wings!*

In her book *Just Give Me Jesus*, Anne Graham Lotz explains one of the differences between turkeys and eagles. "A turkey and an eagle react in different ways to the threat of a storm.

A turkey reacts by running under the barn, hoping the storm won't come near it. On the other hand, an eagle leaves the security of its nest and spreads its wings to ride the air currents of the approaching storm, knowing the wind will carry it higher in the sky than it could soar on its own." Using this song, God was encouraging me to allow the storms of my life—my paralysis—to send me soaring higher than I would have without the storm! It seemed impossible.

Music had always been my lifeline to God, and now God was using music to speak to me! How wise of him to speak to me in my own language! I was learning things about God that I hadn't known before. Reflecting on past months, I could see God's hand—Dorothy finding me when I could have lain on the floor for hours, Mike's company transferring him to Long Beach, the songs in the middle of the night. God was watching over me! For the first time I was beginning to trust that God was really going to take care of me—in practical ways as well as spiritual ones. I knew I was going to be okay, even though the definition of "okay" had changed dramatically.

Another of God's signs to me occurred a few days later when a church member came in carrying two posters. Remembering that "Be Not Afraid" and "On Eagle's Wings" were two songs I often sang at church but not knowing God had been speaking to me through them, she wrote the words of those songs on posterboard and attached them to the ceiling right above my bed. They were the first thing I saw when I woke up in the morning, and I could see them during those sleepless nights when I lay alone in bed with God and my thoughts. The world might say, "What a coincidence that the lady chose those songs!" But I knew God was speaking to me, sending me a message. *Look how much I care, Renée. I sent a lady to hang the words right where you can see them, so that you won't be afraid or discouraged. My love and protection are with you. Trust me.*

I was beginning to realize God cared for me in a far more personal and practical way than I had ever imagined. I knew he cared enough to die on the cross; now I was realizing he cared enough to take care of me moment by moment.

7

Setbacks and Comebacks

About three months after I arrived at Long Beach, I got my first self-propelled wheelchair, the sip-n-puff. It was this huge, honkin' monstrosity that sat high up off the ground and had a huge headrest, big troughs for my feet and arms, big tires and big wheels, a big motor on the back, and lateral supports on each side that fit under my arms so that I wouldn't fall over. Everything about it was big, clumsy, and ugly. There was a straw-like plastic tube that came from the motor, up the back of the chair, and around to the front, so I constantly had this tube in front of my face. Sipping and puffing into the straw allowed me to control the acceleration of the chair.

My first day in it, Therese took me to a long, wide, hospital corridor to learn how to maneuver the monster. She had a remote control in her hand with a cord attached to the chair. I felt like a little remote car by Mattel.

She showed me that she could override me at any time, so I was safe. I thought that was unnecessary. *How hard can it be?* I thought.

"If you 'puff' into the straw," she explained, "you will move forward. If you 'sip' in the air, it will stop. Let's just try it." We practiced a few times, but somehow the actions that went with "puff" and "sip" just didn't automatically compute. Nevertheless, I was ready to go—or so I thought.

"Okay," Therese said. "Puff."

"Puff?"

"Blow!"

"Oh! Blow! Okay." So I blew, and off I went, but toward the wall!

"Sip, Renée! Sip!"

"Sip?"

"Sip in the air!" So I sipped and *voila!* I slowed down.

"Blow, Renée!" And off I went.

As I picked up speed, I started getting the giggles. My cartoon brain completely took over and the Eveready Bunny was on the loose. The more I laughed, the faster the chair moved. Therese had failed to tell me that multiple sips kicked the chair into a higher speed! In seconds, I was flying down the hallway with huge tears of laugher. Totally out of control I watched the horrified faces of nurses and doctors as they jumped out of my way and pulled medical carts to safety. Finally, Therese was able to stop the chair. I think I set a record at Long Beach Memorial that day. To my knowledge, the record still holds. Three carts, two orderlies, and one nurse.

You would think I'd be thrilled to have a chair so that now I could propel myself, but I wasn't. Being in an ugly, unwieldy wheelchair was not my goal. Walking was my goal. I saw the chair as a necessary evil on the way to walking again. It was temporary. I certainly wasn't going to be in that ugly thing for long!

One day a friend and fellow choir teacher, Karen Gauen, came for a visit. I still could speak in little more than a whisper. As we were talking, I noticed she was watching my stomach.

"Karen, what are you doing?"

"I'm watching your breathing pattern. You've got to sing again, Renée. You've just got to sing." As a vocalist herself, she knew that my air supply would be critical.

"What muscles are you using?"

"I have no idea. I can't feel a thing, but something must be working; otherwise, I'd be on a ventilator."

She returned the next day with a weight. She figured the best way to strengthen my diaphragmatic muscle was to make it work harder, so she put a three-pound weight on my diaphragm. From that day forward, I would make sure someone put the weight on me every day, and she continued to increase the weight until I got up to fifty-five pounds! The idea didn't come from a doctor or out of Johns Hopkins, so I think most therapists were skeptical of the value of these weights, but I'm convinced Karen's therapy was instrumental in my vocal power today.

Having endured my halo (who the heck named it that?) for about three months, I was eager to get it off, and several times I had discussed the possibility of removing it with Dr. Parsons, my doctor at Long Beach. He had targeted a few dates but then changed them. One day he walked in and announced, "Good news! Today is your lucky day! We're going to take your halo off!"

Suddenly, I wasn't so sure I wanted it off. I certainly didn't want to endure it being taken off, but my main fear was of the results once it was gone. This contraption had supported my neck for some ten weeks. My neck muscles had not been used at all; I imagined them to be like rubber—incapable of holding the weight of my head. I had this mental picture of the doctors removing my halo and my head flopping over, snapping off my shoulders, and rolling across the floor. Plus, I had experienced so much pain. Every procedure, every movement, every device was painful, and I had had about all I thought I could take.

I was so glad Denise was with me. Dr. Parsons explained the procedure and then reached to start removing the halo, and I just freaked! My eyes got big, and I recoiled in fear.

Dr. Parsons stopped. "What's wrong?"

"Is it going to hurt? Is that pain going to come back? Is my neck going to hold up my head? I don't think it will. It feels so weak! I know I'm supposed to trust you, but I don't think this is a good idea. Let's just leave it on until my neck gets stronger."

"I'm going to numb you, so after that it shouldn't hurt at all," he tried to reassure me. "And as soon as we get the halo off, we'll put on a neck brace to support your neck." I studied the doctor's matter-of-fact demeanor.

Denise and the other nurses in the room all looked completely calm. I was the only one freaking out, so I started collecting my courage, knowing I had to push through. I had tears rolling down my cheeks. *I'm going to do this. I have to do it, so I'm going to do it.* "Okay, Doctor, go ahead. I'm ready. I can do this."

To distract myself, I started humming and soon Denise jumped on the same melody. As they removed the device piece by piece, Denise and the doctors kept a steady stream of reassurance coming my way. After only a few minutes, Dr. Parsons stepped back. "Okay, it's off and your neck brace is on."

"Can I turn my head?"

"Sure, go ahead. Try it," Dr. Parsons replied. So I very slowly turned my head just a tiny bit to the left. It worked! With no pain! So I turned it a little more, which was as far as the brace would permit. Still no pain. Then I did the same thing to the right, and again it worked! I had been in such a state of terror, and now I found that my fear was for nothing—silly, really—so that I let out a giggle. I lay back on the pillow, relieved that another ordeal was behind me. I was one giant step closer to walking out of there.

On the morning of the day that was to have been our wedding day, Mike came in and confronted what we were both thinking. "This isn't where we thought we'd be today, is it?"

It was one of those "Oh well, what can you do?" moments. He took me out of the hospital for the first time; we had a three-hour furlough, which was hard to come by. We didn't have time to drive down to church, so we went to a beautiful botanical garden. Mike thought I'd enjoy getting some sun, and he brought a picnic lunch for us. He pushed me in a manual wheelchair to see all the flowers, then when it was lunchtime, he lifted me out and sat me on the grass. He propped me against him and fed me lunch while he ate his. It was quiet and peaceful; we were together, and we were out of that depressing hospital. Feeling the sun and the breeze on my face was more wonderful than I can describe. I noticed again that life had gone on quite nicely without me. We both tried to put the realities of the hospital out of our minds, to avoid thinking about what today would have been and just enjoy the moment. It was a good time.

All too soon it was time to go back, and suddenly Mike realized we had a problem. How was he going to get me back into the chair? The hospital staff had not yet trained him in how to do transfers from the ground, so it was just trial and error and brute strength. Ever try to lift 125 pounds of dead weight? We laughed as he tried several different options before he clumsily pulled and lifted and got me seated in the wheelchair again.

When he returned me to the car seat, I began to feel dizzy, so he leaned the seat back until I was feeling better. Mike was sitting on the car jam with the door open, and we were just chatting and enjoying being alone. Then Mike got romantic for a minute, and he leaned over and kissed me, a sweet, lingering kiss. As we were kissing, suddenly I broke it off. "Uh-oh! Uh-oh!" Mike pulled away with a puzzled look on his face. "Mike, sit me up! Quick! Get me up! Hurry!" Just as he got me upright, I fell sideways and barfed out the open door all over the grass. After a few heaves he teased, "Glad to see my kisses still turn you on!"

The lowest point came the end of July when I developed a blood clot in my leg and had to be transferred from the

Spinal Cord Unit up to Critical Care. The blood clot was serious. If it broke loose and went to my lungs, heart, or brain, I'd be dead. The three weeks I was there seemed like months. I was losing time, and I wasn't getting any better. What's worse, the staff in Critical Care weren't trained in caring for spinal cord patients, so while they were sweet and meant well, they were clumsy with me. Life was difficult. I became very depressed.

One day when I was particularly disagreeable, Denise and Mike went out in the hallway while a nurse attended my needs. Denise told Mike, "You don't have to stay, Mike. We'll all understand. If you go, she still has us. You don't have to worry because we'll be here to take care of her. Nobody's going to hold it against you or blame you if you can't go through with this. We'll all understand if you want to leave."

Mike responded, "Oh, no. Don't you start, too! Doesn't anybody understand? I'm not here out of any sense of obligation. I'm here because this is where I want to be. I love Renée. That hasn't changed, and it's not going to!" What Denise didn't know was that Michelle and Dad had already talked to Mike privately and made the same offer. When I found out about it, I was grateful my family had given Mike permission to leave. It was amazing that they could unselfishly make him such an offer and equally amazing that he would unselfishly stay.

On a Sunday afternoon during that time, Michelle, Denise, and Mom came in more cheery than usual, and the last thing I wanted that day was cheer. They were chirping all around and fussing over me saying, "Let's comb your hair and put on some makeup and lipstick. Let's put your pretty afghan over you. You'll feel so much better if you'll let us fix you up a bit."

"I don't want my hair combed and I don't want makeup and I don't want that stupid afghan. I just want to be left alone! I know you're trying to help, but can't you just sit down and be still?" They completely ignored my protests and enthusiastically went about improving my appearance, all the time laughing and joking and being all happy. They were really getting on my nerves.

Then an orderly came in with the ultimate bad news. "We're going to take you to X ray." Oh, how I hated X rays. It was frightening because it meant more pain. Being transferred from the bed to the gurney, from the gurney to the X ray table, from the X ray table back to the gurney, the gurney back to the bed—it jostled my neck and was very painful. In my depressed state, I just could not handle an X ray.

"On Sunday?!" I protested. "Since when do I have to be X-rayed on Sunday?"

"I don't make the decisions. I just carry out orders. Let's go." So they transferred me to the gurney and started out the door when Mike came in.

"Where are you going?"

"To X ray. Can you believe they're doing this to me on Sunday?"

"I'll go, too." So he grabbed the IV stand and trailed along and, with Denise, Michelle, and Mom by my side, down the hall our entourage went.

Suddenly I heard music. "The sun is bright and bells are ringing . . ."

"Oh listen," I whispered to Michelle, who happened to be the closest. "They're playing 'Russian Picnic' on Muzak. That's weird. I taught that to my students!" As we rolled on down the hall, the music got louder and louder. Instead of going to X ray, the orderly wheeled me into the lobby. As we turned the corner, there in front of me were all 150 of my kids smiling and singing! I was absolutely flabbergasted! When I saw their beautiful faces, I burst into tears. There were kids everywhere—sitting on the backs of couches, on windowsills, on the floor. Some with big smiles, some with tears rolling down their cheeks, some looking a little apprehensive. Because I was so stunned, I gasped for air, and Denise slapped an oxygen mask over my nose and mouth. Bob Perry, the youth director who helped me get my music program going, was conducting, and he asked with his eyes, "Is she okay? Do we need to stop?"

Denise waved him on, moving her mouth so he could read her lips. "She's okay. Keep going." They did a full-blown concert for me, singing the songs we had learned together, even Brahms! It warmed my heart to see them all, to hear them sing, to know they cared enough to do this just for me. And it was fun to see their excitement at being able to give. It was one of the most special, most touching moments of my life.

They had this planned for weeks. Someone had the idea, and Bob Perry volunteered to rehearse and direct them. Then I almost blew it when I got the blood clot. I was unaware of it of course, but everyone was uncertain about whether my doctor would allow the concert. My condition was touch-and-go, and he feared I wasn't up to it. But Denise persuaded him saying, "We have to look after her emotional health as well as her physical health, and she needs this right now. And it can't happen any other day; parents have switched their vacation plans, students have arranged to be off work. We can't possibly get everybody together again in the middle of summer. This is the only day! I'll be right with her and I'll watch her, and if there's any sign that we're overdoing it, I'll immediately take her back to her room."

He allowed it only because Denise was a nurse.

I was told my students were very upset by my accident. It was unnerving to them to think that someone young like me could suddenly be paralyzed. Kids think they and everyone they love are invincible, immune to disaster, and when it smacks them in the face, it's hard for them to deal with. A wise group of parents decided the best way for the kids to cope with my tragedy would be to find ways for the kids to help me. Rally 'Round Renée was born, a support group of parents and students established to help me in practical ways. For starters, every week they sent a beautiful bouquet of fresh flowers to my hospital room and often visited me in the hospital during rehab. When I was released, their love and support provided many important services. They were a sustaining force in my recovery.

Not long after the concert, Jim Krembas, my principal, came walking in with a young woman. "Renée, I'd like you to meet Julie Barron. Since you're not going to be able to come back as soon as we had hoped, we've hired Julie to be the new choir teacher at San Clemente." There was an awkwardness. Normally we would have shaken hands, but of course I couldn't. "I thought it might be nice for you to see who's going to be walking in your big footsteps this year. I've told her what an excellent program you had going."

I was struggling to react positively. Looking at her was almost like looking in a mirror. Same dark hair. About the same age. Energetic. They pulled their chairs close to my bed, and the three of us talked about the school and the program for about forty-five minutes. I knew Jim was trying to make me feel included, to keep me in the loop, and Julie was pleasant and showed sincere interest in my input. But I did not want to come face-to-face with my replacement. It was like meeting an ex-husband's new fiancée. The marriage was over, and the divorce papers were signed. It was the slap of another colossal loss.

When at last they walked out the door, the dam broke, and I released the tears I had been holding back. Why does life insist on going on when you hurt so much? Shouldn't it stop to wait for you to catch up?

After days of inactivity due to the blood clot, I was relieved when they moved me back to the Spinal Cord Injury Unit where I could work and get stronger. One Monday morning, however, my nurse came in and said, "You won't be going to therapy this morning. You have the beginning of a pressure sore on your bottom, and you need to stay off it. The doctor will be in later to talk to you about it." I don't think she wanted to be the one to tell me how long I'd have to be away from therapy.

When Dr. Parsons came by, he told me I couldn't be in my chair for probably three weeks.

"Three weeks!" I was shocked. "Why so long?"

"These things are serious, and once they get started, you have to take care of them. The only way it will heal is for you to avoid sitting on it."

I had been the model patient. I had done everything they asked, and still I got a blood clot and had to be immobilized for what seemed an eternity. Now another setback was being shoved in my face, and my frustration level started rising. Between my disbelief that it would take three weeks to heal and my confidence that I could find a way around this, I calmly suggested, "How about if I just go to PT for a short time each day in the mornings? Then I'll come back and get in bed for the afternoon. That couldn't do any damage, could it?"

"No. You must stay off it."

"How about just an hour? At least I'd get a little exercise each day. And I'll sit on a pad. I know that couldn't hurt."

"No." He was a brick wall. I couldn't deal with another setback, especially one that would immobilize me for weeks! My tolerance snapped.

"It's really easy for you to sit there and tell me that, isn't it? You get to stand up and walk out of here. You have just sentenced me to another three weeks of doing nothing but lying in this bed, and you don't even care. For just one day I want you to try lying in this bed. I want somebody to strap you down where you can't even wiggle your toes so you can see what it's like. I want you to have to let someone else wipe your bottom and feed you your food and not be able to move. Just try it for one day if you've got the guts. Then you'll see how incredibly difficult this is, and you won't sit there without feeling anything when you tell me I've got to lie here for *three more weeks!*"

That was one of the few times I unleashed my frustration on the hospital staff. Dr. Parsons just sat and listened as I tore into him. Then he gently said, "I do care, and I *am* sorry, but that's just the way it has to be." He added in his usual pleasant voice, "Okay, I've got to finish my rounds. I'll see you tomorrow." And with that, he got up and walked out.

I was more than furious. Hot tears of frustration and disappointment spilled out of my eyes, and I couldn't even wipe them away. I had hit a force I could not budge, and it slammed me against the wall. I wanted to pick up something breakable and hurl it at the door after him, but I couldn't even do that! I had no choice and oh, how I hated having no choice.

For three weeks I lay there while nurses turned me from one side to the other so that the pressure spot would heal and so that others would not develop. I learned that fighting didn't change a thing or help in any way, so I came to accept my confinement. I was determined, however, that even though I'd lost this battle, I would not lose the war. I would walk out of there!

One Saturday afternoon the nurse came in and warned me, "Renée, there are carloads of kids headed this way. Do you want me to let them all come in at once?" For some reason the thought of a crowd made me self-conscious about my appearance. "Hold them up a minute," I told her. "I need to get ready!"

I told Mike, "Honey, could you please get me my blush out of that pink makeup bag over there on the counter?" I could see that he was nervous. "Please just get my blush and put a little on me. Hurry! Hurry! The kids are going to be here in a minute, and I don't want them to see me looking all pale."

Mike went in the right direction, but he continued to look nervous. He'd learned my care, watched them drill holes in my head, and seen me pass out and throw up time after time—all with apparent nerves of steel. Now he was nervous about getting my blush? He shakily opened the makeup case and pulled out the mascara. "Is this the blush?"

After I stopped laughing, I realized there was nothing I could do. I wanted to look good for my students partly because of pride and partly to make them feel more comfortable, but there was nothing I could do. There was no place to hide, not even behind makeup. I felt totally exposed. With a sigh I realized they were going to have to accept me as I was, so I resigned to the inevitable and told the nurse to send them in. This wasn't a battle I had fought and won for good. It was a struggle I'd repeat over and over and over again.

Mike knew how desperately I wanted to go to church, so he finally managed to get a furlough for me on a Sunday afternoon. As we drove down the freeway toward San Juan Capistrano, I could hardly wait. It was like the anticipation of seeing a dear friend I hadn't seen in years. That's the way I felt on the way to church. I always wear my emotions on my sleeve, so when the church came into view, I began to cry. I had been hungry to sit alone in front of my Lord. Yes, I could sit alone with God in the hospital, but it just wasn't the same. We all have our holy places, and mine was church. I had gone to school here, worshipped here, taught school here, and led worship here. This church had played a vital role in every phase of my life. Being back was like sitting at a feast. *Lord, it's so good to be home.*

About four weeks from my discharge, the question of where I would live came up. My parents' house and my brother's and sisters' houses were not accessible to wheelchairs at all, so my parents graciously offered to buy me a condo. They, Mike, and my sisters started the search. They quickly learned that finding a place that can accommodate a wheelchair is not all that easy! Real estate was moving quickly, time was short, and when they didn't find something right away, they started to get discouraged.

However, they worked with a realtor who was a family friend, and she found a place in San Clemente. When Mom and Dad went to look at it, they knew immediately it was perfect. As quickly as they could, they gathered the rest of the family to go see it and pass approval. Mike was with me in my hospital room when the phone rang, and we turned on the speaker so we could both hear.

Denise didn't even say hello. "Okay, Renée. We are standing in a condo in San Clemente. Let me walk you through it. Picture this. Walk through the front door. Really airy. Lots of windows that look out onto the front so you can see who's coming. When you walk in, straight ahead is the living room. To the right there is a little office that could be your music room. Renée, it's by far the best we've seen so far." I could sense the urgency in her voice and knew we were headed toward a decision.

"Okay, thanks. Now put Michelle on the phone. Michelle, what's your take?"

"There's a deck where you can roll out and sit in the sun. It's got a great backyard," Michelle told me. "And there's two bedrooms—a large one with a double door for you and a smaller one perfect for your attendant."

"Great. Now put Mom on the phone. Mom, what do you think of it?"

"There's a little courtyard in front, a place to plant roses. And it's clean, really clean. Just like new. And we met the neighbors. Connie on the right is a singer; she does musical theater. And the ones on the left are very nice. They came over to meet us."

"Wow. Okay, Mom, thanks. Put Dad on."

When I heard Dad's voice, I could tell immediately that he was choked up but trying valiantly not to cry.

"Renée?"

"Hi, Dad." Mike and I both reacted to my dad's emotion by starting to cry as well.

"Renée . . . it's perfect," he choked out. I could tell that was all he could say. Remember, Dad was the strong rancher, the WWII vet, and his was the John Wayne era. Real men didn't cry. I don't know that I'd ever heard or seen my dad cry before. The closest to tears I'd ever seen him was when I was in the ICU just after we'd received the awful news about the extent of my injury. Now, hearing him break on the phone, I realized the extent of pressure and pain he had been feeling while trying to find the perfect place. Having been powerless to prevent the accident or to put my body back together, my dad desperately wanted to provide a place for me—to make it as right as he could. When they looked and looked and came up short, I think he was concerned that he wasn't going to be able to take care of me. And now that he had found a home for me, relief came out in the form of tears.

"Then go for it, Dad."

"Mike, do you want to come down and take a look at it before we decide for sure?"

"Oh, no" Mike responded. "I don't need to see it. If you all like it, I'm sure Renée will love it."

As my release date approached, the staff started training Michelle, Denise, and Mike in my care—how to empty my bladder, evacuate my bowel, and how to transfer me from the bed to the wheelchair or the wheelchair to the bed. This was no easy task, as Michelle learned the first time we tried it. With Therese giving directions and standing behind Michelle to spot her in case she fell, Michelle crouched down in front of my chair, put my legs through her legs so she was holding my legs in her thighs and her hands were free. Still crouched down and bent at the knees, she then got very close to me and leaned me over her shoulder, placing my limp arms around her neck and her arms around my waist. Always a little self-conscious about her hips, Michelle quipped, "Hey, Therese! Think my rear end could look any bigger?" That started the laughter. Michelle secured her arms around my waist and started rocking: one, two, shifting the weight of my body to her legs. On three, she pivoted, and as she did she groaned like she was hoisting a Redwood!

She slung me onto the bed where I landed in a heap, face down, and she fell face down beside me, both of us laughing hysterically. "Houston, we have a problem!" she announced. I think we all learned that the best way to get through these situations was to keep our sense of humor. It was not a time to be taking ourselves too seriously.

But soon the tears needed to come. The day I left the hospital was one of the saddest days of our lives. Mike and I both had thought I'd walk out of Long Beach Memorial. Instead, I rolled out in my sip-n-puff. Reality hit like a thunderbolt. This was it. I knew that outside a miracle, I'd never walk again. I'd be in a wheelchair for the rest of my life. I would always be dependent on someone else to take care of my needs. I'd never drive a car or ride a horse or sign my name to a check or run on the beach. No more singing. No more teaching. No more directing. Hope was gone and the future was dim. What on earth was I going to do with the rest of my life? We rode in silence, each lost in our own thoughts. With Mike's hand on my shoulder, I cried all the way to my new home.

8

Released
to Prison

Somewhere near the end of our one-hour trip down the freeway, I exhausted my supply of tears. Feeling like a baby bird
that had just been shoved out of the nest and couldn't fly, I
was absolutely terrified about what the future held. I was out
of the hospital, but I was living in the prison of my motion-
less body. The thought of resuming life with no body was too
overwhelming to imagine. But as we neared San Clemente,
I was able to distract myself from my anxieties somewhat
when my curiosity kicked in, and I started to get interested
in seeing the new condo.

As we drove into the area, I noticed how clean, fresh, and
new the houses and condominiums looked. Although it was
getting dark by this time, I could still see the white buildings
with slate-blue trim. Flowers were blooming in the yards and
there were lots of trees and grassy areas; the whole complex
looked pleasant and inviting.

Mike parked the car and transferred me into my new manual wheelchair. He wanted me to have the benefit of seeing

my new home from the front door (it didn't matter that the garage entrance was more convenient), so he wheeled me up the front walk, through the gate into the small courtyard area, and to the front door. Denise opened the door and cheerily sang out, "Hi! Welcome home!"

Everything was already in place. My family had completely moved me. My furniture was there and perfectly arranged, the dishes were in the cupboards, the pictures were on the walls (including my favorite posters of the Oregon Bach Festival), curtains were on the windows, my knick-knacks were attractively displayed, and the flowers from my hospital-room boutique were already there. Also, many well-wishers had sent plants and bouquets, so the whole place not only looked like a model home, but also smelled like a florist shop! Having my family around me, seeing all my familiar things, and feeling the outpouring of love expressed in the flowers helped ease my pain and gave me a sense of home.

Wisely, my family had talked it over and decided not to throw a party or invite a crowd of people. After a little while, Mike leaned down and whispered, "I hope you don't mind that we didn't plan a big party. We didn't know how you'd react, and we didn't want you to have to buck up and feign smiles all evening. We just wanted you to relax."

"What you did was perfect," I responded. "I just want to be with you and my family."

It was a loud evening with everyone trying to make this as happy a day for me as possible. There were no whispered voices; this wasn't a funeral. My brother Danny comically informed me, "Renée, you need to know this is absolutely the last time I'm moving that piano!" But under all the frivolity was an unspoken undercurrent of fear. Were we ready for this? Could we really pull this off?

The hospital had been safe—not fun, but safe. I knew what the schedule was each day, and there were trained professionals taking care of my needs. It was their business to anticipate problems and prevent them. If there was ever an emergency, I knew I'd be surrounded in a matter of seconds by hospital personnel who knew just what to do. Plus, in the hospital, I didn't have to face the "normal" world. Others in the hospital were like me; we all had severe paralysis due to spinal cord injury. There is a certain security to being with others like yourself. Now I'd be out in public, mingling with "normal" people.

Mike and my family were equally uncertain. How were we going to do this? Did we have the knowledge we needed to take care of me? Nobody except Denise was a professional; they had only the training they'd received in the hospital. What about emergencies? Did they know what to do if I caught a cold and couldn't cough hard enough to expel the phlegm that was blocking my air passages? What if we didn't recognize the signs of dysreflexia, a serious condition resulting from distention of body organs, like the bladder and bowels, that could actually be fatal?

Equally important was the reality that I had to be taken care of every single day. I could not be left alone. I had to be physically put to bed and gotten up. I had to be bathed and dressed. My teeth had to be brushed and my hair combed. Someone had to prepare food and help me eat. If I needed something, someone had to bring it to me. I couldn't go anywhere unless I was driven, and there was physical therapy three times a week. It was like taking care of a thirty-year-old baby! I was an enormous, time-consuming obligation.

While my family wanted to be there for me, they had lives, families, and jobs of their own. Denise had recently announced that she was pregnant with their second child, so her lifting abilities would soon be curtailed. Just how much could I expect, and how much could they give? And Mike? He was there as much as possible, but how long was he going to be willing to spend his time and energy doing for me what any other woman could do for herself?

The day after I got home, I said to Mike, "Okay, first things first. Take these lateral supports off my wheelchair." The laterals were big, black, cloddy-looking constraints that were attached to the side of my wheelchair and fit up underneath my arms to hold me in place.

"No!" Mike protested. "Those laterals keep you from falling from side to side. Without them, you'd flop over like a Raggedy Ann doll."

"Don't worry. I'm not going to do anything stupid, and I'm not trying to be some valiant, superwoman from the movies. I just want to take off as much of this hardware as possible. Please let me just try."

Against his better judgment, he got the screwdriver and pliers and unscrewed the laterals. When they were off, I told him to push me to the side. He did, and I tried to right myself. I thought that maybe if I used my shoulder muscle to fling my arm out and over, that the weight and the momentum would pull me up. Wrong. However, we did discover that there was no way I was going to fall out. The arms on the wheelchair were high enough that I just couldn't possibly upend myself and topple out. "The worst thing I can do is fall to the side and not be able to get back up, but someone is always here; I'm never alone. So let's just try it for a couple of days and see how it goes." The restraints stayed off.

Until we could interview and hire an attendant, Denise, Michelle, and Mike joined forces. Then we found Yvette, and she was exactly what I needed. She was a breath of fresh air—a pretty, dark-haired twenty-one-year-old who was funny and optimistic. I liked her immediately. She was already trained in spinal cord injury care, but such training is general, so each aide has to be trained in the specific care of her client. Yvette seemed to sense my moods and needs and responded in a way that made me comfortable and reassured.

One of the most discouraging realities was the realization that it took a minimum of three hours to get out of the bedroom every morning. This was the absolute fastest it could be done. Often it was four hours and sometimes longer than that! First there was about thirty minutes of physical therapy—range-of-motion exercises, which stretched my body so that my limbs would remain flexible and not atrophy. At the time, I had a leg bag connected to an indwelling catheter to empty my bladder, so the nighttime bag had to be replaced with the daytime bag.

Next, my attendant transferred me from the bed into the shower chair. The first order of bathroom business was evacuation of my bowel. Without getting too graphic, I will tell you that the whole thing was completely degrading. I mean, who wants company in the bathroom while tending to business? And then there's the time it takes.

My bathroom needs accomplished, it was time for my shower. I sat there stark naked—tummy bulging, breasts flopping, arms hanging useless by my side while Yvette shampooed my hair and washed every part of my body—no matter how private. I couldn't salvage even a modicum of modesty. From my low position in the chair, the steady stream of water from the normal shower nozzle would have hit me right in the face, so we had a hand-held nozzle on a hose. Because my body's thermostat doesn't work properly (another side effect of quadriplegia), I'm always cold, so having the warm water run over only one part of my body at a time left me wet and chilled.

My attendants always seemed to bathe me with elaborate care. They washed between each toe, shaved my legs and underarms, spent several minutes soaping my back, and I couldn't feel any of it. All this detail seemed so unnecessary, and so time consuming! Sometimes I'd get impatient and instruct, "Don't give me the shower you'd give me if I were going to the prom; just give me the shower you'd take if you were late to work!" Of course, my attendants always complied and tried to please me, but then I'd sit and feel guilty for the next half hour wondering if I had snapped at them or hurt their feelings or if they'd quit and leave me with no attendant. When they rolled me out of the shower, they covered me in towels, transferred me to the bed, dried me off, and put my diaper on.

One day when Denise was being my caregiver, she headed back to the bathroom uttering, "Oops, forgot the diaper." When she returned, I was in tears. "What's wrong?"

"I hate that word. I absolutely *hate* that word!"

"Diaper?"

"Yes!"

"Got it," she replied. Thinking, she picked up the box and read the brand name. "This is an Attend. From now on, we'll call them Attends!"

Next task: getting me dressed. First my attendant had to put on my pants, and I was dead weight lying on the bed. If you wonder how it's done, trust me, there's no secret shortcut. Michelle or Denise or Yvette—whoever it was—would just push and pull. Roll me over on one side and pull. Roll me over on the other side and pull. Get on the bed and straddle me—bounce, bounce, yank, and wiggle until the pants were into place. When the pants were up, we were ready for the sip-n-puff. They would physically lift me from the bed and transfer me into the wheelchair, and then put my bra and shirt on.

One thing I really missed that may seem ridiculous was not getting to try on a bunch of clothes. Typically a woman will put on an outfit, check herself in the mirror, make a face, and exclaim, "I look like a sack of potatoes!" And out of it they come. Not me. Not any more. Once the outfit was on, it stayed, no matter how ugly or fat I looked. It was simply too much trouble to change.

Next came the high-top tennis shoes—high tops to keep my feet and ankles from swelling so much. This was another major chore; it's very difficult to push a shoe on someone who can offer no resistance. How I missed wearing pretty shoes. No more cute summer sandals for Renée!

Okay, *finally*, I was dressed. Now it was time to blow-dry and style my hair. At this point my hair was almost dry because it had taken so long to get me dressed, so my cowlick in my bangs was practically impossible to control. My attendants really tried, but they weren't cosmetologists. When you think about it, even our professional hairdressers can't satisfy us all the time! I desperately wanted to grab the brush and do my own hair, but of course that was impossible. My hair almost never looked the way I would have done it. Then they moisturized my face and applied my makeup.

Sometime during this ritual, they brushed my teeth; it was awkward and difficult for someone else to get all those little hard-to-reach places. To top it all off, most mornings I had to blow my nose. I don't have the power to blow, so they'd put a tissue up to my nose, close one nostril, and push on my stomach to push air up and out. Usually this procedure was only mildly effective. What can I say? They did the best they could, and I did appreciate their efforts. It's just not the same as doing it yourself.

By this time we were four hours into the ordeal, and by then it was almost 1:00, and I hadn't eaten breakfast yet!

Feeding myself was another whole ordeal. My attendants would strap a brace with a bracket on my wrist and place my bent spoon in the bracket. If they put my food in a bowl, I could feed myself—sort of. I missed my mouth a lot, so I had to wear bibs, and after eating I'd have food all over my lap and wheelchair so that someone had to do a major cleanup. I felt exposed, ugly, and stupid. I had to be cared for like a baby and I was thirty years old. Life was reduced to this.

Plus, the reality was that all of this care wasn't free. The financial aspect of paying for medical attendants was a major concern. Insurance paid for ten days of medical-attendant care per year. I needed care every day. Good care is hard to find, and it's very expensive. The fear of not knowing how we were going to afford the remaining 355 days each and every year for the rest of my life was daunting and depressing. In addition, I had no income. Although I had long-term disability coverage with my teaching job, the policy required four years of employment before providing benefits. I got hurt at the end of my third year, so I was ineligible for continued wages or any long-term benefits. Always one to look on the positive side, Mike encouraged me to trust in the Lord and take things one week at a time.

While I tired of being confined to my little condo, going out in public was difficult. First of all, by the time I got out of the bathroom in the mornings, most of the day was shot. If we did go somewhere, we had to add thirty minutes to our travel time each way just to get me loaded and unloaded.

When I first came home, we bought an old, blue van with a wheelchair lift—a genuine clunker. Getting me in and out was a major hassle. First they had to get me on the lift and secure my chair. Remembering Dr. Richardson, I was panicked by the lift. The fear of falling, which is germane to all of us, is intensified by about ten thousand times for someone who is helpless. Once I was inside the van, someone would anchor my wheelchair in the brackets in the middle of the van. When Mike was driving, I wasn't sitting beside him but rather way behind him, all by myself. The lift was folded up, resulting in a wire cage-like contraption riding right beside me. Trying to talk was nearly impossible. Between the noisy roar of the old engine, the rattles from the wire cage, and my weak voice, Mike could barely hear me, if at all. I felt like livestock being hauled around. Sometimes from my perch in the middle of the van, I'd bellow out, "Moo! Moo! Mooooo!" We'd laugh, but truthfully I didn't find it all that funny.

I now had to roll in places where I once walked and ran, and as I rolled by people naturally looked my way. I felt like I was on display. I was an oddity—not part of the normal landscape. Some well-meaning observers would give me the "Oh, you poor thing" look, which I hated. However, most adults would generally glance and then look away. Children didn't. They were openly intrigued by the woman in the ugly contraption and wondered how it worked. I wasn't comfortable with myself, but I tried to make them as comfortable as I could by answering their questions and demonstrating my sip-n-puff. The one place I really wanted to go was church, but by the time I was out of the bathroom, the morning service was over!

I spent most of my time in the condo, but occasionally we would go out to eat or to the mall. On these trips, I felt very self-conscious, so I'd keep my eyes straight ahead because I didn't want to see the looks and stares as I went by. I loved it when Michelle brought Brent, her darling three-year-old son. I'd always want him to ride on my lap. I felt like his body concealed mine, and he was so cute that people looked at him and not me.

One Saturday soon after I got home, Mike took me out for a spin in his car. "Mike," I said. "I haven't had ice cream in forever. I'd love some Pralines-n-Cream. Could we stop at Baskin-Robbins?"

"Sure!" So he whipped into the parking lot in front of 31 Flavors. Obviously, it wasn't worth the trouble to transfer me from the car into the manual chair just for a quick trip into the ice cream shop.

"I'll be right back," he said and disappeared.

This was the first time since the accident that I had been left alone in the car in a public place. Suddenly my imagination went berserk. Realizing how absolutely defenseless I was, I began to imagine all sorts of assaults directed at me. *What if some man tries to open my car door and kidnap me or molest me? Or what if someone jumps in the car and starts to drive away with me in it? What if someone just reaches in and yanks me out onto the pavement and steals the car?* Every person who walked by became a potential attacker. Like a whirlwind, my awareness of my vulnerability gripped me and sent me reeling into a state of pure, out-of-control panic.

Seven or eight minutes later, Mike happily returned, proudly carrying my double dip of Pralines-n-Cream. Getting into the car, he took one look at me and gasped in alarm. "What's wrong? What happened?" In those few minutes, I had dissolved into a total basket case. Tears were streaming down my face and I was trembling. Nearly hysterical, I tried to explain what had happened. "I was just so scared here all by myself! There's nothing I could do if someone tried to get in!" He held me until I calmed down, and then we planned practical ways to help me feel safe. Next time he'd park next to the buildings and lock the car. And next time I'd anticipate feeling vulnerable and talk myself through my irrational fears before they got out of control.

Visitors continued to drop by the house, and as much as I loved company, having people see me was difficult. When I saw someone coming, I might know that my hair looked horrible, my mascara was smeared under my eyes, or my clothes had spots from lunch, but I couldn't do anything about it. I was embarrassed when my shirt would be hiked up showing my tummy, but I couldn't pull it down. There was absolutely nothing I could do to make myself more presentable.

Typically, when tragedy strikes, people come at first but then go back to their normal lives. I am absolutely amazed that in my case this just didn't happen. People kept coming and finding ways to help. For example, Rally 'Round Renée provided meals for most of the first year—every single day! But people brought so much food that we soon realized that we had more than we could possibly eat, so we cut it back to three to four times a week. Because of their continued faithfulness, we never had to wonder what we were going to eat or who was going to prepare it.

One afternoon about 4:00, I was sitting alone on the patio in my sip-n-puff, feeling melancholy. I can only equate the feeling to how a surviving spouse feels after the memorial service and burial of his or her spouse, when all family members and friends have returned to their normal lives, and the wife or husband is left with memories and an empty house. As I sat there, I heard laughter and looked up to see two girls wearing San Clemente High School choir dresses. They jumped in a car and drove away, obviously going to a choir event—an event I should have been directing. *Wow. Life goes on without me*, I thought.

At that point, my aloneness and helplessness engulfed me. For months I had tried to keep a stiff upper lip, tried to smile, tried to cope, but all the while there was a reservoir of despair storing up inside. There had been a death—the death of life as I had known it, the death of my movement, the death of my career, the death of my wedding, the death of my usefulness, the death of my future hope and dreams and plans, the death of my body. At that moment I started to grieve. I didn't just cry, I wailed. My neighbor Rosemary was in her backyard, and she called across the fence, "Renée? Renée? Are you okay, dear?"

"It's okay, Rosemary. I just need to cry."

"You sound so awful. Are you sure there's nothing I can do?"

"No, Rosemary, there's nothing. I just have to cry." My cloudburst lasted for several minutes. At the time I felt like I was in a pit of despair so deep that I'd never see daylight again. Later I realized it was necessary to go to that place of mourning so that I could release the grief and start the healing process.

Not long afterward, some of my choir students who had been coming by on a regular basis began to encourage me to come to the fall concert in a few weeks. Because it seemed to mean so much to them that I be there, I agreed. Big mistake. I made a conscious effort to prepare myself for what I was going to see, but it didn't work.

Mike and I slipped into the back of the auditorium just as the music was beginning. After a few minutes, Mike reached over and turned the program in my lap so that I could read what was on the back. Julie had written a note addressed to the choir members. "To my kids," it began. *To her kids? Those aren't her kids! They're my kids! This is the program that I built and the kids I recruited. Where does she get off calling them her kids?* I was furious, and I was hurt. It wasn't easy to turn over to someone else what I had built and nourished.

I realize now that I was misdirecting my frustration. My paralysis was the problem—not Julie. If it hadn't been Julie, it would have been someone else. But at that moment, she had what I desperately wanted—she had my job, and she had my kids. I could hardly stand it.

Three times a week, I had to go to physical therapy at Casa Colina, one and a half hours away, plus loading and unloading time, of course. But who would drive me? My sisters had lives of their own, my students were in school, and almost everybody worked. As always, God had a plan.

One Sunday when I wanted to go to church incognito, Mike and I went to St. Edward Church. Afterwards, we were talking to our friends, Jim and Donna Rosen, who for some reason had gone to the 12:30 service instead of the earlier one as was their habit. They asked how we were managing, and I told them about starting physical therapy and how uneasy I was about having various inexperienced drivers hauling me around in our clunker van. Jim Rosen happened to be six months into a one-and-a-half-year sabbatical after selling his business. He was getting bored, so he volunteered to be my permanent driver. What an offer. The cherry on this sundae was that he took me in style—in his gorgeous, black Mercedes!

Jim learned how to do transfers so each time he lifted me from the wheelchair to the car seat and then loaded my wheelchair in the car. Then he completed the process in reverse when we got to PT. Sometimes he killed time while I was inside, and sometimes he came in with me and chatted while I did therapy. Often he sat with me and fed me lunch. The therapists encouraged patients to sit together, and the normal conversation would be, "What happened to you?"

"Motorcycle accident."

"Hit by a drunk driver."

"I was a construction worker. I fell off a building."

"I was shot."

"Diving accident."

"Football."

"I fell out of bed."

Silence. Always dead silence. Those around the table would suddenly look up from their eating to stare at me. Their unspoken but obvious reaction was, "You shouldn't be like this if that's all you did."

When my therapy session was over, Jim and I repeated the whole transfer process for the return trip home and back into the house. Jim was a great conversationalist and easy to talk to, a delight to be around. He was dependable and flexible enough to roll with whatever mess we were in when he arrived at the condo each time. He not only provided the necessary transportation three times a week for about seven months, but talking to him did me more good than an expensive counseling session. He was literally God-sent!

When I first started my PT at Casa Colina, I learned that the counselor I was assigned, Bonnie, was not only a woman, but she also was a quadriplegic. I was very excited and looked forward to working with her. Who better to understand my frustrations than someone in my exact situation?

In our first session, Bonnie asked me how I got in the chair. As I was telling her the story, I mentioned how God had supplied specific needs at specific times. Her reaction was, "Yeah, we all hang on to something to get us through difficult times." Her comment was like a pinprick, but I didn't think much of it. The next time I saw her, I again mentioned how God's faithfulness had sustained me, and her comment was the same. "We all need to hang on to something during difficult times." The prick was becoming more of a jab. I could see that she had an automatic response.

In the third session I was telling her how Mike wanted to get married. I told her I wasn't sure about it and that I was praying. This time she said, "Yes, we do need to hang on to our little crutches." The prick was now an outright stab. Something snapped in my head. This lady was starting to tick me off. How dare she call my God a crutch!

I stopped the conversation and asked, attempting not to show my displeasure, "Bonnie, would you mind telling me how you got in your wheelchair?"

"I was a student at a community college in New York, majoring in ballet," she said matter-of-factly. "One day in class we were working out on the trampoline, and I jumped too high, fell off balance, and bounced onto the floor, landing on my head." Her tone changed as she continued. "And when I was in the hospital, all these people came in and prayed for me. They talked about God and miracles and faith, and they poured a ton of holy water and oil over me and prayed. And where did it get *me!*" By now her face was distorted in hostility and anger. Her words were venom.

"You know, Bonnie, I'm sorry, but I don't think we can work together."

"What? Why do you say that?"

"Because you obviously have issues with God that you yourself haven't worked out. I can see we're going to have problems when I talk about my relationship with the Lord, and quite frankly that's all I have right now. I can't allow you to undermine my trust in God."

"But we *can* work together."

"No. No we can't. I think you need to work out the anger you have toward God about your accident and paralysis. I'm *very* fragile right now with my emotions and what has happened to me, and I can't deal with any negative influences about God right now. I won't."

Again she tried to persuade me to stay, but I said, "No, I'm serious. There are no hard feelings. I wish you the best, but I need to work with somebody else." With that, I left. In fact, I ran.

She actually scared me. She was a counselor, someone in a position of authority and influence. I was supposed to trust and depend on this lady to give me sage advice and to offer a balanced perspective. I learned that day to be careful about whom I trusted. A title behind a name sometimes means very little. We have to test the water to analyze the quality of the advice we're offered. Whether the relationship is personal or professional, I've learned to be careful whose counsel I seek.

Many of my friends and students visited my home on a regular basis. One was Shannon Bason. She and her parents lived nearby, were actively involved in Rally 'Round Renée, and were very faithful to help me personally in any way they could. One day several months after I got home, Shannon stopped by after school. She sat down in front of me and said, "Renée, I want to ask you about something." I always allowed my students to call me Renée after they'd graduated. Now that I wasn't their teacher and because they'd become my friends, I invited them to call me Renée.

"Sure, Shannon. What's up?"

"I hear you're looking for a weekend attendant. I would like to do that. I really want you to consider me for the position."

My eyes welled up. "Oh, Shan. There's just no way that I could allow you to do that. It's a horrible job. You'd be helping me go to the bathroom, helping me empty my bladder and empty my bowel. It's not pretty. It's not a glamorous job. It's ugly, and it's hard work. You don't want to do that."

She put her hand on my knee. "I know this would be very personal for you. I know it would be hard, crossing over that teacher/student line."

"Yeah, you're hitting the nail on the head! You're my student. You can't wipe my bottom!"

Suddenly she switched from serious to playful. "Aw, come on, Renée. I'll make it fun. We'll crank up the music, and we'll sing, I'll tell you about my love life, we'll do things to distract us from what's going on."

"I don't know."

"I'm sure the first few times will be *very* hard for you, but after that we'll get used to it. And don't forget, I want to be a nurse. What better way for me to have experience than to work with you? I would learn so much!" I knew she was playing to my teacher side to make me more comfortable with the idea. It worked. I was weakening.

"Well, let me think about it."

"Of course. You think about it and let me know."

I talked it over with Mike and my sisters. "Am I stupid for even thinking about this?" I asked them. They helped me walk through the pros and cons, which turned out to be mostly pros. Shannon was very mature for her age, extremely reliable, completely flexible, and she lived close by. I genuinely liked her and enjoyed her company, and she already knew the players—Mike and all my family. She fit in, and that was important. They helped me to believe that Shannon was right; the first few times would be uncomfortable, but after that we'd all get used to it.

"Okay, Shannon, it's a go!" I told her a few days later. She gasped in excitement. "It's going to be *really* embarrassing," I rushed to add. "I'm going to hate it! I want to make sure you know I hate it. I want you to crank up the music loud. I'm going to put a bag over my head and take my mind to Hawaii or France or somewhere—anywhere—and Denise is going to train you." And that's exactly what we did.

The first couple of times were, as expected, absolutely humiliating, but Shannon had a disarming, quick sense of humor and a wonderful way of making me feel comfortable. She worked for me for about two years and became like part of the family.

Shannon was the first in a succession of three ex-students to become my attendants. Dana Hinton and Andrea Imlay, like Shannon, were planning medical careers. By the time they came, I had gone through a few attendants and was more comfortable with the whole process. Because Shannon had been the trailblazer, it was easier with them; however, it was still embarrassing at first. Each time, I did exactly what I had done with Shannon. I put a bag over my head, cranked up the music, and left the training to Denise who, by the way, was very good at it!

As Christmas approached, Michelle and Denise took me on a shopping expedition so I could buy my gifts. When we went into a boutique, there sat this darling little flop-eared rabbit looking up at me, and for some reason that bunny caught my fancy. The look on his impish little face just cracked me up, and I laughed and laughed. I kept going back and looking at him and laughing all over again.

Preparing for that first Christmas was extremely difficult. I couldn't go caroling, I couldn't wrap my own gifts, I could only sit and watch others decorate the tree. It was as if Christmas were a parade, and all I could do was sit and watch it go by when I wanted to march in it like everybody else! I'm often in a mental fight against memories of what used to be, trying to be content with how life is now, but it seems like the battle is more intense on holidays and special occasions. It was Christmas, all the women were in the kitchen preparing our holiday meal, and I sat. When it came time to eat, Mike or my family had to feed me, and while everyone else bustled around cleaning up, I sat again. I felt so utterly useless. Everybody tried to be upbeat and chipper, but it was hard on all of us.

When it came time to open our gifts, my dad got up and went in the other room, then he returned looking proud as a peacock. With obvious excitement he said, "Renée, I made you something so you could open your own presents." He had designed and welded a ripping tool that looked like a miniature pickax, and it worked like a sword. He was so excited to show me how it worked. He placed it in the wrist brace I used for eating. "You can slip the pick into the seam of the paper, and, using your shoulder muscle, yank back, causing the tool to tear the paper." It actually worked! I'll never forget Mom and Dad's thoughtfulness in helping me be as normal as possible.

Christmas is a holiday often charged with emotion. This, combined with the reality that my paralysis exaggerated even the slightest rise and fall in my emotions, had me mentally exhausted. My nerves were on the ragged edge, and my feelings were on my sleeve.

After spending much of Christmas day with the Lacouagues, we said our good-byes and started the forty-minute drive to Huntington Beach where we would have dinner with Mike's family. As we got on the freeway, I turned my thoughts toward Mike's family and became apprehensive. Since the accident, not a day went by that I didn't question why Mike would even think of staying by my side. I had become such a tremendous hassle, or at least that's how I felt. I started to worry about how his family would receive me and what they must think of me as a potential wife for their wonderful son. Fear set in. *There's no way they can want Mike to stay with me.*

I'm not the person I was. I'm like a big ball and chain and I'm keeping him in prison with me. No parents would choose for their son to marry someone with such a devastating disability.

By the time we arrived at Mike's parents' house, I had silently worked myself into believing that I was completely unworthy to be with their son. My self-worth was totally and completely obliterated.

As we entered the Bondi home, we were greeted with smiles and "Merry Christmas!"

Outwardly I smiled, but inside I was falling apart. Mike's family home, where I had been so comfortable before my paralysis, suddenly became an obstacle course for my wheelchair. It was a tri-level home and could not have been a worse design for my circumstances. Any idea of blending in was completely out of the question. Mike first had to enlist the help of his brother Steve and brother-in-law Scott to lift me up the three steps from the front door into the living room. Then an hour later when it was time to eat, once again the three guys had to carry me—this time down three steps to the dining room, while everybody watched and tried to make this as comfortable a situation as possible for me.

Jim, Mike's father, had elevated the dining room table by placing blocks under the legs so that I could fit my wheelchair under it. Sandra, Mike's mother, had thoughtfully placed my adaptive eating utensil by my plate. They obviously had thought ahead, and these sweet gestures demonstrated their intentions to make me feel welcome at their table. But Mike had to feed me my Christmas dinner. *Here I am thirty years old and my boyfriend has to feed me like a baby, and in front of his family! What is his dad thinking? What is his mom thinking? What are his grandparents thinking?*

Even though there was good conversation and family stories around the table, my irrational thoughts were blocking my ability to feel included. My mind was furiously whirling around a center of fear. After dinner it was back up the steps to the living room for opening gifts. Mike opened my presents for me. My stomach was in knots. I couldn't show my gratitude by holding up a necklace for all to see or placing a sweater over my shoulders or jumping up to give the giver a hug. I just had to look at the article in Mike's hands and try to express my gratitude with no body language. From my perspective, I felt out of place. *This is so weird. I've never felt out of place anywhere! I've always enjoyed being around this family. We've had such great times together—fishing trips, skiing trips, volleyball, card games till midnight. Why do I feel so awkward? Get it together Renée. Just relax.*

Still I was unable to see myself as anything but a bother. In my heart, I felt I was no longer worthy to be at Mike's side or a part of his family, and I assumed they felt the same way. For that matter I no longer felt worthy of being by anyone's side or part of anyone's family. These feelings would plague me for years.

When Mike took me home that night, I was physically exhausted and emotionally spent. He pushed me into my bedroom, and there sat that little flop-eared bunny—waiting to cheer me up when I got home. I had been so delighted over that little rabbit that my sisters secretly bought it for me. Knowing I'd need a lift after an incredibly painful day, they didn't put him under the tree but rather left him for a special surprise, just when I needed it most.

On the first anniversary of my accident, I was depressed before I woke up. It marked the fact that I'd been at this for a year and that this situation wasn't going away. This was reality, and it was permanent. While Yvette was doing my range-of-motion exercises, I decided to call Denise. I hadn't talked to her in a couple of days, and the due date for her baby was approaching, so I wanted to check to see how she was doing.

Instead of Denise answering the phone, my brother-in-law answered. It was about 8:30, so he should have left for work already. "Joseph, what are you doing home?"

"We're working on having this baby!"

"Ohmygosh! I'll get off the phone!"

When my phone rang at about 10:15, I was still in the bathroom finishing up. When I answered, I heard Denise sobbing. "It's me. It's me. I'm in the delivery room at the hospital. We have a little girl! We have a little girl! Renée, do you know what today is? Do you know what today is?"

"I sure do!" I was starting to cry too.

"Only God would give us a baby on this day! Now we have something good to celebrate on this day every year for the rest of your life. Her name is Celine, and she's lying right here on my tummy! She was born just a few minutes ago. Renée, she's so beautiful."

Crying, I asked, "Denise, did you induce just to get the baby born on this day? I know you did! You would do that!"

"*No, I did not!* I knew you'd think that. She came completely on her own, I swear. Isn't God just incredible?"

"Oh, Denise! I'm so happy for you! I can hardly wait to see her. I'll be down as soon as I finish getting dressed." A couple of hours later, I was rolling into her room with flowers and balloons. God had turned a ghastly anniversary into a joyous occasion, and it's been that way every year since. There's nothing like celebrating someone else's happiness to get your focus off yourself.

Two of the most unforgettable nights of my life came in June, one year after my accident, when Rally 'Round Renée sponsored a benefit on two consecutive Monday nights to help me buy a wheelchair-accessible van. It was a huge extravaganza at a dinner theater, complete with dinner, floor show, and a huge silent auction. People donated all sorts of things—weekends in the mountains; services such as manicures, haircuts, massages, tutoring; a free studio photo sitting, airline tickets, tickets to Lakers and Chargers games, and several paintings by Rick Delanty. There was electronic equipment, gift certificates, homemade items—you name it. It was overwhelming. The crowd had come early for cocktails and the silent auction, so by the time I got there for dinner, the place was electric.

There was only one way into the room without steps, so I made my big entrance from the kitchen, with Mike and Jim May on either side of me. When I came through the swinging door, the spotlight hit me, and the crowd of some 350 people both nights spontaneously gave me a standing ovation—just for showing up!

The entertainment was The Young Americans. The first half was the current group. These kids were so talented, so young and handsome and energetic. They were absolutely phenomenal. By the time they left the stage, everybody in the place was tapping their feet, clapping their hands, singing whether they had a voice or not, and wishing they were twenty years younger!

By contrast, the second half of the performance was the "old" Young Americans from Tibbies. These people had not performed together—had not even been together—since we performed ten years earlier. Remember that a YA performance is characterized by fast movement and high energy, and then consider that these were very talented but frankly somewhat out-of-shape adults. Also remember the evolution of music from the late '70s to the late '80s, and you'll get the picture; the second half of the show was far different from the first, but equally entertaining!

The Tibbies group did the same show we did ten years earlier with the same band. There were five guys and five girls, great energy, lots of clapping, and audience participation. I remember one performer particularly well—Reggie Burrell, who sings backup with Gladys Knight. The performers were working hard—really hard—pushing their bodies to do what used to be a whole lot easier! At one point Reggie came up to the microphone to talk to the audience. "Is everybody out there having a great time?"

"Yes!"

"Okay, now I want everybody to put their hands together." By this time the audience was rockin' and rollin'. They were ready to dance in the aisles. But also by this time Reggie was drenched with sweat. He couldn't have been wetter if he had been baptized—the Baptist way. All of a sudden he jumped off the stage, grabbed a towel from a busboy, hopped back on stage, and wiped the dripping perspiration off his whole body. "Dang, Renée!" he exclaimed. "I'm just too old for this!" The crowd loved it!

During the standing ovation, Mike and my sisters lifted me onto the stage in the shadows and rolled my wheelchair over to the piano and Jim May. They quickly elevated my feet onto an ottoman to keep me from getting dizzy. This was the first time I had sung publicly since my accident, and I didn't know how it was going to go.

As the cheers, whoops, and whistles for the performers continued, the spotlight fell on me. A hush fell over the audience. I began simply, a cappella. "Let us break bread together on our knees . . . ," with the Young Americans backing me up. "When I fall on my knees with my face to the rising sun, oh Lord, have mercy on me. . . ." The backup vocals were so pure and warm that the blend created a blanket of unity that permeated the room. When I finished, the crowd stood in a cheering, applauding ovation. It was really sweet of them, but truthfully my voice wasn't all that good. Oh, my tone was fine, and the amplifiers sure helped. But anyone who knows music knows that my power wasn't there anymore and that I had to breathe far too often.

While Jim played softly I addressed the crowd. "Every time I thought about all of you and all you are doing and all that you have done, how you give so freely and so cheerfully— everything from Shannon's wanting to be my attendant, to meals, to all the visits and phone calls, to the flowers and cards, to driving me to physical therapy, to making this night a reality—I tried to think of a song that would express what I feel. When I couldn't, I decided the next best thing was to do what you've always seen me do. I decided to sit by the piano and sing with Jim."

Noticing that I needed time to catch my breath, Jim took the microphone and told the audience how we met. "I looked across the piano, and I saw a pair of the biggest . . . blue eyes."

"Eyes?" I quipped. Everybody roared.

"We did this tune from *Cinderella,* and it's become our song," he continued. "We do it every time we perform together."

I added, "And when you hear the song, you'll realize how ironic it is that we're singing it now. It's supposed to be funny, so remember that when I get to the last line."

I began singing "In My Own Little Corner." When the last line came, the audience was riveted. "Just as long as I stay in my own little corner, all alone . . . in my own . . . little . . . chair."

"While I don't feel at all lucky to be in this wheelchair," I said, after finishing the song, "I am more than lucky—I am blessed—to be surrounded by all of you here tonight. Thank you for coming, thank you for being here. May God bless you as much as you have blessed me."

The two benefits brought in $38,800. Soon I was sitting right beside Mike in our new silver Dodge Caravan. It cost $38,400. We paid cash for the van and the special ramp modifications, and we still had $400 left over for gas money. How incredible is that? Yet another amazing example of God's faithfulness.

Many people go to their grave never feeling loved or appreciated, never knowing if they've had an impact or made an impression on anybody else. Although my body was broken, my spirits were soaring. I wish every person in the world could experience and feel the gift of love that I was given those two nights.

9

Going to the Chapel

The question kept coming up. Were we going to get married, or weren't we? Mike said many times he wanted to marry me the minute I got out of the hospital, but I just couldn't let him do that. I felt that we needed to deal with the realities of me living life in a wheelchair outside the hospital before we'd know for sure. When I came home, we didn't know for certain whether he and my family could take care of me! How on earth could we make an intelligent decision about marriage?

I had more doubts than the sky has stars. What did I have to offer Mike? How could I be his wife, his companion, his best friend when I couldn't share the things he enjoyed like biking, playing volleyball, hiking, backpacking, and camping? What about normal, mundane wifely responsibilities like cooking, cleaning, doing the laundry? (Remember, I was raised with a mother who got up at 5:00 and cooked breakfast for everyone on the ranch!) Even in the late '80s, I needed to do my fair share. I couldn't do any of those things.

What of the physical side of marriage? To put it plainly, we'd never have a normal sex life. How important would that be to Mike? Was it fair to Mike for me to marry him?

Another major consideration to me was his family. "Mike, your family," I said quietly. "They're probably having a hard time with this."

"I suspect you're right," he said, thoughtfully. "I haven't asked them directly, but they love you, and I know they'll respect my judgment."

The seeds of unworthiness where Jim and Sandra were concerned began to take root. Although Mike told me otherwise, I had my own interpretation. Even though I felt loved and accepted before the accident, I figured things had to be different now. Parents want their children to have the very best. Was I the very best for Mike? In my eyes, absolutely not. My paralysis was robbing me of the joy of feeling like I would be a welcome addition to the Bondi family if Mike and I went forward with our wedding plans.

"Mike, I can guess how they must be feeling. If you had been the one to break your neck, my dad would have sat me down and said, 'I know this is going to be very difficult, but we're talking about the rest of your life.' No parents' first choice for their child would be that they marry someone in a wheelchair. I'd be shocked if your parents weren't concerned. Who wouldn't be?"

Before my accident I had looked forward to having a loving relationship with Jim and Sandra; now my insecurity had me wondering whether that was possible. Nearly a year after my accident, I still interpreted everything they did (or didn't do) through a filter of feelings of unworthiness.

Jim and Sandra had no instruction manual for how to help us get through a situation like this, so we all just groped our way through. If I needed some water in my cup, they'd call for Mike. If I needed my adapted eating utensil out of my backpack, they'd call Mike. If my wheelchair needed to be moved, they'd call for Mike. At the time I interpreted these actions as a lack of acceptance, but years later I realized this wasn't the case. Actually, they were trying to be sensitive to my feelings. "How would Renée feel if we, as her future in-laws, spooned food into her mouth?" they asked themselves. "How would Renée feel having us rummage through her personal things in her backpack or purse to locate her adaptive eating utensil? How would Renée feel having us adjust her clothing?" To them, having Mike assist me seemed more appropriate, so that's why they called for him.

What a mess. Looking back, I can see that my instigating a little honest dialogue would have solved a lot of misunderstandings. Instead of wishing they'd read my mind, I should have just asked for their help. And perhaps they could have asked whether I'd be comfortable with them helping me, but at the time we were all walking on new and unfamiliar ground. I didn't want to call attention to just how helpless I was, and they didn't want me to feel embarrassed. The situation makes a good case for open communication. If we had talked things through, we might have avoided a lot of misinterpretation. Sometimes silence is anything but golden!

When Mike and I finally made the decision to move forward, it was not a dramatic moment. We had had our big moments when Mike proposed before my accident, when he gave me my ring, when we danced at the San Clemente prom. In Mike's eyes, our wedding had never been cancelled, just postponed.

One Saturday afternoon in the spring, Mike and I were enjoying the sunshine on my deck. He looked at me and said, "So, when are we going to set the date for our wedding?"

I turned to him, rolled my eyes, and asked, "How can you say that? Mike, do you really want to go through with the wedding?"

"Absolutely!"

"Well, I can no longer tell you that you don't know what you're getting into, because you certainly do by now. You're really serious, aren't you?"

"Of course I'm serious. It's your body that's broken, not you. You're the woman I fell in love with, and yes, you're the woman I want to spend the rest of my life with. We're a team."

"You know we probably will never have children."

"Children would have been wonderful, but I don't need a child to be complete. I only need you. I love you just like you are, wheelchair and all." We sat in thoughtful silence for a few minutes, and then he added. "You know, this may sound weird, but if this had to happen—if you had to be paralyzed—then I'm glad it happened two months before our wedding rather than two months after. If we had already been married, then I might have felt trapped—like I was in a situation I couldn't get out of. But since it happened before, I now have the choice."

"I understand that. If I had been paralyzed after our marriage, then I always would have wondered if you stayed with me only because of your vows."

"So now you'll never have to wonder. I have a choice, and I choose to be married to you."

"You're *sure* about this?"

"Completely." When I looked into his eyes, I could see his resolve. I knew he wasn't trying to convince me of something he didn't feel. For him, it was settled. He was going to stay with me forever because that's what he genuinely wanted to do.

"All right," I said, a little reluctantly, and that was that. The next day we made a couple of phone calls and set the date for October 21.

My family was amazed and Mike's family, as Mike had predicted, respected his decision. Jim simply asked, "Mike, do you know what you're doing?"

"I know exactly what I'm doing."

"Do you really?"

"Yes, Dad, I do. I've thought long and hard about this and I'm completely committed to Renée. She's the one I want to be with."

"Okay then."

Later Jim and Sandra would relate the story to Steve, Mike's younger brother. His comment was, "Of course Mike is going to marry Renée. That's the way you raised us." What a tribute to Jim and Sandra as parents, and God bless Steve!

Our wedding plans were back on. Most of the work had been done the year before, so we merely had to pick up the ball and start running again. We had the teal bridesmaids' dresses, the flowers had been selected, the decorations planned, the caterer chosen, the band hired. And I already had my wedding dress. When Mom and I had gone shopping for my gown before my accident, I had narrowed it down to two; one had a sensational front, and the other had a breathtaking back. I chose the one with the stunning front. When you're sitting in a wheelchair, the back of a dress is totally out of sight; it's the front that people see. When I realized I had chosen the perfect dress without knowing what my circumstances would be, the lights came on! *God knew I would be in a wheelchair on my wedding day, and he directed me to make the right choice!* It was another realization of how interested God is in the details of our lives.

We did have to make a few adjustments to our wedding plans. For one, in the year that had elapsed, scores and scores of people had become involved in our lives who had not been before—all of the Rally 'Round Renée group, doctors, nurses, therapists. They all deserved to be invited, and we wanted them to come. After all, if it hadn't been for their assistance, Mike and I may not have been getting married. However, when more people attend the wedding, the reception has to be expanded! We accepted the gracious offer of our good friends Art and Gaye Birtcher to have our reception in their gorgeous estate, but it couldn't accommodate seven hundred people! Finally, we decided to have two receptions—one with light refreshments in the church gym immediately after the ceremony and a sit-down dinner later for about three hundred of our friends.

Scott Wyatt, who smuggled the puppy into my hospital room, accepted our invitation to be an usher. We also asked Cameron Brown, who sat outside my ICU window at night, to be an usher, but he was playing football at the University of Colorado, Boulder, and had a game that day, so he couldn't come. We were disappointed, and so was he. However, Kevin Busch, another special student, stepped in. Shannon Bason was our guest book attendant.

A few days before the wedding, I began to get nervous. "Mike," I said. "I'm afraid that if Mom and Dad push me down the aisle in my wheelchair as we planned, I'll break down and cry, and they won't be tears of joy. I'll see you standing at the front watching your bride in a wheelchair instead of walking, and I'll lose it. I don't think I'm strong enough to do that. What would you think if you and I came down the aisle together?"

"I'd love to do that!"

So I approached Mom and Dad. "When we're going down the aisle, I'm afraid I'll start to cry, and that'll cause Dad to start crying, which in turn will get Mom teared up. It could be a real mess. And there will be poor Mike at the altar on his big day watching all of us blubbering and falling apart. What would you say if Mike and I came in together behind the two of you?"

My dad spoke right up. "Whatever it takes. We don't care where we are in the line-up. Whatever makes the two of you happy, then that's what we'll do!"

Mom readily agreed as well. "Well sure, of course."

"But I'm your last daughter. It's your last chance to walk down the aisle. Are you sure?"

"We don't care about that kind of stuff. It's your day. We just want it to be what you want."

The day of the wedding, my attendant and my sisters had the monumental task of getting me dressed. We had set the ceremony for 1:30 so we could get me to the church on time. It was the usual marathon morning in the bathroom, then they started the dressing ordeal.

All the time I had a battle going on inside. On one hand, this was my *wedding day!* On the other hand, *this* was my wedding day? Who on her wedding day has to have someone else brush her teeth, shave her legs, and put on her bra? It was a mixed bag of emotions, for sure. But I made up my mind to look only at the good. I couldn't have been happier with the man God had given me to marry, and I was going to be surrounded by family and friends who loved us. Although it wasn't like I had planned—rolling down the aisle instead of walking—nevertheless it was the best it could be under the circumstances. I made a deliberate decision to enjoy the day and push back the "shoulda coulda woulda" thoughts.

They got my wedding dress on me, which was no small feat, and transferred me to the chair for the beautification process. Lydia, my hairdresser even before the accident and a dear friend, fixed my hair and applied my makeup while Denise fed me yogurt and fruit for breakfast.

Because I already had my wedding gown on, they draped me in sheets and a cosmetic gown. Without the drape, one stray fleck of mascara or a dropped blush brush would have meant disaster! Late in the morning, Mike came in. He was already dressed in his tux, and he looked so handsome, and so happy! He leaned down and gave me a kiss, then he pulled a small box out of his pocket. "Happy wedding day," he said with a smile. He opened the box so that I could see an exquisite blue sapphire and diamond necklace—a stunning wedding day gift.

Mike drove me to the church in our van, and we went straight into the gym for family pictures. Soon we heard a traffic jam developing outside as cars were pulling into the parking lot, and I began to get excited. It was obvious that an amazing number of friends and well-wishers were coming to support us.

At the appointed time, the bridesmaids and groomsmen went into the church to begin the processional. Mike and I waited outside. When the wedding coordinator gave the signal, Mike's parents went down the aisle first, followed by the bridal party—Dorothy Henry, my roommate at the time of the accident; Debbie Wilcox, my previous roommate; and Pam, Mike's sister. Their escorts were, respectively, Danny, my brother; Mark Sanders, Mike's high school friend; and Scott Hill, Pam's husband. Next came the ring bearer and flower girl—Brent, Michelle's four-year-old son, and Natalie, Pam's four-year-old daughter. Next were Michelle and Denise, co-matrons of honor, with the best men, Steve, Mike's brother; and Alex Alvarez, his good friend. Finally, Mom and Dad went down the aisle together.

When everybody had disappeared into the church, I heard the blare of the trumpets (I *had* to have trumpets!) proclaiming our entrance with the beautiful march *The Trumpet Volantaire*. With my fragrant bouquet of stargazer lilies and white tulips lying in my lap, I took a deep breath, looked up to Mike, and said, "Well, here we go!" The doors opened, and we heard Steve announce, "Will everyone please remain seated." Our church has the appearance of a cathedral; it's grand and regal, and it was packed with over seven hundred guests.

We went down the aisle side by side, with Mike pushing my chair with only his left hand. When we got to the front of the church, we stopped; Mom and Dad stepped into the aisle, gave me a kiss, and Dad firmly shook Mike's hand. Then Sandra and Jim kissed me, Sandra embraced Mike, and Jim gave him a tight hug and whispered, "Mike, I'm proud of you."

While we were exchanging kisses, I realized that the congregation was starting to applaud. Mike turned around, looked, and then bent over and reported to me. "They're all standing, Renée. They're giving us a standing ovation!" I think they were applauding because Mike and I had, in the fullest sense of the phrase, made it down the aisle!

There are about four steps that transition from the aisle to the altar, so Mike turned me around to face the audience, and then he, Steve, and Danny lifted me, chair and all, onto the upper level. As they did, I spontaneously squealed, "Wheeee!" Surprised, everybody laughed.

When we got turned around and settled, I looked up at Father Martin, expecting him to be starting the ceremony. But he was crying! He tried to speak, but the words couldn't get around the huge lump in his throat. He wiped the tears and tried again. He attempted to speak several times while everybody patiently waited for him to gain his composure. Finally Michelle leaned over to him and whispered, "Here's a tissue." He laughed, and I think the diversion helped him break the cycle. When he finally began, he said, "In all my years of officiating marriage ceremonies, I've never been this emotional. These kids have been through so much. This is truly a special day."

Then just as Father Martin began the actual ceremony, Michelle leaned over and whispered to me, "Dr. Palmer just walked in; he came all the way to the front and is sitting in the front pew." I turned and whispered it to Mike, who turned and winked and gave him a concealed thumbs-up. Funny, when people come late to a wedding, they usually slip inconspicuously into a back pew. But Dr. Palmer walked all the way to the front, his gift rattling in a Nordstrom bag, and he claimed the front-row seat I had promised him.

For the wedding ceremony, we wanted a full mass with lots of congregational singing. Imagine seven hundred voices filling the sanctuary when they sang "On Eagle's Wings" and "Here I Am, Lord." The harmony was so melodious and their voices so robust and fervent that it gave us chills. Longtime friends from Young Americans gave us the gift of music in their special solos. The highlight for us was when Michelle and Denise sang "Be Not Afraid," with the congregation joining them on the chorus.

When we said our vows, Mike got down on one knee so that he'd be at my level. I heard the congregation simultaneously sigh, "Aaaaawwwwwww." After we promised to love, honor, and cherish each other for better or worse, for richer or poorer, in sickness and in health, we prayed this prayer together: "All powerful and living God, we now kneel before you, very happy, but a little nervous. We feel you brought us together in the beginning, helped our love grow, and, at this moment, are with us in a special way. We ask that you stay by our side in the days ahead, protect us from anything that might harm this marriage, give us courage when burdens come our way. Teach us to forgive one another when we stumble. We ask finally that, in our old age, we may love one another as deeply, and cherish each other as much, as we do at this moment. May you grant these wishes which we offer in the name of your Son, Jesus Christ our Lord. Amen."

The service continued and at the sign of peace, when the congregation turns to pass a gesture of Christ's love to each other, Mike turned to me, kissed me, and said, "Christ's peace be with you, Renée. I love you." Then he turned and walked down the steps to greet our parents.

Father Martin and the bridal party had gone down to do the same. Sandra, seeing me on the altar all alone, boldly stepped out of her pew and walked up the steps to the altar. Leaning over to give me a warm hug, she said, "I love you, Renée. May the Lord's peace be always with you." As she walked away, my heart was melted. I looked up at the cross behind the altar and said aloud, "Thank you, Jesus."

The ceremony ended with a choir of special musicians and friends singing John Rutter's beautiful arrangement of "The Lord Bless You and Keep You," the song I had used to close every performance when I was directing the San Clemente High School choirs. As we left the altar and headed back up the aisle, there was another standing ovation with lots of cheers and whistles.

At the gym reception, it was absolutely wonderful to greet those who had cared enough to come—church musicians, faculty, SCHS students and parents, Mission School students and faculty, nurses, physical therapists. Steve gave a beautiful best man's toast, and it was just a wonderful time to mingle and chat while the guests munched on the refreshments.

Later, when we arrived at the Birtchers' Rancho de Dios and saw the reception layout, I gasped. It was *Sunset Magazine* beautiful! The reception tables were spread in a beautiful natural setting of large trees nestled on the beautifully manicured lawn. The caterer not only outdid himself with delicious food, he presented it with flair and style. There were stations throughout the setting—a table with Italian cuisine, a station with French delicacies, a table with fruit and cheeses—each one decorated with special touches of elegance.

When the wedding party came down the walk, the band emcee introduced each couple, then he said, "Ladies and gentlemen. May I present Mr. and Mrs. Michael Bondi!" Again, there were enthusiastic cheers and shouts. We joined the party and fell in among our guests. We wanted to make sure we got to talk to each one who came. Several from Mike's office in Denver were there (amazing how many Martin Marietta executives had pressing business in L.A. that weekend!); Tia Conchita, my aunt from Ainhoa; all the Rally 'Round Renée gang; colleagues; students; parents; YA alumni; church members; and of course family. The turnout was amazing.

When we cut the cake (six tiers!), Mike put my hand on his, and we cut it together. Mike did the garter thing—very tastefully, I might add, and Steve caught it. For the throwing of the bouquet, Danny had designed a catapult for the arm of my wheelchair, and when the time came, all the girls gathered behind me. With flowers in the catapult, evidently I hit it with my elbow a little too hard because, instead of the bouquet making a nice arch and falling gracefully into someone's waiting hands, it shot back like a torpedo and hit my nine-year-old niece Erica right in the stomach. "Well, I guess I caught it!" she exclaimed in surprise!

Instead of a first dance, which obviously would have been a bit difficult, I arranged a surprise for Mike. My sisters got me positioned in front of the band, and the emcee announced, "Mike, come up here. It's time for the first dance!" Of course, he was a bit confused, but Michelle ushered him up and sat him in a chair beside me. The band started playing, and I began singing "The Wind Beneath My Wings." Although my voice was weak, my sentiment was strong.

Although I didn't realize it while I was singing, there wasn't a dry eye anywhere. After the applause, everybody was still quiet. Finally, someone yelled out, "That's it! No more! We're out of Kleenex!" Everybody laughed, and the festive atmosphere returned. Later when everyone was dancing, some of my students coaxed Mike, and he took me out on the dance floor and spun and twirled me around in my chair. Then my students took turns "dancing" with me. Although it was incredibly awkward for me to dance, I chose to go out onto the dance floor. I knew it would make my guests smile, and after all they needed to laugh as much as I did.

By then it was close to 10:00 P.M. The party was winding down, and I was getting tired. Mike and I thanked Art and Gaye, said our good-byes to our family and friends, and walked back up the path to our van. As we pulled away from the beautiful Rancho de Dios, Mike and I knew we had begun a new chapter in our lives. We were basking in the love and support that had been extended to us on that most special of all days. With that kind of love, with our love for each other, and with God's unwavering faithfulness, how could we feel anything but hope and anticipation for our future?

As we drove back to our condo, we realized we were hungry. In our excitement, we had never eaten, so we drove through Del Taco. Now, every year on our anniversary, we hit Del Taco in remembrance of our unforgettable wedding-night dinner. It's a tradition.

When we got home and went into the bedroom, Michelle and Denise had been there again. They had replaced my old comforter and sheets with the new ones we'd gotten in our showers. They had turned down the bed, put mints on the pillows, flowers on the nightstand, and a point on the toilet tissue! They had prepared our honeymoon suite.

We didn't leave on our wedding trip until a week later. Our original plan had been to go to Hawaii for our honeymoon; however, with my paralysis, we decided that a Mexico cruise could work better—just so we'd always have a room accessible to us for my care. When my bladder needed to be emptied, I needed a place to lie down and be catheterized.

I didn't want Mike to spend his honeymoon taking care of me, and besides I wanted someone to go along to do my hair and makeup so I'd look decent, so we decided to take along an attendant. My normal attendant was unavailable, so I asked my friend Brenda if she'd be interested in going on a cruise free in exchange for being my attendant. She readily agreed. "I'd love to go along! I'll do your care then make myself scarce so you and Mike can be alone."

There was one more hurdle. We couldn't afford to pay for Brenda to have a private room, and it wouldn't be fair to expect her to share her cabin with a stranger whom the cruise line would assign to her, so we asked if she could find a friend to go along. Unfortunately, not one of her friends was available, and with the wedding date only a couple of weeks away, Mike and I were sweating it. Not knowing what else to do, Brenda stood up one night at choir practice and made the announcement: "I'm going with Mike and Renée on their honeymoon as her attendant. Anybody want to go and be my roommate?"

Early the next morning, Brenda called. I was still in bed, and my attendant was doing my range-of-motion exercises. She turned on the speaker phone. "Renée, I've got someone to go with me on the cruise!"

"Yea! That's wonderful! What a relief!" I was ecstatic.

"But, before you get too excited, I need to tell you who it is. It's Florence Klein."

"Florence Klein?"

"Yeah, I asked in choir last night, and she volunteered."

"Florence Klein? My old boyfriend's mother is going with me on my honeymoon?" I was still trying to process what I'd just heard!

"Yeah. Renée, she can afford it, and she really wants to go. Is it okay?"

"I'll have to run this one past Mike."

When I told Mike that night, he laughed. "You're kidding me. This is weird! This is really weird. But okay." He had gotten to know Flo at church. She was a very likable lady. The only negative was that she just happened to be the mother of Jerry, my ex-boyfriend. The next day I called her and we laughed over the unnaturalness of the whole situation. "But I really can go," she said. "Is it okay?"

"What the heck. Why not! Just don't be in my room at midnight, okay?"

"You can count on that!"

So it was set. We had our reservations, our itinerary, our wardrobe, and our foursome. I was ready. Or was I?

The sadness started on the way to the port. It was a beautiful, clear day in California, but the clouds were gathering in my spirit. We arrived at San Pedro Harbor—Mom, Denise, Brenda, Mike, me, and a van full of equipment. When they wheeled me out of the van, I saw the ship, and I let out a big sigh of resignation. I felt no excitement. I turned and watched as the other four people started unloading, and unloading, and unloading all my stuff. Suitcases full of medical supplies, my manual wheelchair, my shower chair, my battery charger. *It takes four people just to get me on a ship. What a joke.*

Mom asked, "Renée, do you want to put this jacket on, or do you want me to stick it in a suitcase?"

"I really don't care!" I snapped at her. She winced.

"I'm simply trying to help."

"Just get me out of here!" I screamed. I rolled around the corner behind the parking structure, and I exploded. "I am so sick of having to be nice! I'm sick of having people around me every minute of every day! I'm sick of having people help me do every stupid thing. I even have to have people come with me on my honeymoon!" When I said honeymoon, it went from anger and rage to sorrow and grief. Then the tears started. Mike came around the corner.

"This is so stupid!" I told him. "This is our honeymoon, and we have to have all these people here. Who in the world takes two extra people—one being her ex-boyfriend's mother—

on her wedding trip! And all this stuff! Why should anybody have to take all this stupid stuff on her honeymoon? It looks like a portable rehab center! Why can't we just have a normal honeymoon like anyone else?!

"Now Mom's mad at me because I bit her head off, and I have to go back and apologize to her when I don't feel like apologizing to anybody for anything! But I have to so it'll make her feel better, but I'm sick of apologizing! Every time I turn around I'm having to say please or thank you or I'm sorry! And I'm so sick of having to worry about what other people think when I'm so ticked off! I hate living like this! I hate it! I hate it! I hate it!"

Mike held me until I got it all out of my system. He knew that words weren't going to help; there was nothing he could say to change anything. Just then the foghorn on the ship bellowed, a loud, startling blast that brought me back to reality.

Meanwhile, Denise and Brenda were putting my equipment on the ship. Seeing me break down, Denise was upset. When she got to the door of the ship, the crewman wasn't going to let her on. In no mood to be told no, Denise told him very firmly, "Look, this is my sister's honeymoon, and she's in a wheelchair. She can't move, so I *am* going to board this ship and set up her room. There's no way I'm going on her honeymoon with her. I'm just going to take her stuff on, then I'm coming off. You're going to have to trust me on that." He let her pass.

When my tantrum subsided, I rolled back around the corner. "Mom, I'm sorry. I just hate this." She understood, but she was still kind of upset.

"I was just trying to help."

"I know it." Then I started to weep again. "Mom, I'm *really* sorry. I'm just mad that my honeymoon has to be like *this*! I shouldn't have snapped at you like that. You were trying to help. I wasn't mad at you." She hugged me and we made up. Then she hugged Mike, whispered, "Good luck!" and we were off on our honeymoon.

Our first port was Mazatlan. When I went to disembark, I was told that I had to go down to the lower deck and get off where they loaded and unloaded the freight. Once in the town, I was bouncing along on the cobblestone street, being jostled so much that I thought I was going to bounce right out of my chair. Mike and I looked at each other and said, "What were we thinking? Mexico in a wheelchair?"

In Cabo San Lucas, we had to moor in the bay and use lifeboats to transport us to the dock. My first instinct was to stay on the ship, but then I thought, *Heck no! This is our honeymoon! I want to do everything!* This was our last stop, so by now the crew knew us, and they assured me they could get me off the ship. Not being one to watch the parade when I could be in it, I decided to do it. If I had known, however, what I was getting myself into, I might have chosen otherwise.

There was a long gangplank that stretched from the ship to a lifeboat. The deck of the ship was probably three stories high, and the waiting boat was way down there at sea level. Because the gangplank was so narrow, the crewmen took the wheels off my manual wheelchair. One crewman was in front of me and another was behind, and Mike walked backward in front of them to be the spotter. In other words, he was there to catch either crewman if one started to fall!

I was on my back, looking up at the sky. One time I turned my head and looked downward. Big mistake! I saw nothing but space and water. Knowing that if I went into the water I wouldn't be able to move and would quickly sink, I was terrified. I kept my eyes up and prayed. The men slowly inched all the way down the makeshift bridge to the waiting dingy. When they had me safely aboard, everyone in the boat and everyone watching on the ship clapped and cheered. I think they were as uneasy and nervous as I was!

One night of the cruise was formal night. When Brenda was getting me ready, I broke down in tears. I was wearing a formal of sorts, but it just didn't look elegant or beautiful in my wheelchair. Brenda held me close while I dissolved in her arms. Throughout the rest of the honeymoon, I tried not to be disappointed and was generally successful, but there were moments when my emotions just crashed through the veneer.

We did the things people usually do on cruises—watched floorshows, sunned on the deck, played bingo. One night I sang "Wind Beneath My Wings" in the talent show. We enjoyed breathtaking sunsets, balmy weather, and great food.

Our honeymoon was nowhere near what I'd always dreamed it would be, but it was as good as it could have been under the circumstances. We were married and we were together; that was the most important thing. We had a good time together relaxing, laughing, sightseeing, and eating! We came to understand that intimacy is not sex. Intimacy is holding and loving and listening and caressing. It's about being loved and giving love in return.

10

A Home
of Our Own

While we had been making wedding plans, things began to happen. I never knew what the next phone call would bring or what I was going to be called upon to do. About ten months after my accident, I got a phone call from Pastor Jim Farley, the minister at the Presbyterian church where I had recruited some of my choir members. "Renée, most of the kids in our youth group go to school at San Clemente High, and they're still struggling over your accident. Would you consider being our guest for an interview at a Sunday morning service? You could update the kids on your progress and answer questions I'd ask you. They need to see you, to know that you're okay."

"Uh, sure," I replied slowly, still trying to take in what he said. "If you think it would help, I'd love to come. How much of the service would you like me to do?"

"All of it. Actually, we have two services, so we'd like you to do both if it's not too taxing on you. And we want you to sing. The kids need to hear you sing."

"Oh, I really can't sing—not like I used to. How would it be if I brought my sisters to sing with me? Would that work?"

"That would be great," he replied. "How about Sunday after next? I'll announce it from the pulpit next Sunday and put it in the bulletin so people will know you're coming."

When we hung up, I sat and thought about what it would be like to speak in front of a whole church and to see my kids again—in a different setting and under different circumstances. *That was certainly a call I never expected to get, but I think it'll be good; it'll be fun.* I looked forward to seeing my kids and trying to help them.

Although I'd been on stage and in front of audiences literally hundreds of times, I was nervous that Sunday morning. This was different. I wasn't doing a show; I was sharing my heart. This wasn't an act with props and costumes and a script to follow; this was authentic. I wanted my kids to see that I was adjusting, and I especially wanted them to know that even in tragedy God had been faithful.

The pastor told the congregation the details of my accident for those who weren't familiar with the story, and then I gave an update—how long I was in full-time rehab and where I was living. I thanked everyone who had visited or sent cards or provided meals or prayed. He asked me specific questions about my progress and prognosis, and then he asked, "How are you dealing with this emotionally?"

"Well, I cry a lot," I said with half a laugh. "I just have to take it day by day. I can't allow myself to get sidetracked by what could have been, nor can I spin my wheels wondering what's down the road for me. It takes all my energy to keep it together just for today."

"That's good advice for all of us," he agreed. "Are you angry at God?"

"If you were to ask, 'Have you been angry?' I would say yes! I've been through that emotion as well as any other feeling you'd care to suggest. But am I angry at God? No. I just get angry or maybe a better word would be 'frustrated' over the situation. Do I blame God? No. That would be silly. God didn't push me off the bed. I can't blame him for something that was a tragic accident. However, I did expect him to fix it, and I got pretty ticked when I realized he wasn't going to—at least not like I wanted. He evidently has other ideas about what 'fix it' means."

"What has this experience done to your relationship with God?"

"Oh, that's easy to answer. I'm closer to God than I've ever been. When I could walk and take care of myself, God was a part of my life, but I'd have to say that the role I allowed him to play was minor. Through this, I've seen God taking care of details—practical things, like Dorothy opening my bedroom door in the middle of the night, and like Mike's company giving him a job in Long Beach. I've felt God's presence and heard his voice in the middle of the night. Before this, I never knew God was involved in the everyday details of our lives. More and more every day I'm learning how much He cares and that I can trust him to make beautiful music of my life again."

To conclude Michelle, Denise, and I sang "We Will Rise Again." At the end of the service, I felt cleansed and at peace. It was great fun to share my experiences and feelings, and talking about God's presence in the midst of my pain acted as a catharsis. I found it's true that when you hear yourself say something, your words and thoughts are cemented in your own mind.

The congregation was very responsive; I could sense their empathy and hear their laughter, and many came by to tell me how much my testimony encouraged and inspired them. When you share what you've learned about God, it helps others see God too. I felt so good about the whole experience that looking back, I think I had an inkling that this was the beginning of something. The spark of a ministry was ignited.

Having heard about my appearance at the Presbyterian church, another church called a few weeks later, and I did much the same thing. Invitations slowly began to trickle in. I was in no way seeking to become a public speaker; that thought never entered my mind during those first few years. I accepted invitations if I could, but I never tried to open any doors.

The first Christmas after our wedding, Austin Buffum, who had hired me at San Clemente High, called and invited me to sing a solo in the Christmas cantata at South Shores Church in Laguna Niguel where he was music director.

I gave him my usual response. "Thank you for the invitation, but I really can't sing very well anymore." Nevertheless he said he'd drop the music off for me to look over. The song was "People Need the Lord," and the words were incredible. Once I saw the music, I cried. "I'll do it," I told Austin, "but you're going to need a really good sound man."

The afternoon of the concert, Andrea, my attendant, did my makeup and hair and got me into a dress. As I was getting ready, I noticed that Mike was acting kind of funny and that Andrea was taking unusually long. When it was time to go, I couldn't get Mike out of the house. He kept forgetting things and going back to get them. I was in the manual chair, so I couldn't move from the spot where I was parked. Finally Mike said, "Okay, let's get in the van." But instead of pushing me into the garage, he pushed me out the front door. As we came out, I heard a large group of people singing "Jingle Bells."

We came into view of the street, and there in front of me were giant candy canes, snowmen, bales of hay, a stage, Christmas trees, a sound system, musical instruments, and thirty Young Americans singing in full costume! All the neighbors were in the street; everybody in the neighborhood had known they were out there setting up—except me! When I saw them, I was torn between laughing and crying.

"No way!" I exclaimed. "You've got to be kidding! This is too wonderful!" I was completely blown away. They did a full forty-five-minute concert just for me. They danced, sang, joked, and changed costumes many times. I never knew what was coming next—the rolling of a snowman, the appearance of Santa Claus, beautiful Christmas music with fully chore-

I was born on
June 21, 1958.

I'm the baby in this
smiling brood. Left to
right are Danny,
Denise, and Michelle.

ird grade and it's
ficial—my nickname
"Lumpy"

Senior picture,
1976. Move over,
Brady Bunch!

Barrel-racing
with Tar Baby

Goofing around with my sisters
Denise, then Michelle, and I'm
on the bottom. Why am I
always on the bottom?

Young Americans Tour, 197

Ooh la la, I'm in France!

San Clemente High School Choir (1986)

Chaperoning the prom with Mike the night before the accident

Trying on my wedding dress (1987)

Family photo on the Lacouague Ranch (1987). Standing from left to right are Danny, my parents John and Marie, and Denise. Michelle's sitting on the left, I'm sitting on the right.

My first day-trip home from the hospital

Mr. and Mrs. Mike Bondi

Mike knelt to speak his vows

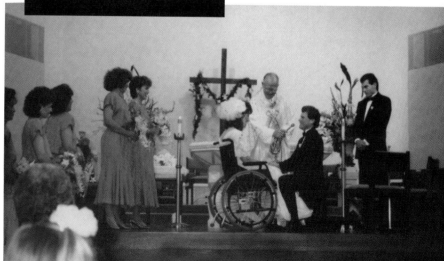

Mike makes it
to his dream
spot—Alaska

My dear friend
Jim May

eeting Pope John Paul II

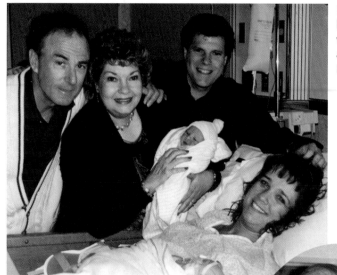

Daniel James Bondi, born March 20, 1995, with grandparents Jim and Sandra Bondi, Mike, and me

Father Martin and baby Daniel

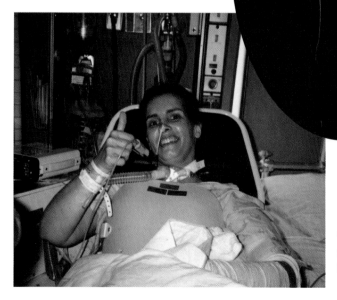

Thumbs up from my sister Michelle

Feeding Daniel in his special sling

My parents, John and Marie Lacouague

Daniel having fun at our neighborhood park

Daniel resting in Mom's lap

In the studio recording *Let It Rain* (2001)

Still smiling—me, Denise, and Michelle

Our family today

ographed moves. The kids danced and sang with the energy they would have expended on an audience of thousands.

By tradition, the final number in YA Christmas concerts is always a gorgeous arrangement of "Silent Night," sung a cappella and beginning with a solo. But no one ever knows who the soloist will be until that night, when the director hands the microphone to one vocalist. It was always a big deal to see who would be put on the spot.

When the program was drawing to a close, Milton, the YA founder and director, walked over to me. "We're going to do one more number. As you remember, the picking of the soloist is always important to the cast. Renée, we'd appreciate it if you would sing the solo for us this evening."

"Oh, you guys!"

Mike held the microphone to my mouth. Fighting back tears, I took a deep breath and sang. "Silent night, holy night. . . ."

The kids started crying, and so did the neighbors. My voice was being amplified all over my neighborhood! After the concert the kids gathered around, and I thanked them profusely.

"You guys bring such joy to my life. How did you ever think to do a surprise concert?"

Milton answered. "I've always wanted to do a living Christmas card, but this time of the year is always so busy I've never been able to do it. But this year, we had this weekend and time to do three. So I sat down with the kids, and together we decided who we would like to sing to, and you won! After we leave here, we're going to sing for Andy Williams."

"You guys, this has been more than wonderful," I said. "The music brought back such memories. And thank you for choosing me to do the solo." I looked at Milton and quipped, "I never got to do it before!" The kids thought it was hilarious. I chatted with the kids for a few minutes and then they had to be off to their next concert, and I had to be off to mine.

What I learned later was that Mike had conspired with Austin to give me a false time that I needed to be at church. Even after the neighborhood concert, we had plenty of time to make it for our sound check. When Mike rolled me into the church and I saw Austin, I gave him a look that said, "You were in on that!"

"Pretty wonderful?" he asked.

"Oh, I think you could safely say that. It was fabulous!"

Not long afterwards, my principal from San Clemente High School called. "We want you to come back to teach next year. What do you think?" I was flattered, and I wanted more than anything to accept his offer.

Students who still came by for visits encouraged me. "Miss Lacouague, you just thought we were watching your arms when you directed. Really, we were watching your eyes and your facial expressions. You can do it. Come back!"

But I knew it was too soon. Physically, I couldn't handle the pace I'd need to keep, nor the paperwork, nor the emotional stress. I still had months and months of rehab ahead of me, and the bottom line was that I had little movement. There was just no way, so I very reluctantly declined.

I wanted to go back to work so badly I could taste it, and the invitation from SCHS intensified my desire. How I missed working with kids, directing beautiful songs, instilling in kids the love for music. While I was still stinging over not being able to return to teaching, Father Martin came by one afternoon. "Renée, we want you to start some youth choirs at the church."

"Thank you for the offer, but there's just no way," I said. Although I had graduated from the sip-n-puff straw to a joy stick, I was still in that humongous chair with my arms in troughs.

Starting the youth choirs sounded like so much fun, but I could see only my limitations. Realizing I'd have to miss yet another opportunity, I began to cry. "How can I teach this way? I can't do it. There's no way. By the time I get the page turned, the song will be over. I just can't do it."

Prepared for my response, Father Martin said, "We'll get you a couple of volunteer moms. They can turn your pages, take roll, and pass out the music. You can just teach. They can even drive you from your home to the church. It's an hour and a half once a week. Let's just try it."

His argument was convincing. With that much help, and since it would be only one afternoon a week, maybe I *could* do it! I began to get excited. "Let me talk to Mike and my family," I told him.

When I told Dad, I didn't get the reaction I'd hoped for. "I know why you want to do this, but didn't you hear what Dr. Palmer said? He told you clearly that your life will never be the same again. The doctors have been studying cases like yours for years, and they know best. You can't do this, Renée. You need to start accepting this and quit trying to do the impossible."

"I'm sure Dr. Palmer never thought I'd have as much stamina in the chair as I do, and he was wrong about that. Who's to say I can't do this? Dad, look at me. I'm thirty years old. If all I'm going to be able to do for the next fifty years is sit in this chair or lie in that bed, then just go ahead and put the gun to my head now. I have got to do something worthwhile. Why are you so against me trying?"

"Because I don't want you to fail. I don't want you to hurt any more than you already have. You've been through enough."

Dad was from the old school. If a doctor said something, it was as valid as the Bible and as binding as the constitution. Doctors were infallible, and what they said was law. You didn't question what a doctor said; you just followed instructions. He was also struggling to overcome an old point of view, common to people in his generation, that cripples didn't go out in public or live productive lives. But this viewpoint was now in conflict with what he saw and felt for me. Of course he wanted me to have a full and productive life, but he thought I was in denial and wanted me to accept my fate and be content with it. Although I wished he felt differently, I understood.

Fortunately, everyone else, especially Mike, encouraged me to go for it, so I called Father Martin and accepted. I started three choirs—one elementary, one junior high, and one high school.

Teaching without my body was definitely a challenge. When singing an entire song, there'd inevitably be trouble spots I needed to address when we had completed the piece. The normal thing would be to put circles in pencil on the sheet music where the two or three areas of concern were so that I would remember, but because I couldn't use my fingers, I'd have to keep a running list in my brain: *top of page 3—tenors came in too late; bottom of 4—enunciation; middle of 8, second score, third measure—altos flat.*

It took real concentration. When setting the tempo, I had only my voice. You'd think that once the tempo was set the choir would stay on course. Not true. Without direction, a group tends to drag or race ahead, so I learned to use my shoulders (all those shoulder shrugs finally came in handy!) and the little bit of arm movement I had to pick up the pace or hold the tempo back.

When I had my body, if there was a student having a lapse of self-control while I was teaching, I'd just keep on teaching and walk toward the student and stand there while I finished my point. The student would get the message and I didn't have to interrupt myself or create a scene. It worked well. But I couldn't get up to the back row in my wheelchair, so I learned to use my eyes. Also, sometimes I'd stop and say something like, "Okay, here's the scoop. You've got a choir director with no hands, so I have to rely on you to be a partner with me in this endeavor. You have to discipline yourselves."

For the most part, they were wonderful. They even disciplined each other. I often saw elbows fly when someone was talking out of turn. And there was the ever-present problem of getting the pages turned on time. But we made it work.

Like at SCHS, the numbers quickly began to grow. During one rehearsal, I had the roll book in my lap and was counting the number enrolled. I mentally counted, "148, 149, 150!" One hundred and fifty? That was the same number of students I had at the high school! Wow! God gave me back just as many students as I had lost! He didn't have to do that; I would have been totally jazzed with twenty!

I remembered Julie Turner when she told me that God speaks to her; I had wondered what God sounded like. I immediately realized that these 150 choir members represented God's voice speaking to me loud and clear. "Don't worry, Renée," he was saying. "I'm in this with you. I'm inside of you. I'm beside you. I'm in front of you, behind you. I'm right in the middle of this with you. Be not afraid."

I worked out a schedule for volunteers to drive me to choir practice each week, and the designated volunteer would come to my house and then drive me in my van. The situation was always a little bit disconcerting because the volunteers were driving an unfamiliar vehicle; some had never even driven a van before, and because I have absolutely no trunk control, a smooth drive was a necessity. One day Peter Huber, one of my church choir kids, came to drive me, and this to tell you the truth was pretty risky. We stereotype teenage drivers for a reason!

Sure enough, he took a right corner a little too fast, and the momentum threw me right into his lap—face down! He was afraid he had hurt me, but I wasn't at all hurt. I was just completely embarrassed to have my head in the lap of one of my senior boys! With no trunk support, I couldn't even get up. "Okay, Peter," I said, "don't take this the wrong way. Just get me up out of your lap!" Not knowing what to do, Peter was trying to get me out of his lap with one hand while guiding the car to the side of the road with the other. By the time we came to a stop, we were both laughing at ourselves and our ridiculous predicament.

I was only working part-time, so I could continue in physical therapy three days a week. I loved Tina, my PT at Casa Colina, but because we became such good friends over the months, we chit-chatted and too much of my physical therapy time was wasted. Also, the long drive was getting old; I needed to find a therapist closer to home. I asked around for recommendations and found Jim D'Agostino, a wonderful therapist in Oceanside, forty minutes south rather than an hour and fifteen minutes north.

He was just what I needed. He worked my muscles to the max, squeezing out every ounce of strength. Sitting on the mat, I worked and worked until I could throw my arm backward with my shoulder, lock my elbow, and catch my weight. Frequently Jim would "slap me around," shoving me sideways with deliberate force to make me catch and bring my torso upright. Next, he'd put me on my stomach and make me do push-ups using my elbows and lower arms. As I progressed, he'd apply resistance, and eventually he actually lay across my shoulders and made me lift him.

I went to therapy on Monday, Wednesday, and Friday, and on alternate days I nursed aching, sore muscles. Little by little, inch by inch, I got stronger and regained some use of my upper arms. Without Jim's regimen, I would be able to do much less today than I can.

About a year after our wedding, Mom and Dad came over to our house together. "We want to talk to you about something," Dad began. "Mike, with your hour commute each way and long hours at work, Mom is pretty worried about Renée being so far away. If there were an emergency, it's a fifteen-minute drive on the freeway to get here. It's scary for her. Although you haven't been out to the back of the ranch, I'm sure you know they've cleared the rest of the trees and have started building scores of houses out there, and they're just about finished. We think you should buy one and move closer to us. Another option is that you could build your own home up on the five acres we kept, but why do that if one of the floor plans in the development would work?"

"Yeah, right!" Mike and I just laughed. At that time, the housing market was booming; prices were incredibly high. "Dad, there's no way we can afford that; some of those houses go for a small fortune."

"Well, Mike, how much do you think you could afford?" Mike got out his calculator, did some figuring, and came up with a house payment he thought we could handle, which gave us a ballpark figure of how much we could afford to pay for a house.

Dad made an offer. "Okay, as your inheritance, we'll match that, bringing you to a figure that just might buy you one of those houses. Construction is complete, the landscaping is going in, and this week they're paving the streets. They've not been able to sell the houses like they thought, so next weekend there's going to be an auction. Between now and then, we'll go look at what floor plan would work for you and which lot with that floor plan will give us easy accessibility. We'll bid on that one and hope it comes in under our limit."

"You've got to be kidding!" I responded. "It's an incredible offer, but we can't accept your money. You've worked hard for it, so take it and enjoy retirement."

"Renée, you need it now. Why suffer until we go when we could help you right now? Just know you ain't getting anything when we die!" he said with his dry laugh.

During the next few days we considered their generous offer, and we realized this was for their peace of mind as well as for us. At the time, Denise and Joseph and Danny and Vicki lived on the hill too, so being all together would eliminate a lot of trips back and forth when they came to help me.

When we drove out to what used to be our picturesque ranch the following Saturday, I got a jolt I didn't expect. Where there had been rolling hills with orange groves and shade trees and pastureland, there were now houses and sidewalks and stop signs. The family ranch in rural San Juan Capistrano looked like the rest of Orange County—tract houses dotting the landscape as far as the eye could see. I was very upset.

As Mike backed me down the ramp of the van, my eyes fell on the hill where Danny used to have the perfect fort. As kids, we had played on that hill, using the cave for our hideout. Now, new houses almost obliterated it. It was the last straw. When Mike got me onto the ground, I told him, "Get me out of here!" He pushed me around behind the van, and I lost it. I cried for yet another loss. It felt like my childhood had been stripped away. I looked at the hill and cried. Looked away and cried. Looked back and cried still harder. In my mind's eye I could see the peaceful hills that used to surround the ranch house. I relived riding over the hills on Tar Baby. I knew with my head that it was necessary (Dad had needed to sell), but my heart ached. It was another death.

Another disturbing reality was that Mike and I were moving back to the ranch so Mom and Dad could help take care of me. Before the accident, the plan was that someday Mike and I would move onto the ranch and take care of Mom and Dad, not the other way around. It just wasn't working out at all the way it should have, which gave me something else to cry about!

Deciding I'd had enough time for my meltdown, Mike came back to me and held me close, allowing the tears to flow. He always seems to know when to offer words and when to let me purge. Sensing that I was trying to rally, he said, "Renée, let's go take a look at the model your mom and dad think we ought to get. They think you're really going to like it."

Three out of five of the models had two stories, so there were really only two floor plans that would work for us. The best of the two had an open arrangement with wide halls and few doors, and it even had a large front bedroom, with a huge window that looked out onto the street, that could serve as the office. We then went to see the actual house; it backed right up to the "Lacouague Compound" at the top of the hill.

I loved the openness, and as I sat in the living room and looked out the back slider, I could see orange trees! We could easily put in a ramp that would lead right to Mom and Dad's back door. It was perfect. But would it sell under our ceiling? We decided we absolutely would not exceed our budget. We would only bid on the one, so we had only one crack at it. We were trusting that if God wanted us to have it, then it would work out.

The auction started at 3:00 P.M. under a gigantic tent that had been erected for this purpose. About half the size of a football field, it looked like a spaceship had landed on our ranch—totally out of character. As we entered the tent, I was still crying. All day I had fought to keep my composure, but to no avail. I was hiding my red eyes behind my sunglasses. Many people there were from San Juan and wanted to stop and talk, but try as I might, I could not get it together. I was a full-blown basket case.

Wisely, Dad gave our bidding paddle—number fifty-four— to Mike, who was visibly nervous. "Never have I spent this much money by just waving my hand!" he said. I looked at Dad and cautioned, "No emotional buying, Dad. We cannot afford one dollar more than we agreed upon. We can't get carried away."

The bidding went very quickly. The auctioneer ran through each house like a game show host on fast forward. One whack of the gavel, and one by one each home was sold. Many times there were little cheers of celebration as the new owners rejoiced. The houses seemed to be going for more than we could pay, so it didn't look good. Mike got more nervous with the coming and going of each house. Anxiously we waited. Our house was one of the last to bid, the very last one of our floor plan. If we got it, we got it. If we didn't, it was all over. There were no second chances.

Finally, our model came up, and we were off to the races. There was just one man down front—number twenty-six— who was bidding against us, and back and forth it went. Quickly, the auctioneer barked out each level.

"Give me $100,000. Who'll give me a $100,000?" Paddle fifty-four went up.

Immediately, "Give me $120,000. Who'll give me $120,000?" Paddle twenty-six went up.

"Who'll give me $130,000? $130,000?" Paddle fifty-four up.

"I need $10,000 more. $10,000 more!" Paddle twenty-six up.

The price rose as quickly as the auctioneer's cadence. Mike kept his cool while the rest of us sat on pins and needles. Finally, Mike raised his paddle for three thousand under our limit! The auctioneer slammed his gavel down. "Sold!"

Mike screamed like the kid in *Home Alone*. I was stunned. "Oh my goodness! We just bought a house." We looked at Mom and Dad, and the celebration started. "We got it!" Handshakes, high fives, hugs, and laughter.

Smiling broadly, Dad stood up, puffed out his chest, put his cap back on, and said matter-of-factly, "Good deal." It was vintage Dad. Mom giggled. "Oh, my hands were sweating. Well, good. I think this will be very good for you both."

Later we learned there had been an investor there that day who had brought others to bid on houses as investments. This investor knew Dad and had recognized me. He told his colleagues, "See that couple down there? The lady in the wheelchair? That's the original owner's daughter. She needs this house for accessibility, so please don't bid against them." That's why there was only one man bidding against us. He was not a part of the investor's group. God always makes a way!

One month later, we moved into our new home.

Fast forward two years. We were enjoying our new home, but the backyard was nothing but dirt with a two-foot drop from our living room to the ground below. After buying a house, who has money to put in the backyard? My family could walk down to me, but I couldn't get to them; however, accessibility was better than it had been. At that time I was on the Board of Directors for The Young Americans. One night when Mike and I were working in the office, I found an envelope containing 125 raffle tickets I was supposed to have sold for $2.00 each, the grand prize being a new VW Jetta. I had forgotten all about them, and the money was supposed to be turned in within a few days. I had totally dropped the ball.

"Uh, Mike, dear? How would you feel about giving a donation to The Young Americans?"

"Maybe. How much?"

"$250.00"

"Whoa!" He nearly choked. "Heftier than I thought! Why so much?"

"Look," I said, showing him the raffle tickets. "I royally screwed up. These accidentally got buried. Could we possibly donate the money? There's no way I can get them sold."

"Well, I just balanced the checkbook, and we have a little extra. You really have to do this, huh?" The next day, a former student came over and stamped all 125 of the tickets with our name and address, stuck them in an envelope, and mailed them off with our donation. I never thought about them again.

A few weeks later, I had an awful nightmare. Although I was still asleep, I was so frantic that I woke Mike up, and he had to shake me to wake me up and stop the dream. "What's wrong? What was it?" he asked.

Through tears I told him, "I dreamed that our house was on fire and I couldn't get out the back slider!"

"That's it! We're putting our backyard in. I don't know how we're going to pay for it, but that's a sign. It's dangerous that you can't get out of the house!"

As usual, I started crying. "Don't overreact. It was just a dream. We can't afford to put in the backyard. I can get out the front. It was just a dream!"

But his mind was made up. "I don't know how, but that yard is going in. We'll pray and ask God to provide it. It's just going to happen."

Two days later, we got a phone call. "Is this Renée Bondi?"

"Yes, it is."

"Are you sitting down?"

"Yes, and if you knew me, you'd know I was sitting down," I said, laughing.

"You've just won yourself a new VW Jetta!"

I screamed!

We sold the Jetta for ten thousand dollars and used the money to put in our backyard. Our dear friend Mike Imlay, who is a landscape architect, designed a wonderful layout for us, maximizing what little backyard we have. There's lots of cement so I can move around, plenty of grass, great shrubs, lovely trees, beautiful flowers, and best of all, a ramp up the hill to Mom and Dad's. How many times and in how many ways has God provided for us! There seems to be no end to God's provision for us or to the creative ways he demonstrates his love.

11

The Sounds
of Music Again

About that same time, early in 1991, Robert H. Schuller's organization called out of the blue and asked me to appear in their Sunday morning services and on the *Hour of Power* television broadcast. We set the date for February. It was a big opportunity for me—a true honor to be invited. I confess, however, that I wasn't sure if it was something I should be doing. I didn't know much at all about Dr. Schuller. I knew he got his start doing a drive-in church, that his Crystal Cathedral was world renowned, and that his approach to church was innovative and revolutionary.

On the morning of my appearance, Mike and I were discussing my uncertainty as we drove up I-5 toward Garden Grove on a rainy Sunday morning. In addition to my curiosity about Dr. Schuller, I was concerned about all the logistical considerations that people who aren't in wheelchairs don't always think about—like how am I going to get on stage without being a spectacle? Who's going to run the sound? Will my weak voice carry over the orchestra? Does Dr.

Schuller know enough about me to ask pertinent questions? Do I respond with long answers or short answers?

It was all a big unknown, and I was almost regretting that I had accepted. Then as we came around a corner we saw a perfect, brilliant rainbow! It was right in front of us—one end piercing the ocean and the other disappearing behind the hills. It was breathtaking!

Mike and I looked at each other as if to ask, "Are you thinking what I'm thinking?" Mike confirmed it. "Looks like maybe God is telling us we're on the right track!"

Once inside the Crystal Cathedral, I quickly realized that my fears were completely unjustified. We were taken to a well-equipped private room where I could get ready. Someone came in and told us exactly what I was to do and what to expect. Dr. Schuller's wife, Arvella, came in to say hello. She was very warm and kind; in fact, the entire staff was completely professional, friendly, and helpful. Right away, I knew that I had nothing to worry about.

I didn't meet Dr. Schuller until I was on stage, but he was a gracious, warm host. I had been told that the interview would be only five minutes long, so I knew that my answers to Dr. Schuller's questions would need to be short and concise. This was my first television interview, and I was aware that time would be limited, so I consciously made the decision not to have diarrhea of the mouth.

Dr. Schuller asked me pertinent questions like, "How did you get in the chair?"

I responded with a thumbnail description, "After going to bed on a seemingly normal night, I woke up about 2:00 in the morning in midair, falling off the foot of my bed, onto my head. Boom!" I looked at him, waiting for the next question, but he was looking at me, waiting for more details, so I went on. "I tried to get up, but each time a pain cut into my neck like a knife."

"Go on."

"Within a few minutes my roommate Dorothy opened the door and found me on the floor." So the interview went—

me giving short answers, and he looking at me with interest, waiting for more.

"I understand you're married now."

"Yes, Mike and I were engaged, and our wedding was just two months away when I broke my neck. But he hung in there with me, and we got married one year after I got out of the hospital. There wasn't a dry eye in that church!"

"Wow. In this day and age, you don't find men like that very often. Tell me about Mike." I knew we were running way over on time, but it was only because he kept asking for more. I was surprised later to find that Dr. Schuller had allowed that five-minute interview to last twenty minutes!

I closed the interview with "Here I Am, Lord." I chose this song because from the beginning of this ordeal my prayer was for God to use me. Even lying on the floor minutes after breaking my neck, I was praying, "I'm your instrument; I'm your tool. Use me, Lord." And here I was, on international TV, being used by God! The other reason I chose this song is that it is not too hard to sing. Here again, I had to work around my lack of power and shortness of breath. Thank God (literally!) for the powerful sound system at the Crystal Cathedral!

While I was leaving the stage, Dr. Schuller said to his congregation, "I have never had a guest who has touched me more deeply with the love of Jesus Christ than Renée Bondi has, and she's lovely enough to be one of my four daughters!" What a loving, gracious man! Since then, I've returned to the *Hour of Power* about twice a year, and it's always a blessing to me.

The summer of '92, I got a phone call from Gordon Paine, the choirmaster for Helmuth Rilling who was coming to L.A. to do a series of concerts with the L.A. Chamber Orchestra. Helmuth had commissioned Gordon to put together a choir, and because I had sung with the Oregon Bach Festival for five seasons, he called to invite me to be a part of it. "We'll be doing the *Bach Mass in B-Minor*, which you have performed several times."

I said, "Gordon, you know what happened to me. I'd have to take six breaths to the other singers' one. I just wouldn't be any help. Thank you, but I just don't think my voice can handle music at that level. I do pretty well on the lighter stuff, but I just don't have the breath control for classical music anymore. I'd be okay on the long notes, but my voice just won't handle those sixteenth-note runs. I'm not what you need."

He replied, "You're exactly what we need."

"I know it's a courtesy and I appreciate it, and it would be so much fun to sing with everybody again. Tell you what. Send me the music and I'll take a look at it." He did, and I called him back to identify the sections where I would and would not be of help.

Gordon listened but pressed on. "Okay, let's do it," he said.

We had a couple rehearsals at Cal State Fullerton. I didn't think Helmuth knew I was there. It wasn't like I was close to him; I was just a voice in the choir. Just like he always did, Helmuth came in and got right to work. But at one point he looked up to say something to the altos and saw me. "Renée!" He came over and gave me a big hug, and then at break he talked to me at length. Gordon told me later that it touched Helmuth greatly to see that I was back on my feet again, so to speak.

The night of the concert found us in Royce Hall, UCLA, performing in front of a sold-out crowd. A full orchestra was on stage. I was in the front row at the end of the alto section, wearing a black skirt and a white, long-sleeved blouse like the others, but with an abdominal binder underneath so my diaphragm would have something to push against.

The orchestra began. Fellow choir member and good friend Linda turned my pages. My eyes were glued to Helmuth—back and forth from conductor to music. I concentrated more than ever on breathing, precise pitch, calculating the intervals just right, gasping for air like an Olympic swimmer. I did not dare make a mistake. Self-doubt crept in. *Adding much?* I slapped myself, mentally. *Just go for it! Yes, I am!*

Two and a half hours later the concert ended, and the audience broke into thunderous applause. Helmuth took several bows. The concertmaster stood up. Applause. The soloists got their acknowledgment. They went off stage. Applause, applause. They came back on stage for another bow. Applause. They went off stage. The audience was begging for more. Helmuth swept back on stage. Applause. He acknowledged the orchestra and they stood. Applause. Helmuth turned to the choir. Applause. Helmuth left the stage and came back on stage. Bows and applause. He walked off yet again, and the crowd gave us a standing ovation and stomped their feet. Helmuth returned, and the audience broke into wild cheers.

I started crying. Although no one ever pays attention to the choir, much less to an individual member, it was a big moment for me. It marked a huge step in my recovery. I had done it. I was back. I was singing Bach again and holding my own. Linda and my friends near me were crying too because I had done it, so there was this big drama going on between the appreciative audience and the stars of the evening, but playing out on the back of the stage was a mini-drama to which the audience was oblivious.

Helmuth and the soloists were presented with the traditional huge bouquets of flowers while the applause continued. The conductor and soloists exited. After a long wait Helmuth returned by himself with a red rose from one of the bouquets. He bowed. Hair tousled and wet, face aglow with moisture and fatigue, Helmuth turned and started making his way through the orchestra. I could hear his thick German accent as he picked his way through. "Excuse me. Pardon me. May I get through here? Excuse me." This was totally out of protocol. You could sense everyone wondering, "Where is he going? What is he doing?"

Once he cleared the orchestra, he walked straight to me and presented me with the rose. My jaw hit the floor. The choir turned to me, the orchestra turned and stood, and together they gave me a standing ovation. It was unbelievable. I was a wreck—a total and complete wreck. Quite frankly, it is every choir member's dream to get acknowledged. Soloists get recognized, but never anyone in the general choir. And here it was—me, Renée, just a little, insignificant choir member in my wheelchair, receiving a standing ovation from Helmuth Rilling, probably the most noted Bach conductor in the world, the soloists, the orchestra, the choir, and a thousand in the audience—all standing for me. What a moment.

When it was over, Linda and the choir members helped me off the stage. Backstage, dozens came by and offered their congratulations, expressing their delight that I was back again. Then I heard, "Miss Lacouague? It's really you!" Holly Zell, one of my students from San Clemente High, just happened to be at the concert. She had needed it for a college class and didn't even notice I was in the choir, which is not unusual because Royce Hall is so big the audience can't see individual faces. "I didn't know you were here until the conductor gave you the rose. I'm so proud of you!" So we sat there and hugged and bawled.

As if getting a standing ovation from the musicians I most respected wasn't honor enough, God gave me the added blessing of sharing the evening with one of my special students. As Jeremiah said in Lamentations 3:22–23, I could say, "His compassions fail not. They are new every morning: Great is thy faithfulness."

After Rally 'Round Renée's first year, when they did the big benefit to raise money for the van, they continued each year by doing subsequent fundraisers to pay for my attendant care. What incredible generosity. When it was time for benefit number four, someone called to set up a time when the committee could come over and discuss plans for that year's event. "Oh, you guys, there's no way I can ask you to do this again—no way I could let you. You've done three, more than anyone could ask or dream—and it's so much work for you!"

"Well, we're going to come over and talk about it." They wouldn't quit easily.

We were sitting in our family room, and they charged into making plans. "Okay, let's do it at the Coach House. Renée, what if your Young Americans friends do the first half and you and your sisters do the second half? If people know you and your sisters are going to sing, that'll be a big selling point. And if your sisters help you, it won't be so much on your shoulders. We'll do another silent auction. Maybe your youth choirs at church could sing."

I just froze. "You guys, evidently I'm not communicating clearly enough. I cannot let you do this again! I can't! It is so much work for you! You've got families and children who need you. I just can't let you do this!"

Monica Hunnicutt, a mom of one my SCHS students, stood up, and she was angry. "Would you just be quiet and let us do this for you. Come on! This is ridiculous, Renée." With that she walked right out of the room. A shocked, embarrassed hush fell over the room. No one knew quite what to say, how to continue, or whether to continue, for that matter.

"I'm so confused," I said through tears.

Debbie Bridgeman, a former guitar student of mine, knelt down in front of me. "Renée, we are just frustrated that you are trying to shut us down. We know why you're doing it, but we *need* to help. Doing for you is part of our healing too. When we walk out of this house, we literally walk out of this house. We get in our cars, and we go on our merry ways. You're the one who's left in this chair. Doing these benefits helps us as much as it helps you."

I cried all the harder. "It's difficult to keep receiving over and over again. I don't know how to do it gracefully."

"We understand how you feel, but you're worrying needlessly. Just trust that we're doing it because we love you and because it's something we enjoy doing. When we get tired of it, we'll let you know." The fundraiser was scheduled, and my fourth year of attendant care was covered. Undoubtedly, God uses willing people to be his arms of love.

Why is it so hard for some to receive? Is it that we sincerely feel bad when someone is helping us and we know we'll probably never be able to repay them? Or maybe it's a pride thing; we all want to be self-sufficient, and we're embarrassed that we need help. Perhaps it's that we've been taught from childhood that we need to be givers and not takers. Whatever the reason, being on the receiving end over and over again was unnatural and awkward for me.

Debbie's comments helped me understand that those who love us want to help; it's their gift to us. If we refuse, we deny them the opportunity to be God's hands to us, and we may make them feel awkward for even trying. While it still feels unnatural sometimes, I've tried to learn the art of receiving gracefully and of finding special ways to express my appreciation.

One beautiful spring afternoon, Jim May came to visit. After a long run on Broadway, Jim was coming home to L.A. to open *Les Misérables* at the Schubert Theatre. I hadn't seen him in several months. We caught up on each other's lives and discussed his new house in L.A. As usual, we laughed a *lot*. It was great to be with my old friend again. After dinner he said, "Hey, when are we going to finish that recording?"

"Oh, Jim. I shouldn't even try to sing anymore because it's not the way it was. I definitely can't sing well enough to record."

"Well, let's just try it." He went over to the piano, sat down, and started playing the beginning of "Be Not Afraid."

Why didn't he play "In My Own Little Corner" or "The Sound of Music" or any number of other songs that we had done together? He had no idea how special this song was to me. Although it crossed my mind as being unusual, I was focused on projecting. I wanted to give it all I had and see what I could do. So I started singing.

> "Be not afraid. I go before you always.
> Come, follow me, and I will give you rest."

To my complete surprise, my voice was powerful! I could sing long phrases without taking a breath! My voice was almost as strong as it was before the accident! I tested it to see if it would hold.

> "If you pass through raging waters
> in the sea, you shall not drown.
> If you walk amid the burning flames,
> you shall not be harmed.
> If you stand before the power of hell
> and death is at your side,
> know that I am with you through it all. . . .
>
> "Be not afraid. I go before you always.
> Come, follow me, and I will give you rest."

Right then, in my living room, I realized that I could sing— I could *really* sing! My voice wasn't weak or throaty or breathy; it was forceful and healthy! "Wow! I *can* sing again!" I almost squealed.

"You can do this!" Jim nearly shouted. "You really can!"

Jim—a tall, forty-year-old man—stood up from the piano bench, came over to me, dumped his head in my lap, and we sobbed for joy. We both recalled the day in the hospital when I had to lie down to get any sound out at all and how we had cried together that day. Now we were crying together for the opposite reason—for joy!

My voice was restored. It was a marker. The doctors had said I'd never sing again, and now my voice was not only respectable, it was good enough to record! God had done a miracle. Jim didn't understand it at the time, but I knew what I knew. Without God, this would have been impossible.

We quickly picked up the project to complete the recording. I called Tony Anstead, who initially suggested the project years earlier, and he became our producer. Much of the legwork had been done before the accident, so I had only to rent a studio and get the musicians together. With E. J. Stanton, a young, aspiring composer, I wrote three of the songs on the album: "You Are the One," my tribute to Mike; "Only

Me," my song about the pain of the injury; and "Inner Voice," the title track. Jerry Klein played guitar and his brother Dave played bass. Rob Williams, a friend from Young Americans, drummed, Jim was at the piano, and Michelle and Denise sang backup on "Mansion Builder." It was a lot of fun making music with these special people again!

However, it wasn't all roses and sunshine. I wore an abdominal binder around my stomach that would act as a support for my diaphragm, giving me just a little more power. On about the sixth day of recording, Mike was helping me into bed one night when he suddenly stopped and stared. "Oh my gosh. Look what you've done!" The binder had been cutting into my skin all week, but of course I couldn't feel it, and by the time Mike found it, it was bad. The skin was cut and bleeding; it was ugly—an open pressure sore. The next day we gauzed it and put foam between the binder and me. Because it got as bad as it did, to this day it is still prone to breakdown, and I have to be careful with that area. After four years I finally understood why Dr. Parsons confined me to bed for three weeks because I had the beginnings of a pressure sore. I hate being wrong.

One night, exhausted from the day's work, our recording engineer Michael turned to Mike and asked, "What's the run going to be?"

Mike responded, "I think about three thousand copies."

"What?" I asked incredulously.

"Yeah, I think three thousand."

"You're kidding! Who's going to buy this thing? Just the little old ladies who go to the early service, and there are only thirty of them!"

"I've been praying," Mike said, "and I feel that the Lord is saying three thousand."

"Then you should probably come up with a record label for yourselves; you need a name and a logo," Michael said.

I laughed. "Record label? We're not Capitol Records or Word. We're just doing this for our church. Why do we need a name?"

"You should be able to catalog it."

So Mike and I were driving home at 2:00 A.M. trying to think of a name. "Probably Capo something," I said. San Juan Capistrano was always shortened to Capo by the locals. "How about Capo Records?" I suggested.

"That's too close to Capitol Records, don't you think?"

"Trust me. We're not going to be confused with Capitol Records, okay? But if that's too close, how about Capo Recording?" So, it was settled, and Capo Recording was launched.

"Wouldn't it be something if we made enough profit on this recording to pay for your attendant care?"

Mike is such the dreamer, I thought. *Profit? For one, there's not going to be any profit! And even if there were, there would never be enough to pay for my attendant care. Please! We'll take this loan to our graves! We'll end up giving these things away as Christmas presents for the rest of our lives!*

Early the next morning I called Rick Delanty. "Rick, I know you're leaving for school this morning, but I need a logo, and I need it . . . within two days. Can you do it?"

"Sure, what do you want?"

"Well, we're going to be called Capo Recording. It's a Mike thing. He thinks we're going to sell all these CDs and cassettes. I don't care what it looks like. Whatever you can come up with will be fine, I'm sure."

The very next day, Rick came back with the design. He used an arch to represent the Mission and in the middle was a bell and a musical note "for fluidity," he said, "so that people will know that even though you're paralyzed, you're still moving." It was much more profound than anything I could have come up with! I loved it.

To introduce the CD, we did a kick-off concert at the church, and the parishioners and community came out to support us in full force. We sold Mike's three thousand copies of *Inner Voice* in the first four months. In fact, the demand was so great that we made a second run, and a third, and a fourth. Mike was right, and I was amazed. To this day, the profit from my recordings completely covers the cost of my attendant care. Our God is a very practical God!

Not long after we finished recording, I was slated to perform at World Youth Day in Denver. The hub of the event was Mile High Stadium where all the big names were performing, but I was asked to sing at one of the overflow auditoriums. It was a wonderful experience—wonderful to see thousands upon thousands of young people on their knees in worship. The week culminated with mass given by Pope John Paul II at Cherry Creek Park outside of Denver on the last day at 10:00 A.M.

Every TV and radio broadcast warned people about the congestion and how crowded it was. People had been camping out there for two days. The park's capacity was already maxed out and the August heat was so oppressive that people were already dehydrating. The night before the event, Mike, my friend, Lydia, and I discussed it and decided that the best thing for us to do would be to watch the mass on TV. The wheelchair would be a problem in a place like that, and our plane reservations back to California were for 4:00 P.M. with the airport on the other end of town.

The next morning, however, I woke up about 8:15—wide awake, and my mind went right to Cherry Creek. I went through the reasons not to go, but my spirit kept saying, "Go! Just go!" Just then Mike was waking up. "Honey, I think we should go," I said.

"What?"

"Let's just go! Let's try it! What do we have to lose? Worse case, we can't get there and we turn around and come back and watch it on TV. When else are we going to get a chance to see the pope?"

With Lydia beginning to wake up, Mike responded. "Let's go!"

They flew into action. Mike worked on me while Lydia showered, and then Mike announced, "Trade places, tag team! Lydia, you're it!" Lydia took over my care while Mike got dressed. We were out the door in forty-five minutes—

record time for me! Mind you, I didn't look like much. All I had on was shorts, a tank top, sandals, and no make-up, but we were on our way.

Surprisingly, the freeways were wide open! Evidently, everyone had listened to the media warnings, and we went flying down the interstate. We expected a line miles long to get into the handicapped shuttle parking lot, but we drove right in and found drivers to be so idle that they were sitting on the curb smoking cigarettes! Lydia lined up a shuttle while Mike reassembled my motorized wheelchair, got me in it, and we arrived on the scene at 9:55—just five minutes to find a place to sit. We were ecstatic that we had made it until we looked up and saw the stage—or the dot that we thought was the stage—easily one and a half miles away at the other end of the park. The "park" was more like a dirt field, and the sea of people made the scene look like a Christian Wood-stock—beach chairs, blankets, coolers, shorts, tank tops, sun-glasses, hats and visors, the smell of sunscreen, and water bottles. People with disabilities were supposed to sit up on a knoll in the back where the breeze was better.

About a half mile down, there were jumbo media screens so people who were far from the stage could see the pope close up. When Mike turned around from tipping the shut-tle driver, he saw that I was already flying down the hill, leav-ing a cloud of dust behind me. "Let's go!" I hollered, and we took off for the screens. I was hitting potholes and bouncing around in my chair. At the screen, we hit a wall of people and decided that was as good as we were going to do. Within a couple of minutes, a lady wearing a staff shirt and with a darling French accent approached me and said, "Oh, honey, you shouldn't be here."

"Please don't make us go all the way back to the disabled area. We worked really hard to get here. I've got water and I won't be stupid."

"No, no, no. You should come down here!" she said as she pointed toward the altar.

I started to protest, "No, we're fine here, really." I didn't want any special favors, or at least I thought I didn't!

But Mike was behind me whispering, "Honey, shut up! Let her take us!"

I quickly changed my response. "Sure! Thank you! Let's go!"

We dashed off, scrambling to keep up, as we followed our guide to the next jumbo screen. She left us there, telling us that this was as far as we could go, so we got all settled in and were feeling very lucky to be there. It was but a few minutes before another staff person—this time a huge man with a German accent who looked like a bar bouncer—came toward us. "You shouldn't be here!"

"Oh," I moaned. "The other gal brought us up this far."

"No, no, no," he persisted. "This will not do. Follow me."

Again, my first response was, "No, that's okay," but again Mike was elbowing me and reminding me to follow!

By then the music and opening procession had started, and we were moving really fast, following this big bouncer guy because we weren't supposed to be in the aisles. I had the wheelchair cranked up, and Mike and Lydia were racing along behind. Suddenly a huge mud puddle loomed in front of me, and because of the wall of people on each side, there was no way around it, and I couldn't go through it. It stopped me short. All of a sudden, some big, buff teenage guys saw our dilemma. "You need a lift across?"

"Yeah!" They grabbed my wheelchair and, taking me totally by surprise, they hoisted me high in the air, like they were lifting me over a car instead of a mud puddle! "Wheeee!" I squealed! I landed, yelled, "Thanks, guys!" and off we went again.

The bouncer guy took us through security and behind the stage. "Now," he said, "you can sit here," and he walked away. We had moved so quickly through the crowd that we didn't know where we were. We looked around and saw that we were under a covered area, behind the stage completely by ourselves. We looked at each other, asking, "How in the world did we get back here?"

Suddenly, another man approached, this one looking like an FBI bishop—black clothes, Roman collar, the bishop chain, sunglasses, and a security ear piece. "You guys need a place to sit?"

"Oh, no, we're fine," I said timidly, while Mike talked over me.

"Yes, we do!"

"Follow me." While he led us up a ramp, we could hear thunderous noise and applause and singing and clapping. Later we found out there were three stages—the center stage was the altar, stage left was the choir and orchestra, and stage right was the VIP stage for cardinals, bishops, and other church officials. When we came up the ramp, we found ourselves sitting among the bishops and cardinals. There I am wearing a tank top, sandals, no makeup, and I'm sitting on the VIP stage!

The pope was less than twenty yards away, and we were looking out over the sea of people where we used to be. At that moment the pope began: "As we start all things in our lives, we begin today in the name of the Father, and of the Son, and of the Holy Spirit. Amen."

Our heads were spinning. Mike, Lydia, and I kept looking at each other, silently saying, "Can you believe this!" As far as we could tell, we were the only uninvited guests on the stage, and what's more our seats were under the shaded portion!

Pope John Paul II gave a fabulous message to the youth, encouraging them to use their untapped talents and gifts for the glory of God. It was beautiful. To worship with people from all over the world and to hear half a million youth singing, "We are one body, one body in Christ, and we do not stand alone" was an amazing spiritual high. After the post-communion prayer, I looked at my watch and gasped and whispered, "It's almost noon! We should get going!"

But how on earth could we leave? We were on the platform with *the pope!* We had a plane to catch, and we hadn't even packed or checked out of our hotel. We were a mile and a half from our shuttle, and there were no fewer than five hundred thousand people, who also would be trying to leave. We *had* to get going, so we quietly slipped down the ramp, and still there was nobody behind the stage. We paused, trying to get ourselves collected and figure out how to get back to where we had started. Suddenly, the FBI bishop appeared again—forever scanning to make sure all was secure. He leaned down and, still searching the area with his eyes, he said coarsely, "You wanna meet the pope?"

"What?"

"Do you wanna meet the pope?" he repeated.

"You've got to be kidding!"

Again, Mike talked over me. "Yes, we'd love to!"

"Follow me."

He took us to a roped-off area near the stairs behind the center stage. He instructed Mike and Lydia to stand behind the rope and told me, "Sit here, in front of the rope. When mass is over, the pope is going to come down those stairs."

Excited but confused, I looked at my watch, and Mike said from behind me, "Don't worry about the flight. This is the chance of a lifetime! We'll figure out something later."

The mass ended with a big "going forth to serve" anthem, and when it was over, we heard the sounds of an audience on a spiritual high. Applause. Whistles. Whoops and shouts. "Praise the Lord!" *"Viva el Papa!"* People from all over the world were united in a common bond.

We could see people moving up on the stage. The FBI bishop came back and told me to move out about ten feet closer to the stairs.

"Are you sure?"

"Move, Renée!" I heard Mike say.

"Okay, sure! Thank you!"

About two hundred people were congregating behind the rope, and I was all alone way out in front, about twenty-five feet from the stairway. When I could see the pope on the landing, the FBI bishop came back. "Okay, move out another ten feet. When the pope gets to the bottom of the stairs, call out his name."

I moved out, thinking, *Call out his name? What do you call the pope?* I was getting panicky about what to say! But when he stepped onto the grass, I remembered how to address him. "Holy Father!"

Pope John Paul II stopped, looked, smiled, and slowly walked right over to me. I looked up to him and, fully aware of his love for the youth of our world and moved by his interest in them, I said, "Thank you so much for loving our young people."

He smiled. "Oh, that's not hard to do," he said with his thick Polish accent. "Can I pray for you?"

"Oh, please do!"

He put his hands on my head, and I began to weep. Pope John Paul II was praying for me! Even more significant than the pope's blessing was the fact that God had orchestrated the whole thing—the sudden decision to come, the deserted freeways, the empty shuttles, the officials who led us closer and closer, our seats on stage, and finally being the only person singled out to meet the pope! I had an overwhelming sense that through all of this God was saying again, "I'm here, Renée. I'm with you. Be not afraid."

Pope John Paul II silently prayed over me for maybe forty or forty-five seconds. He removed his hands from my head, and I smiled into his beautiful blue eyes—full of peace and warmth. It was like looking into the eyes of the ultimate grandfather. He touched my shoulder, and then he was escorted away. The FBI bishop came back and said, "You have to stay right there for security reasons." I turned and looked at Mike whose face was also streaked with tears, and he came to stand beside me.

A few minutes later the papal secretary came back to me and said, "The pope wanted me to give you something." He handed me a beautiful rosary with a papal seal on it. Mike said, "We have something to give to the pope."

"We do?" I said.

Mike pulled out one of my *Inner Voice* cassettes from the backpack on my wheelchair. "We'd like him to listen to this on the plane trip home."

The secretary accepted the cassette. "I'm sure he'll be very appreciative and that he'll enjoy listening to it."

After we watched as the military helicopter swept the pope away, we were finally cleared to leave about 1:45. To have any chance of making our flight, we had to figure out how to negotiate the crowd and the distance between us and the shuttle parking lot. It would take a miracle to get out of there in less than an hour.

Suddenly, a first-aid truck appeared, moving slowly through the crowd. "Get behind that truck!" Mike instructed. The vehicle "parted the Red Sea," and we drafted right behind it all the way to the shuttle. We started at the furthermost point, but we were in one of the first shuttles to pull away. When we arrived at the parking lot, Mike threw me and the chair into the car, and we hit the freeway, elated to have beaten the crowd out of the park!

We flew to the hotel. Mike and Lydia ran in, gathered our things, packed our suitcases, checked out, and in no time we were racing across town to Stapleton International. They were already boarding when we got to the gate, and the gate crew was not happy to see me coming. I'm supposed to board first, before the plane is occupied.

When the flight attendant was pulling me down the aisle in the aisle chair, he happened to stop right beside Bishop Driscoll, the bishop of our diocese. "Hi, Renée! Did you have a good time?"

"Oh yes. And do I have a story for you!"

12

The Decision

In the weeks and months after the accident, when I was learning to cope with "the new me," my biggest question was, "What kind of wife can I be for Mike?" Following that was the question, "Will I ever be a mom?" Would I be equipped to have children?

The doctors assured us that my chances of carrying and delivering a healthy baby were good, but I knew all too well that being able to give birth doesn't qualify a woman to be a mother. Could I be a mom from a wheelchair? What would I do if my child darted into the street? What if he reached for a hot pan on the stove? And what about the everyday responsibilities? I could never change a diaper, give him a bottle, or scoop him up into my arms to kiss away his tears. Was it selfish of me to want a child? Would it be fair to bring a child into our home when my ability to care for him would be so limited? And what about Mike? Would he come to resent me because of my inability to help? Most of the responsibilities would fall on his shoulders. But on the other hand, would it be fair to Mike not to give him a child? The questions and doubts were endless, and there were no clear-cut answers.

Before we got married, I did not give Mike false hope. I told him that I couldn't see myself being physically or emotionally capable of dealing with the pressures and demands of parenthood. If I put the situation in terms of a percentage, I'd say we had a 10-percent chance of my feeling comfortable with having children. Mike knew that if he chose to marry me, he probably would never have children, but he wanted to marry me anyway.

During our four years of marriage, the subject came up occasionally, but there was no pressure to make a decision. After all, we were still young, and we needed time to learn to cope with the challenges life had dealt us already; there would be time to decide about children later. But one day I woke up and I was thirty-five years old.

The issue came to a head one night after we'd been to a big family dinner. After the meal we adults were, as usual, lingering around the table, chatting and visiting, when someone asked, "Hey, where'd Mike go?" I went and looked outside, and sure enough there he was romping and playing with our nieces and nephews. Mike is just like one of them, and they adore him. I've never seen anyone who can stir up a bunch of youngsters like he can. He loves children, is energized by them, and gets just as wound up as they do.

As a teenager, Mike was a camp counselor several summers, and he frequently volunteered at the local YMCA and at the local boys and girls club. As I sat and watched them playing together, I thought maybe we could have a child. *Mike would be such a wonderful dad,* I thought, *and even though I don't have arms, hands, or fingers that work, I do have a lot of love, guidance, and nurturing skills to offer.*

While I was contemplating the possibility, I also considered our different personalities. When I was growing up and as a teenager, I was never Miss Maternal, never a little kid person. I never wanted a Betsy-Wetsy doll, never got all gushy when looking at someone else's baby, and I surely didn't care to cuddle one of the creatures. If someone handed me a baby, I was very uncomfortable; I never knew where to hold it! Instead of responding with tenderness, I had more of an impatient "What do I do with this thing?" feeling.

However, while I wasn't very comfortable around little kids, I had enormous compassion for adolescents and teenagers. That's why my first choice was to be a high school choir director, not an elementary school teacher. Many people seem to shy away from older kids, especially those of junior high age, but I find them fascinating and delightful. Getting close to my high school students came naturally to me. I admired their energy, their intensity, their propensity to dream high. I loved being involved in their lives—hearing their problems, sharing their plans, encouraging them to pursue their dreams. I didn't need hands and fingers to draw close to a teenager. So maybe if Mike could handle the early stages, I would be of more help when our child got to be eleven or so. I was beginning to see that having a child was a possibility, but it certainly was not a probability yet.

At home that night, I brought up the subject of children, and we had a long, long discussion. We weighed the pros and cons, dissected the reality of our responsibilities from every possible angle, and prayed together. Mike told me, "We've made a lot of decisions together, but I think this is one you have to make alone. Only you know how tough you are mentally. You have to be totally at peace with a yes. Otherwise, I might have a child, but what would be the point if at the same time I had a wife who was having a nervous breakdown from the pressures of trying to be a mom from a wheelchair?"

"But what about twenty-five years from now?" I persisted. "Will you come back to me then and say that we made a mistake in deciding against children? Will you say, 'Renée, there's an emptiness in our lives, in our marriage? We've missed something special because we didn't have a child'?"

"Absolutely not," he said emphatically. "We'll make this decision and move on and not look back. We can't be second-guessing ourselves years from now.

"I want you to know that I don't need a child to make our marriage complete and whole," he continued. "You know I love children, but I will be content if the decision is no. So, remember that I'm not pressuring you toward a yes, but it is time to make a decision. We're thirty-five. If we're going to have a child, we need to get started. If you decide not to, we can make other plans—travel maybe. We could go to Alaska, and you could show me Europe. We could focus on other things, find another direction."

Mike was right. We had to come to terms and decide. He virtually left the decision up to me, but I wasn't ready to choose. This was far and away the most important decision I would ever make—even more important than our decision to get married. It would forever change our lives, and it would be irreversible. You can always trade in a car or sell a house, but a child is forever.

Of course, the decision came down to one question. "What would God have us do?" At that point, I was totally without direction, so I started to pray like I had never prayed about anything before—begging God for a clear answer. I don't think I had ever truly surrendered anything to the Lord until this; I don't know if I really knew the meaning of the word "surrender." This really mattered, and I had no idea what to do. There wasn't one detail about the decision that I didn't talk to God about—many times. I was totally surrendered, submitted to him, totally open to either answer. What was his will?

The need to make a decision—the right one—occupied not only my prayer life, but much of my thought life as well. I tried to turn every stone in my quest to make the best choice. There were questions about my emotional toughness. How could I watch someone else put a bow in my daughter's hair or teach her to play the piano? Would my toddler love my attendant more than me? Could I deal with him seeking her attention, care, and comfort instead of mine? Would he know which one was mom? When he got a little older, would he be ashamed of me? After all, I would be different from the other mothers.

I considered not only the present but also the future. I didn't want us to grow old without someone to love and to love us. I watched my parents and how much they enjoyed their children and grandchildren. And the biggie: What if I died first, without children? I couldn't stand the thought that Mike would be left with no one because I couldn't—or wouldn't—give him children. I wanted desperately to protect him from such loneliness in his senior years.

The only ones I asked for advice were my sisters. I was nervous in approaching the subject with them, first because of my paralysis, and second because they well knew I wasn't a baby person even before my accident. I had no doubt that had I not been paralyzed, if I'd announced my pregnancy to them, they would have found it irresistibly funny. The thought of Renée with a baby would have been too hysterical for my sisters to miss.

The circumstances being what they were, I was worried. Would they think I was being totally ridiculous? I felt vulnerable as I timidly ventured, "What would you think if Mike and I had a child? Is that just the stupidest idea?" I should have known better. As I launched into my litany of questions and insecurities, their faces lit up. They were all for it!

"Renée, the time of infancy passes very rapidly," Denise said. "Children are babies for such a short time. The stage when you'd need your extremities the most will go by quickly."

"And we'll be your hands until the baby gets older—for as long as you need us," Michelle eagerly offered. Over the course of several months, as I would be hashing over potential problems, I would run ideas past them; I trusted them and knew they'd never lead me astray. Their candid responses based on their experience were enormously helpful, and their approval and support left me reassured that maybe we really could make it work. Yet, having a child still felt like plunging into a pool of icy water.

Surprisingly, during this time Mike and I hardly talked about the subject. A few times he did ask casually, "So, where are you with the baby thing?" And I'd reply, "I don't know. I'm still praying about it, but I just don't know. I'm not ready to decide yet." Mike would say okay and nod understandingly.

I prayed for nearly a year, and still I had no clear direction. I waited for a FedEx letter from God, but it didn't come. He didn't drop a sign, speak to me in a dream, or illuminate a Scripture to give me the go ahead. But neither had he placed any roadblocks in my path. During this time of seeking, in my quiet times with the Lord I would say, "Okay, Lord, do you want me to have a child?" Then with an open heart I'd wait to see what would come—a sense of peace or a sense of uneasiness.

Then I'd test the other scenario. "Okay, Lord, do you want us to remain childless?" Sit. Wait. Listen.

I went back and forth like a ping-pong ball between these two questions, being patient and quiet, until I began to feel a peace when the pendulum was at yes and an anxiety when it was at no.

I thought I had no preconceived notions, but frankly I was surprised at what I thought I was hearing. I said to the Lord, "You're kidding! Do you really mean this? Are you telling us to have a child? If you're not, you've got to stop me, change my sense of your direction, or I may make a terrible mistake here!" But no change came, so one night, being sure of nothing except that I had analyzed this decision from every possible angle, I mustered my courage and told Mike. "I've been thinking and praying for a good year now. This is weird, and you're not going to believe it, but I have an 80-percent peace about having a child. I don't think I'll ever have the other 20 percent."

The look on Mike's face showed that he was astonished. His eyes danced with excitement. In his heart of hearts, he thought I'd say no. He had prepared himself for a no, planning to pursue other interests.

"So maybe we should just start trying. It's the only way we'll ever know if it's truly God's will," I continued. "You know how many couples are unable to get pregnant; that might be us. So let's give God a chance to give us a child. If I get pregnant, then God's answer is yes. If I don't, then it's no."

"Really? Are you sure?"

"No, but I'm more sure than not."

Mike's excitement was restrained and cautious. I think he didn't want me to feel like I had permanently locked myself into a decision, and there was no changing my mind. He wanted to leave me an out, a chance to renege.

We sat with the decision for a week. I retraced my footsteps for him through my journey to the decision. Always we returned to the one truth we could depend on. If it was God's will for us to be parents, he would equip us with the tools we needed to meet every need of our child. We simply left it in God's hands.

One month later I was pregnant!

I thought I might be, so without Mike knowing it, I dropped off a specimen at the doctor's office where, "coincidentally," Dorothy Henry worked. I told her the reason for the test, and she beamed with excitement. "Maybe I'll drop by your house tonight with the results," she offered.

About 5:00, the doorbell rang, and there stood Dorothy and her daughter, Jennifer. In they came, giving each other knowing glances, trying to act nonchalant but failing miserably. They handed me an envelope and helped me open it; inside were two balloons, a pink one and a blue one, along with the results of my pregnancy test. Positive! God had sent Dorothy and Jennifer to deliver my FedEx letter!

I was in a state of shock—period. I couldn't believe that after an entire year of agonizing and praying, now my fondest dream but in a way my worst fear was suddenly a reality. I was totally awed because I knew God had spoken loud and clear. As thrilled as I was that Dorothy and Jennifer brought the news, when Mike got home, I was ready for them to go. I wanted to be alone with my husband when I shared the news with him. Not too subtly I chirped, "Thank you for coming! Let's get together again real soon." They got the hint and quickly left.

When we closed the door, I told Mike, "Let's go in the living room and sit down. I have something to tell you." We walked in, he sat on the ottoman, and I pulled up as close to him as I could get.

"Mike, I just found out we're pregnant!" Mike grabbed me in a big bear hug. He held me and we cried and laughed together. "Here we go!" I laughed.

"I'm so excited!" Mike responded.

"I feel like we're at the top of the roller coaster!"

"No turning back now!" he exclaimed.

In our laughter we turned to each other, and almost at the same time we said, "Be careful what you pray for!"

Eager to make our announcement to my family, we set off for Mom and Dad's house. When we went in, as usual Mom was working at the kitchen table and Dad was snoozing in his easy chair with the newspaper over his face. Suddenly, I began to realize that this might not go too well. I hadn't even mentioned to them that we were thinking of having a child. I didn't intentionally leave them out, but I think I knew without asking what their response would be, and I wanted more than anything to hear clearly from God on the subject. Now, realizing this was going to hit them like a ton of bricks, I was regretting that I didn't prepare them at least a little. My exciting news was going to be more like a bombshell.

There was no way to go but forward, so I took a deep breath. "Well, I'm glad you're both sitting down, because we have some pretty big news," I began. Then I smiled broadly and exclaimed, "We're pregnant! We're going to have a baby!"

Instantly, my dad's eyes shot to Mike, staring at him in disapproval and even anger. Mom got the "mom" look—taken totally off guard but trying to be happy for her daughter, not knowing if she was pleased or not. Disturbed by Dad's gaze, I said, "Dad, you're glaring at Mike. He did not pressure me in the least to make this decision. We didn't come to it lightly or without weighing all of the pros and cons. We've agonized about this for over a year. It's what we want, and we made the decision together."

"But, isn't your life hard enough as it is?" he asked.

"We know it's not going to be easy, but we've thought through everything. We see what your grandchildren mean to you guys, and we don't want to grow old without children and grandchildren of our own. Can you understand that?"

We talked at length, telling them how painstakingly we had come to our decision, and Dad began to soften. His initial reaction came only out of his love for me and his fatherly inclination to protect me. I knew that. I was only sorry that I had blindsided my parents instead of preparing them.

Next, we went to Michelle and Denise and their families, a short walk from Mom and Dad's. Even though I had gone to my sisters for advice, I never told them we had decided to go ahead. Now there was a bit of a problem; they just happened to live next door to each other. Who do we tell first? We couldn't choose, so we decided to tell both at the same time. We stopped on the sidewalk in front of their houses and started screaming at the top of our lungs: "Everybody out! Michelle! Denise! Doug! Joseph! Kids! Everybody get out here! We've got something to say!" Immediately, people came tumbling out of the two houses, not knowing what all the racket was about and looking rather baffled and curious. When they were all in the yard, I loudly announced, "Well, we're pregnant!"

Both my sisters screamed in delight. Denise froze, anchored in her tracks, tears streaming down her face. "Thank you, Jesus. Thank you, Jesus." Michelle, on the other hand, tore out toward me and made a flying leap. Somehow she landed right in my lap, straddling me, with her feet dangling out over the arms of my wheelchair on either side. She was laughing and crying and pounding on my shoulders. The other family members surrounded us, giving hugs, offering congratulations, expressing their delight and excitement. Soon Mom and Dad came out and joined in the celebration; I think it helped them to see everyone else so excited.

This baby was a big deal, a really big deal, not just for us, but for the whole family. Looking back, I see that my pregnancy was a milestone. It marked the last obstacle to a "normal" life. When paralysis happens, it doesn't happen just to the victim; it happens to the whole family. The members of my family weren't spectators; they were in this thing with me.

So the announcement of this baby was symbolic. Life *could* be complete from a wheelchair. The announcement screamed without my saying it, "I can lead a normal life! I am okay!" It was a different kind of okay than we would have chosen, but nevertheless we were okay. After almost seven years, we were getting on the other side of this thing. We had walked on the edge of defeat and despair, and were now beginning to dance on it. We had faced the monster and conquered it, if not physically, then definitely emotionally and spiritually.

Who would have imagined that the monster was about to rear his ugly head once again?

13

The Monster
Takes His Best Shot

As we entered 1995, things were rolling along really well. Due to my pregnancy, I stopped my speaking engagements at Christmas, so in the first couple of months of the new year there was no hectic, crazy schedule to meet, and I had lots of free time to relax and get ready for the baby, who was due in March.

On Sundays Mike and I often drove out to Rancho Santa Margarita to browse and shop for baby things, and we were all excited when we found a blue-and-white-striped comforter set, trimmed in darling teddy bears. I had dozens of teddy bears that people had brought to me when I was in the hospital and rehab, so a friend from church, Oscar Rosales, father of one of my favorite techs at Mission Hospital, built shelves for the nursery, and we put teddy bears everywhere. Life was blessedly peaceful as we prepared for our baby.

Even though we really preferred to wait until delivery to know the gender of our child, we took the practical advice of my sisters and others and went for the ultrasound. "After all," they said, "You're having five—count them—*five* showers! It's harder for you than most to return pink for blue or blue for pink, so if you don't find out now, this kid will be wearing green and yellow for years!" It was good advice.

Somehow I'd assumed we'd have a girl, but when I heard the technician say, "It's a boy!" the first thing that came to mind was that Mike would have a son to go backpacking with, to do "guy" things with, and to be close to as he was with his own dad. Secondly, I instantly saw that God had protected me from a lot of tears in being unable to do mom things with my daughter. I would have missed the little things, like fixing her hair and tying it in a bow as a finishing touch, painting her nails, preparing a tea party for just the two of us, helping her get dressed in her lacy little girl dresses.

I pictured us with a girl and then with a boy, and immediately I saw that a boy was good and right, actually perfect for us. All the way home, Mike and I kept saying to each other, "God is so good! He's giving us a boy—a son!" Daniel James would be his name, we decided—Daniel after my brother, Danny, and because every Daniel we had ever known was good natured, characterized by both strength and gentleness. Mike's middle name is James, which was the name of his father and grandfather. Our son would be the fourth generation to carry the name.

Everybody, it seemed, was getting ready for the baby. My high school friends, my Young American colleagues, and the Rally 'Round Renée crew all gave me showers; our church held a couples' shower for us; and Mike's office threw a party for him. Once again we were blown away by all the love and support that came our way, and Daniel James had every possible necessity and convenience that any baby could need, plus he had enough blue to last for four years!

As the date drew near for him to make his first appearance into our family, the crib was in place, the bassinet was ready, and the tiny little clothes were washed and folded. Although I still felt a little apprehensive, our home and our hearts were ready to welcome him.

My pregnancy was absolutely normal except for one potential problem—autonomic dysreflexia. This is a serious condition that all people with spinal cord injuries have to beware of; it can occur when any body part is distended—like the bladder and the bowel if not frequently emptied, or the uterus. If autonomic dysreflexia hits, the blood pressure quickly shoots dangerously high, and in extreme cases this can result in stroke or coma. Therefore, women with spinal cord injuries have to be carefully monitored when they're in labor. To further complicate the situation, not every hospital and medical staff is trained and equipped to diagnose and treat the condition. I couldn't pop into any hospital; I had to go to Mission Medical Center in Mission Viejo, where I was expected. Actually, at Mission, each member of the staff on every shift had to take special classes to prepare for me. That's how technical and serious it all was.

Fortunately, I had a dress rehearsal before the scheduled delivery date. Because of the fear of autonomic dysreflexia, I was monitored from home for the last six weeks of pregnancy. Twice a day someone attached a monitor belt around my belly, which traced contractions. After an hour, I'd push a button on the belt that would send the message to a lab in Phoenix where the results would be evaluated. Then a nurse would call me with the report. One evening early in March, when she called she said I was having some contractions and, to be on the safe side, I should go to the hospital.

When we drove up to the ER, the same ER where I was taken when I broke my neck, there was an ambulance parked there with the back door open. The sight triggered seven-year-old memories of when I was the passenger, and the tears began to flow. The sadness was in remembering what it was like when I arrived that night seven years before and in sympathy for whomever the ambulance had brought in on this evening.

I got my act together, but when I was placed in an examination room and saw the familiar dots on the ceiling, it all flooded in on me again. I thought I was past all that, but sometimes ghosts of our past just won't die. As it turned out, it was a false alarm and I was sent right back home. I'm convinced, however, that God orchestrated the whole experience so I wouldn't have to relive the past on the morning of Daniel's delivery.

It was Sunday morning, March 12, eight days before my scheduled delivery date. I was eating breakfast in the kitchen after my three-hour dressing ritual when I saw Mike and Denise approaching the back of the house. When they came in, the looks on their faces provided the first suggestion that something wasn't right.

Denise began. "Renée, I need to tell you something." Her mouth had that pinched look that told me she was struggling for composure.

"What? Mom? Dad? Did something happen to one of them?"

"No, Mom and Dad are fine." She paused. "It's Michelle," she said as tenderly as she could. "She's had an accident; she took a spill on her ATV."

I looked into their faces, desperately needing to see that the accident was harmless. But there was sadness in their eyes. I was terrified of the truth, but I demanded to hear it anyway.

"Is she okay?" My eyes darted back and forth to each of them for answers, for reassurance. "She *is* alive! Tell me she's alive!"

"Yes, she's alive." Denise paused and took a deep breath. "But her back is broken."

Something within me snapped. "No! Is she paralyzed? Please tell me she's not paralyzed!" I said, sobbing.

They dropped down beside me, put their arms around me, and whispered the most revolting words I've ever heard. "Yes, she's paralyzed. From the waist down."

The monster had struck again. His blow was almost more than we could take.

I was hysterical. How could this happen to two of us in the same family? I screamed and cried and had no control of myself. Mike and Denise were still on the floor beside me. I desperately needed to feel their embrace, to be hugged close, but because my chair was in the way, their attempts to embrace me were ineffectual.

For a long time we remained three heads together, united in our grief and despair. It was the worst day of my life, even worse than the day I broke my neck. Because I'd been there and done that, I knew all too well what Michelle faced. I didn't think I could stand it.

"I want to go see her," I told Mike. "Take me to the hospital."

"I don't think that would be a very good idea," Mike cautioned.

"She's pretty messed up," Denise added.

"What do you mean?" I asked. Surely the news couldn't get any worse. But it did.

"She's on a ventilator," Denise told me.

"Oh, God," I wailed. "Permanently?"

"Both lungs were punctured." My stomach turned. My beautiful sister on that hideous machine.

"We're very lucky that she's alive—that she's still here," Denise explained. For one fleeting second I was grateful, but then the reality of her paralysis washed over me again, and I was inconsolable.

Again, I told Mike and Denise that I wanted to go to the hospital, but they were adamant. "There's nothing you can do, and she's mostly comatose. She looks awful, and it would be very difficult for you to see her like that. It might be too much for you. If you were to go into labor while you were there, that hospital won't know what to do with the possibility of dysreflexia. Besides, Michelle won't even know you're there. You've got to think about the safety of the baby." I conceded, even though I didn't like it and wasn't at all convinced they were right.

A little later, Mom came down, and when I saw her—so lost and helpless—my grief doubled. No matter how old we are, there's something about seeing our parents' sadness that disarms us of any semblance of composure. "I'm so sorry! I'm so sorry!" I kept repeating. It was just so unfair that my parents had to see *two* of their daughters in chairs. Wasn't one enough? The unfairness engulfed me as I cried for Michelle, for her husband and sons, for Mom and Dad, for all of us who were victimized yet again.

Later, I went up to see Dad. Always big and strong in stature and character, my dad now looked thunderstruck. I could hardly stand seeing him cry. "Here we go again," he sobbed into my hair. Nothing more needed to be said.

The accident had happened the afternoon before I received the news. Michelle was vacationing with her family in Imperial County near Yuma at the Arizona border, and they were riding their three-wheel all-terrain vehicles (ATVs) across the enormous sand dunes in the desert. As was their usual formation (Michelle described it as "ducks in a row"), Doug, her husband, went up the hill first to find the best and safest path, and he veered off to the left; Brent rode up and veered to the left too; then Jordan took the same route. But when Michelle went up, she gathered a little too much speed and had to pass Jordan on the right. To avoid Jordan, at the top of the hill she went off in the opposite direction, down the face, the steep side of the dune, which was about sixty feet or six stories high.

An experienced rider of over ten years, riding the face was commonplace to Michelle. She knew that the soft sand would roll along with the bike, creating a mini-avalanche effect. Bushes were few and far between in the dunes, but unfortunately there was one right in her path—a big one about ten feet in diameter. Had it not been there, there would have been no problem.

The avalanche was sending her bike left, but for some reason she cannot explain she decided to go right, cutting across the avalanche of dust to maneuver around the bush. But her bike wouldn't respond. She hit the bush and was propelled into the air.

She landed face down in the sand with her left arm pinned under her. Being in the medical field and having dealt with my paralysis, she carefully began to take stock of her injuries. Starting at her neck, she mentally examined each part of her body to see if it was working. Head, arms, fingers, trunk all seemed to be intact, but then she realized she couldn't feel her legs—nothing below her waist.

In a matter of thirty seconds, Doug got back to her. "Are you all right?" he asked.

"No. Don't move me," she instructed. "I can't feel my legs. I can't move them. I think my back is broken. You've got to get help."

He wanted to remove her helmet and turn her over, both to make her more comfortable and to examine her for injuries, but again she wisely insisted that he not move her at all. She was completely alert and already fully aware of the seriousness and of the probable permanence of her paralysis, and she decided that the best thing she could do would be to concentrate on remaining calm.

They had to decide how to get help. They were three miles from the nearest road, and it was only dirt and gravel. They had deliberately chosen this area because it wasn't as popular for bikers; it was almost deserted. Michelle lay near the bottom of a dune and couldn't be seen except from close range. Doug didn't want to leave her, but the boys were so young; Brent was nine and Jordan was seven. Finally, they made the awful decision to send Brent for help. Doug took his older son to the top of the nearest dune and helped him get his bearings; he needed to go mostly south, back to their camper. Brent knew only too well that he could see where he was going only when he was on top. Here again is where the hand of our faithful God began to be evident. Just the night before, the area had experienced one of the biggest rains in years, washing away old tracks and leaving the sand moist. Brent had the tracks of their bikes to help him find camp. He took off on his cycle, but when he had gone only about a mile, in his panic to get help for his mother he crashed. His bike was too heavy for him to get back on its wheels, so he left it and started off on foot.

Just then, a stranger riding alone just "happened" to come along. Riding alone is completely against the cardinal rule of riding the dunes, and coming upon another person in the dunes is extremely rare. But at just the right moment, Larry intersected Brent, and after hearing about the situation, Larry—an angel, we're convinced—took Brent back to Michelle's accident scene where he stayed, helped, and even prayed with them.

Meanwhile, before Brent and Larry returned, Michelle said to her husband, "Doug, go get help." Realizing that he was caught in a life-and-death situation, he made the agonizing choice to leave Michelle with only their seven-year-old. Reluctantly, he left on his ATV and before he had gone far, he found a man setting up camp and convinced him to drive out to the ranger station about ten miles away to tell them of the accident. At last, the wheels were set in motion for the rescue.

Meanwhile, Brent, exerting all the maturity his nine years could compose, positioned himself on top of a dune to be a marker for any rescuers who might come. Michelle could hear him crying, pleading over and over again. "Will somebody please help! Will somebody please help my mom!"

The younger son sat down at his mom's side and took her hand. Michelle could feel that her lungs were not functioning at full capacity, that her breaths needed to be shallow and easy. This indicated to her that she had internal injuries in addition to her broken back. As Jordan sat next to her, he asked, "Mom, does it hurt?"

"No, not so much. I'm just having a little trouble breathing."

"Mom, are you going to die?"

"Well, I don't know, son," she responded honestly and calmly. "But, if I do, it's okay, because that means that God wants me in heaven."

The ways of God are truly amazing. In addition to the rain and to Larry, a dune buggy club just "happened" to be in the area and somehow found out about the accident. They provided an empty buggy for the ranger to carry Michelle, and they also perched their buggies on the tops of dunes between the road and the accident scene so that the ranger could go straight to her. The ranger arrived and called for the ambulance and EMT. When at last the EMT arrived, fortunately a very professional and competent lady, she cut Michelle's clothes off, positioned the board, and gave directions to Doug and the others on how to turn her. When they got her half turned, the EMT yelled, "Stop!"

It was apparent that the arm pinned under Michelle's body had been badly broken just below the shoulder; she immobilized it, and they finished placing her on the board. Just then they heard a beautiful sound, the *fwop, fwop, fwop* of a helicopter. It was only because of the rain that the helicopter could land so closely; ordinarily, the whirling blades would have created such a sandstorm that no one could be near. Doug and five other men picked Michelle up on the board and, keeping her level, which was no easy task, they carried her to the top of that huge dune where they slid her into the helicopter. Instantaneously, it was airborne again.

Michelle had lain in the sand for two and a half hours before the rescue was complete. By her strength and determination not to give in to the temptation to panic, she had remained perfectly calm and composed. As the helicopter lifted off, she felt the cool oxygen on her face and realized she could now relax. "Lord," she prayed, "I give this whole situation to you." She then closed her eyes and went to sleep. They took her to a small hospital in Yuma where they stabilized her and then airlifted her to San Diego. She had punctured both lungs, ruptured her spleen, broken numerous ribs, snapped the humerus bone in her left arm, and totally shattered five vertebrae in the middle of her back.

From the emergency room, Doug called Father Martin and then Mom who called Denise. It was about 9:30 P.M. when my sister knocked on our sliding glass door. She motioned for Mike to come out, so he told me he had to go up to Denise's to help them with something. Denise filled Mike in on the details she had. Together, as they cried for Michelle, they tried to decide what to do about me.

With Daniel's scheduled birth only a week away, they thought it best not to alarm me until they learned more of the facts. They knew that as soon as Michelle arrived in San Diego, she'd be taken to surgery to repair her internal injuries, and they'd know more by morning. Mike called my doctor who reassured him that the shock probably wouldn't trigger labor or interfere with the pregnancy. They knew only too well that the news of Michelle's accident would be a devastating blow to me. At about 10:30 P.M., Denise and Mom went to the hospital, and Mike returned home. Although I had no idea, he didn't sleep at all that night. He deserves an Oscar for his performance.

The next morning, Mike went to Denise's while my attendant was dressing me. Denise informed him of the devastating news, and he and Denise made what was suddenly a long walk to where I was eating breakfast.

The next few days were a flurry of questions and of waiting for news from the ICU. I still wasn't allowed to visit Michelle in the hospital. My limitations were blatantly in my face. I hated being paralyzed even more because I couldn't help Michelle in even the simplest of ways, like getting her a drink of water or brushing her hair out of her eyes. But even though I couldn't help, I wanted to be with her anyway, to see for myself.

I didn't know then how God had aided in Michelle's rescue and didn't fully acknowledge that it was a miracle she was alive. I knew only that we had loved God with all our hearts and that in spite of that he had allowed this awful tragedy to hit our family once again. Anger began to boil within me.

On Tuesday, while Doug was with Michelle, our good friends and neighbors, the Andersens, had all of us Lacouagues over to their house for dinner, a sweet gesture of compassion and an attempt to alleviate our pain. After dinner we were all trying to be upbeat for each other and for Michelle's sons. In light of my sister's fight for life, the whole idea of a cheerful family get-together was more than I could take; it was artificial and hypocritical. I suddenly couldn't stand being there one more minute and had to get out, so I told Mike I needed to leave, and we made a hasty exit.

Entering our house, I stormed into our bedroom and totally went to pieces. "Get Denise and Danny over here! You guys aren't telling me the whole truth. I need some answers!" Danny and Denise came right away, and I was completely out of control. I screamed. I cursed. I cried. "You're not telling me the whole truth! I've got to know! Don't worry, I can handle it! Is Michelle dying? Are you keeping anything from me? Why can't I go? What is so awful that I can't see? You tell me the whole truth, and do it *right now!*"

Danny was good at this sort of thing. Being the fire chief, he often had to break the awful news to people that there had been an accident. His experience kept him calm in the face of my outburst. Danny knelt beside me. "We are telling you the whole truth," he reassured me. "Michelle is stabilized. Her injuries are very serious and she's got a long road ahead of her, but barring infection or other complications, she's going to make it."

Denise, sitting on the edge of our bed, reminded me, "We're just so lucky we still have her. With the extent of her injuries, she shouldn't be here." Her look communicated, "God has spared us," but wisely she didn't say it. I wasn't feeling particularly delighted with God right then. I felt he'd let us down, even betrayed us. How could he allow this to happen to our family again? Denise knew better than to give me spiritual platitudes, but I got her message.

Looking into Danny's eyes and listening to Denise's serene reassurance got me calmed down. I just needed to know that I knew the worst of it; then I could work on dealing with it. Ignorance breeds fear, and that's what brought on my outburst, so they agreed that I should go to the hospital.

The next day, Mike drove me in the van to see Michelle, and on the one-hour drive to San Diego, we were nervously chit-chatty, avoiding thinking about or talking about what we were about to see. As we turned off the freeway, I began to get anxious, not knowing what to expect. When we entered the hospital, my stomach began to churn.

We stopped at the ICU desk. "Hi, I'm Renée Bondi, Michelle Smith's sister. I'm here to see her." Someone had already told them that this wasn't the first time this had happened to us. They looked at me with sympathy that indicated, "Oh, your poor family." With Mike by my side, I rolled down the line of cubicles and curtains in the ICU. I looked in one, saw a large lady, and started on, but the nurse said, "Your sister is in here." I backed up and looked in again, in disbelief. My small, delicate sister looked like she weighed three hundred pounds. I never would have recognized her. Her body was so traumatized that it was blown up like a balloon.

I rolled up beside her bed. "Hi, Michelle. It's me, Renée," I said. She was glassy-eyed and almost comatose. Her eyes looked in my direction but couldn't focus. There seemed to be no recognition. Surprisingly, I didn't fall apart. I think it was just that I was so glad to be with her and to have her with us, and if there was any understanding in there, I didn't want her to see me dissolve. I continued to talk to her. "This is quite a hotel room you've got here—all the attention you need around the clock. Not bad, huh?" I just wanted her to hear my voice, to know that I was there.

The other family members had been there almost constantly, and I was afraid that maybe she thought I didn't care. We stayed about an hour, and on the way home there was no idle chit-chat. Mike loved Michelle like a sister too, so he shared my grief and understood better than anyone else how I felt. We were very quiet, lost in our own thoughts. Occasionally, one of us would break the silence. "Unbelievable" was our most frequent comment.

I went to the hospital every day after that until the day before my delivery. I talked to Michelle as though she could understand. On Sunday I told her, "I'm going to have the baby tomorrow. I'll send you pictures so you can see him."

The whole thing was just one big yuck. I was incredibly depressed.

When Mike and I arrived at the Mission Hospital about 6:30 Monday morning, March 20, we went through all the paperwork and preliminary tests and procedures. I was placed in a lovely delivery room with two nurses. Usually there is only one, but the doctor didn't want me to be left alone even for a minute. They hooked me up to two heart monitors, not one, in case one failed. They took no chances. By 10:30 the pitocin, a labor-inducing drug, was dripping, and Dr. Stadler said, "It's all on board. Just lie back and relax. It'll probably be late afternoon or early evening. I'll check back often."

This is when any pregnant woman in the world would have traded places with me. I literally felt no pain. Nothing. The only way to tell if I was having a contraction was to watch the monitor. Ironically, pain probably would have been good for me at that point because it might have taken my mind off Michelle.

On what should have been one of the most exciting days of my life, I couldn't get my mind off my sister. Here we were bringing a life into the world while she was fighting for hers in an ICU sixty miles away. I couldn't help but think of the beautiful smile she had whenever someone approached her. I thought of her caring way of making others feel special and loved. And perhaps the most haunting memory was of her landing in my lap and pounding my shoulders when we told her we were pregnant. That was so Michelle.

Denise was with Michelle while I was in labor, and under the circumstances I wouldn't have had it any other way. But I missed them. Were it not for Michelle's accident, there was no question they would have been at the hospital with me. Their encouragement had played such a vital role in bring-ing us to this point. It was unfair that Michelle was cheated out of even knowing that this was the day.

As thankful as I was that Michelle was alive, I was already mourning the death of another era in our lives. Things would never be the same again, just as things were never the same after my accident. There in the birthing room, I cried off and on all morning while Mike sat by my side. About 1:00 he got up and walked over to the window and gazed out. I looked at his back and realized, *This is the most special day of his entire life, the day of the birth of his first child, and his wife is a complete disaster. His wedding got completely blown out of the water because of my accident, and now I'm letting Michelle's accident ruin this day for him as well. It's not fair to him at all.*

I made a conscious decision to focus on him and not on Michelle. "Mike," I said. "I've got to get Michelle off my mind."

He turned and looked at me. "How can we do that?"

"I don't know." I thought a minute. "Want to watch a video? When Dorothy packed my bag last night, she stuck in *The Lion King.*"

"Why not?" He smiled. So Mike started the VCR and crawled up beside me. There we were, in the birthing room, sitting side by side watching *The Lion King* together. About half an hour later, I got goose bumps around my neck. That always meant that something, usually of a personal nature, was going on in the lower part of my body. "Excuse me," I said to the nurse. "Am I having a contraction?" She looked at the monitor and replied without concern, "Yes, you are."

Back to Simba. About five minutes later, the goose bumps still hadn't gone away.

"Am I having another contraction?"

"Yes, you are. Maybe I should check you."

She came to the foot of my bed, lifted up my hospital gown, and instantaneously got wide-eyed with shock. "Oh, my gosh! There's the baby's head!" she almost shouted. She turned to the other nurse and with a firm, controlled voice, instructed, "I think it's time to get the doctor," meaning, "I really don't want to deliver this one!"

The other nurse ran out the door, and Mike ran for the phone. He dialed. "Hello, Mom? The baby's almost here!

Bye." He dialed again. "Hello, Marie? The baby's almost here! Bye." By that time Dr. Stadler was racing into the room pulling on his gloves, and the nurses were busy strapping my legs into the stirrups.

"Well, looks like this little guy is coming on the next contraction!" he said.

"Next contraction?" I reacted. "Oh my gosh! Mike, hurry up! Hurry up! Come here! Come here now! Here, here, all the way up here by my face!" Mike rushed back to my side, put his face next to mine, cheek to cheek.

I cried, "Mike, we've got to pray." Knowing that the birth of the baby was only seconds away, I panicked. "Lord, our family can't handle *one . . . more . . . thing!* This baby has to be *perfect!* Dear God, *please* make sure this baby is *perfect!*"

That's all the time we had. Dr. Stadler got this big grin on his face and exclaimed, "Here he is!" He held up Daniel James Bondi for all to see.

"Is everything there? Doctor, check him. Make sure he has all of his fingers, all of his toes. Count them!"

"Yep, everything's perfect."

"Mike, double-check him. You count, too!" Dr. Stadler placed Daniel on my stomach for inspection, and Mike counted each tiny little finger and each tiny little toe out loud for me to hear.

"He's perfect," Mike reassured me. "He has everything."

I could barely see him through my tears. We could hardly believe it. After months of praying and seeking and after months of pregnancy, suddenly here he was! "We did it! We did it!" We celebrated and congratulated each other. But I must confess that in the middle of the excitement and "We did it!" was also just a trace of "What have we done?" Daniel James was so important. Could we really do this?

They cleaned him up, weighed him, and wrapped him tight in his blanket. He was seven pounds, eight ounces, and nineteen inches long. They placed him on my lap and he lay there contentedly, like a little angel. I looked him over. He had sweet little lips, a round button nose, tiny little ears, and a lot of dark, brown hair. Any baby is a marvel, but because of all the unusual circumstances that surrounded Daniel's birth, he was an exceptional gift from God.

"Mike, do you want to hold him? Do you want to hold your son?" I offered. He picked him up tenderly in his arms and beamed down at him and then at me. "Unbelievable."

Just then I heard a familiar deep voice ask, "Is there a baby in here?" and in walked Father Martin. "Oh my gosh!" I gasped. "You're kidding!" Father Martin had been at every important event in my life—my confirmation, my accident, our wedding, and now at the birth of our son. He had been called to the hospital to visit someone in ICU, and as he was walking out the door to leave the hospital, "something" stopped him. He remembered that this might be the day, turned around, walked back in, and asked at the desk if we were there. He just "happened" to walk in five minutes after Daniel arrived. What a "coincidence" that out of all the people who could have walked through that door, our very first visitor was our pastor. It was a moment.

To us, Father Martin was God's messenger, communicating his affirmation and blessing on our family. He was the first one besides Mike and me to hold our baby boy. There was a warm glow in the room. Thank you, Jesus.

Then Mom and Dad came. They'd been to Michelle's hospital all morning and returned home to wait for Mike's call. I knew Mom had been on her knees; she and Dad had been really worried about the delivery. I'd seen no hint of joy in her face for the last eight days, but when she held Daniel, she just lit up! Dad was a riot. He was the proud grandpa, shaking hands with Mike and congratulating him. I knew that Dad had great respect for Mike and what he put up with in being married to me. He didn't say much, but he smiled a lot. I knew what he was thinking: "I'm not sure if I agree with all of this, but you did it. He's got all his fingers and all his toes. Good job. I'm proud of all of you."

Mike's parents, Jim and Sandra, were the next to arrive, slipping into the room with big smiles of anticipation. Tears welled in my eyes when I saw Mike hand them their newest grandchild. They beamed with delight at their first glimpse of Daniel James. "Congratulations! We are so proud of you both. He's beautiful! Look at all that dark hair!" A stream of relatives, friends, and parishioners started visiting and lasted the two days we were there. There were flowers all over the room, cards, and baby gifts galore.

Even though this hospital stay was for the happiest of events, the thought of staying there all night by myself made my stomach lurch. I remembered all too well that the hardest and scariest part about being in the hospital is the long, sleepless nights. I asked the doctor if Mike could stay with me. He said it was an unusual request, but under the circumstances he gladly allowed it. So they brought in a recliner, and Mike stayed with me and the baby both nights. We were a family.

What had seemed to be the worst timing may well have been the best. Daniel's arrival provided diversion from Michelle's tragedy, but my awareness of my sister was just as real and close as our new baby. For sure, it was the best of times and the worst of times.

14

Rage Turns to Peace

We brought Daniel James home when he was three days old. Looking at him, I was full of amazement. He was a miracle—a tiny little person but completely whole.

Eager to see me enjoy motherhood to the fullest and recognizing the need for physical contact, Denise adapted a No-Jo baby sling so that I could hold Daniel and be close to him. She laid the sling on my lap, pulled the straps around me, and then looped them around the back of the wheelchair so that his weight pulled on the wheelchair and not on me, which would have pulled me forward. Using the harness, I nursed Daniel for the first two weeks until my milk dried up—whether from the stress of Michelle or from neurological dysfunction we will never know. After that, someone would prepare Daniel's bottle and place him in my lap, and I could use my arm to balance the bottle against my body, keeping the nipple in his mouth until he was old enough to reach for it himself.

I cherished those times of holding my darling son, looking into his eyes, and watching his tiny little hand curl around my fingers. My heart had never known such joy. I was in awe that the Lord had allowed us to create such an amazing little person. Mike took two weeks off work so that he could be with us and enjoy those precious first days of Daniel's life.

Jim and Sandra came too and moved into the loft for the first week. They were very careful to let Mike be dad and me be mom in spite of my disabilities, giving me the opportunity to do what I could. They never tried to take over but were wonderful to get up in the night and bring Daniel to me to nurse, to take care of meals and household tasks, and to watch Daniel while Mike took me to the hospital to see Michelle.

But on our first trip to see my sister, we took Daniel with us so that we could show him to her. Because of her punctured lungs, she was still on the respirator, and although she was slowly making progress, her condition was still very precarious. Mike held Daniel up to her face. "Look, Michelle," I said. "Here he is! Your new nephew—Daniel James." Michelle smiled weakly but couldn't talk due to the ventilator. She would have been ecstatic if things had been normal.

Michelle was robbed of the joy of sharing this special event. I was sad and bitterly disappointed that we all had been denied what should have been a highlight for our family, and I was even more angry because I knew the road Michelle would have to travel in recovery and rehab. There was nothing fair about this.

Speaking of nothing fair, a couple of days after Daniel was born, a large, popular L.A. radio station picked up the story of Daniel's birth. Dad had made his usual weekday morning trip to Harry's for coffee with his cronies and was listening to the radio on his way home when he heard, "I'm looking at an article in the *L.A. Times* about a quadriplegic woman down in Orange County who just gave birth to a baby boy. Can you believe this? Now, aren't we taking disability rights just a bit too far? How is she going to care for this baby? That's just totally irresponsible and selfish. What gives her the right? She's probably going to go on welfare, and we're going to have to pay for day care for this kid because she can't take care of him herself. What do you think? I want to hear from my listeners. Do you agree that people like this shouldn't be allowed to have kids? Call in with your opinion."

Hearing the talk show host's tirade, my dad quickly realized, *He's talking about Renée and my new grandson.* The realization that his precious family was being berated publicly on the radio unleashed his pent-up emotion, and Dad was overcome. He pulled over to the side of the road, laid his head on the steering wheel of his truck, and wept. He didn't want to hear more, but he had to know what people were saying, so he continued to listen.

"We've got our first caller. Debbie down in Laguna Niguel."

"Sir, you have absolutely no idea what you are talking about." The ire in the woman's voice was obvious. "The woman you're talking about is my son's choir director at church. I challenge you to get off your high horse and come down here, and I will personally walk you into a rehearsal so you can see what she gives these young people. You are assuming that because she doesn't have use of her fingers to pick up a beer like you would, she has nothing to offer. Well, you have it all wrong."

"Thank you. You have a right to your opinion, but you obviously have a personal interest in this that keeps you from being objective. Next caller. Cathy in Dana Point."

"I completely agree with the last caller. Renée taught my daughter at San Clemente High School, and you better check your facts, buddy, before you get on that microphone and start pontificating. Renée was one of my daughter's favorite teachers because she cared deeply for each one of her students. She has more going for her being paralyzed than most of us do being able-bodied."

On and on it went. Out of about twelve callers, eleven were friends and parents of ex-students who called in to support me and to rip into the talk show host. Only one person agreed with him. The opinionated, pompous host had never met us and knew nothing of our agony in making the decision, nothing of the preparations we had made to deal with parenthood. He didn't make the effort to check us out to see if we were really capable of pulling this off. He knew one fact, and from that he developed an ironclad opinion and called it truth: I am quadriplegic; therefore, I have no right to have a child. With little information, he publicly ridiculed us, and it hurt deeply. Dad wiped his eyes and drove the rest of the way home.

We knew we would need help, so we quickly found a wonderful live-in nanny for Daniel. Aurora lived in the loft for about six months, and then she came during the daytime only. Our primary concern was always for Daniel's safety; we made sure we were doing everything just right.

It was hard to sit and watch while someone else bathed Daniel and changed his diaper. About not changing diapers someone might say, "Yeah! You weren't missing a thing!" But like most moms, I wanted to do everything for my son. Danny removed the middle shelf from the changing table so that when Daniel was being changed, I could roll up and be face-to-face with him. I'd talk to him, put my arms on the table and stroke his cheeks with the back of my hand, sing "Danny Boy" to him, and make all those undignified noises that one makes when talking to an infant.

Physically I could do little for him, so I seized every opportunity to be near him. I wanted him to see me and recognize that I was Mom—not Aurora, not Janet or Christi, my attendants. They would be there only temporarily, so it was important for his feelings of security and his mental stability that he not be overly attached to them. I realized that Daniel needed to recognize that I was permanent in his life and know that I'd always be there for him to turn to.

After four weeks in the hospital, Michelle's lungs healed at last, so they removed the ventilator, and she was moved to St. Jude's Medical Center in Fullerton for rehab. However, when she started to do her exercises, she realized her broken left arm was not working properly. In the surgery soon after her accident, doctors had inserted rods in the bone, but they were not anchored to the bone, and the result was something they call a "nonunion," meaning it didn't adhere and heal. The rehab staff needed to teach Michelle how to function as a paraplegic, but temporarily she was actually a triplegic, so they couldn't teach her many of the skills she needed to learn, like transferring herself from the wheelchair to the bed or toilet.

I was very torn. When I was at the hospital with Michelle, I was worried about not being home with Daniel. When I was home with Daniel, I felt guilty for not being at the hospital with Michelle. I was frustrated and never satisfied. I had a newfound appreciation for what Michelle and Denise did for me when their babies were only eight and nine months old.

To make matters worse, when I was at the hospital, I was of no earthly use. Denise was wonderful. She was a nurse who knew what to do for Michelle, and she spent many nights in the ICU with her. Denise could go in and identify problems or potential difficulties. She could make Michelle physically comfortable—reposition her body, move her pillow, wash her face. She knew how a hospital operated and how to get things done. And she had legs and arms that worked so she could get Michelle whatever she needed. All I could do was sit. I couldn't water her flowers, arrange her cards, wash her hair. I couldn't even physically get to her— crawl up on the bed and be close to her.

Sometimes I'd go with Michelle to therapy and cheer her on. I'd see her struggling as her sleeping appendages flopped around. I had been right where she was, so those lifeless legs looked hauntingly familiar. I knew what they didn't do, and I knew how frustrating it could be. I couldn't stay too long with her because, knowing how she felt, my heart would break for her, and I'd react by getting angry.

I remembered the hundreds of times Michelle worked with me. I remembered how when she was trying to put my high-top shoes on feet that gave no resistance, she would slap my feet playfully and say, "Come on, feet! Wake up! Get moving!" We'd laugh, but there was truth to her humor. I wanted to do the same for her—to slap her feet and make her laugh. We three sisters had always expressed our affection for each other with playfulness and animation. Now I could only sit by and watch. Just rip my heart out and throw it on the floor.

I knew how alone Michelle felt; everyone else could walk out the door, and I remembered what it was like to lie in bed and watch everyone else leave. Since I couldn't do much for her physically, I wanted at least to be an emotional support. Sometimes I would say to her, "Michelle, I wish I could do more for you." I was her sister; you'd think that a desire to do more for her would be understood, but I believe it's important to come out and say what we're feeling and thinking. Sometimes we assume that others know how we feel, but I've learned that we can't depend on that.

It seems like our mutual plight should have brought us closer together, but it didn't, at least not at first. She didn't complain much or share her fears and frustrations with me, and I sensed her holding back. Later she told me she would have felt guilty grumbling to me when she still had use of her hands. I told her, "Please, don't feel that way. When you're paralyzed, it's all relative. If I had my hands, I'd be griping that I didn't have my feet. It's all paralysis, and we're both in wheelchairs. You can rip at me anytime you want, because I totally get it!"

Now she knows that I want her to use me as a sounding board, and I use her too! But in those first months, communication was awkward. I felt so paralyzed. I had never felt my paralysis more than during Michelle's hospital time. And it killed me. Frustration and resentment became part of my composition. I was boiling inside, day and night. I can honestly say that during my own ordeal, I was intensely frustrated but never truly angry. But now it was Michelle, and our family was going through this nightmare again.

What's more, Michelle and Denise were the ones who had stuck with me through everything. They had attended to my every need, both physical and emotional. Michelle didn't deserve this! To see her in that bed, going through the same thing we had just beaten, I had had it. I didn't want to play this game anymore.

The more I thought about it and the more I dwelt on the unfairness, the madder I got. I was furious. I was engulfed in anger at God, in a way that I'd never been before. I was so out of control it was scary. I was cussing like a sailor. I was shaking my fist (figuratively, of course) in his face and accusing him. "Why did you let this happen? Isn't one member of our family enough! You could have stopped the accident. You could have protected her from a broken back. Why didn't you! Don't you care? *Where are you?*"

I was not only angry with God; I was mad at everyone around me. Anger engulfed me. It was like a boil, feeding on its own infection until finally the pressure caused it to open and drain its abscessed core. Because of the hardness of my heart, I lashed out at innocent people around me. No one could move fast enough or slow enough. Whatever anyone said, I jumped on the other side. Whatever anyone suggested, I was opposed to it. I had no qualms about biting the head off of anyone who got in my way. I had a right to be mad, and no one was going to appease me. The festering anger that I was fertilizing grew into a full-blown case of bitterness, and the bitterness turned me into a contemptuous hellcat. I knew it, but I didn't care.

So, what do you do with this kind of anger? Well, for about two months I just sat in it and let it rule. After all, I had a right to be angry, right? No one would blame me, right? Then came a day of reckoning. Mike and I had to be out of the house by 10:00 A.M. Any parent knows that with an infant, you almost never get out of the house on time. Throw in a wheelchair, and it's just about impossible. I was screaming at Mike, "Hurry up! We should have been in the van ten minutes ago! We're late everywhere we go! You should have gotten up an hour earlier! Why can't we ever leave on time? Let's move!" Mike stepped into the hall and glared at me. Like a defiant fifteen-year-old, I glared back. Our eyes locked. For a few seconds, we stared each other down.

Suddenly I stepped back and looked at myself, at who I had become. The picture came into focus. There stood the man I loved with all my heart, the man who had loved me enough to marry me in spite of my wheelchair, the man who was the father of our child, the man who was doing his best all alone to get three people out of the house, with sadness in his eyes. I had just callously thrust a spear through his heart, piercing him to the core. Instantly, I saw myself as he must have seen me, and it was not a pretty picture.

"Got it," I said to him, thoughtfully. "I got it." I bowed my head right there in the hallway and started crying. I wept tears of shame and confusion. "Oh God," I sobbed. "I surrender this anger. I ask you to replace my anger with your peace. I knew it at one time. I don't know it now. Please take this anger and replace it with your peace. I surrender it all. Look at me. Just look at me! I'm a total mess. I don't know what to do with this. From the top of my head to the bottom of my useless toes, every fiber within me is screaming with anger.

"But Lord, I'm tired of it. I'm tired of being so irritable, so I'm asking you to take it from me. Lord, I give up my right to be angry. I surrender it to you. Take it from me and replace it with your peace. Please forgive me for not trusting you and for the ugly way I've acted. I'm so ashamed. Forgive me for lashing out at my husband. Lord God, keep me from damaging our relationship. Cleanse me now from the inside out, and fill me with your peace once again. Give me the strength I need to be part of the solution rather than part of the problem. Lord Jesus, I just desperately need your peace."

The longer I prayed, the calmer I became. When it was all over, I was drained. Doing business with God on that level is exhausting. But I had taken a critical step; I had consciously and deliberately surrendered my anger. When we got to the garage, I said to Mike, "I think I'm all right now. I got it all out. I'm sorry I blew up. Are you okay?"

He hugged me. "I know how difficult this is for you. We'll work on it together."

I didn't immediately feel any different; I didn't get results instantaneously or even overnight. It was a process. I continued to surrender my anger daily—five or six times a day, in fact. It was a daily discipline, and it wasn't easy. My carnal side still needed to hang on to the anger because, after all, I had a right to it. But the Holy Spirit inside me told me I had to give it up, and then he gave me the courage and strength to do it—over and over again.

One day about two months later, I was enjoying lunch in a restaurant with my friend Linda. She said something that cracked me up, and I started laughing so hard that I totally lost control and couldn't stop. When I started to recover, I suddenly realized what had happened. *You did it, Lord! You really did replace my anger with your peace!* I was much lighter; I was feeling genuine joy again, and I recognized the source of my freedom. I knew God had done something supernatural in my life. Never would I have been able to break the cycle of anger and resentment on my own; it took the breeze of God's Holy Spirit moving in my soul.

Philippians 4:7 was becoming real to me: "And the peace of God, which passeth all understanding, shall keep your hearts and minds through Christ Jesus." I didn't understand how I got in this wheelchair, and I certainly didn't understand how two sisters in one family could end up in wheelchairs in separate accidents seven years apart. I still don't! But the peace that passes my human understanding *will* keep my heart and mind because, when I bowed my head in that hallway and surrendered my anger to God, I invited God's supernatural serenity to overpower my natural confusion. My heart and my mind are all I have left; I don't want anybody messing with them but the King of Peace.

As the weeks passed and the time approached for Michelle to come home, the whole family began making preparations.

The bad news was we had been through this before. The good news was we knew what to do, and that helped a little, albeit a very little. It was surreal that we were again calling the businesses that we had once called for me, this time to help with Michelle's adaptation.

Just before her accident, Michelle and Doug had bought a new van. For some inexplicable reason, except that it was a God thing, they bought it with a tow package, which is necessary for a wheelchair conversion. So, while she was still in the hospital, Doug took the van to Arizona and had a ramp installed and the hand controls transferred to the steering column. He also built a ramp into their mobile home, which was up on the hill close to Mom and Dad where they had moved a few years earlier. Doug also widened the doors inside the house and adjusted anything else he could.

When Michelle came home the end of May, she was scared to death. Life was going to be so different in a wheelchair! How could she adjust? The mother instinct was paramount for her. She wanted to be the nurturer, the one who cared for her household, not the one being cared for. With her left arm still useless, fulfilling that role was almost impossible at first. It was a very scary time for her. We hired an attendant to get her up in the mornings, and, thrilled that I could do *something*, I organized an army of volunteers who took turns going in each day to help her with household responsibilities—folding clothes, cooking, changing the beds.

As the church and the community had done for me, they now rallied around Michelle. They held two fundraisers to help finance her attendant care, and they set up an address— ironically, the same post office box as mine had been—for people to send contributions. Our family will forever be indebted and grateful to the hundreds of people who supported us with their prayers, with their time, with their talents, and with their money. Their efforts sustained us financially and, equally as important, helped our mental and emotional health more than they'll ever know.

Michelle's boys never missed a beat. They were so thrilled to have Mom home that it didn't matter that she was in a wheelchair. Perhaps they were so used to me in my chair that it helped them not to be repelled by hers. One of the hardest things for Michelle was not being able to sit on their beds with them at night to read them their bedtime stories. Many times Doug put her to bed first and the boys came to her for their goodnight kisses. She missed tucking them under her arms for that special time before they went to sleep. When life as you have known it changes, it's surprising what you miss the most.

The surgery on Michelle's arm was crucial. With Denise's leadership and expertise, we consulted three doctors before we felt we had found a surgeon who was skilled enough to pull it off, an arm specialist who had done this particular procedure about 160 times compared to the other two doctors' dozen. He inserted a plate without disturbing the indispensable radial nerve, which controls the function of the wrist, obviously vital to Michelle's ability to transfer herself. The surgery was a complete success, and after two months' recuperation, she was ready for physical therapy.

She chose my therapist, Jim D'Agostino, in Oceanside. However, during the months of immobility, her shoulder had frozen and would no longer rotate, so she had a few strikes against her when she began her therapy. Michelle's first visits were grueling and painful because while Jim is an outstanding therapist, he works his patients hard. Not to be deterred, Michelle attacked the therapy with enthusiasm, seizing every opportunity to improve her function so that she could be as normal a wife and mother as possible. She was unstoppable.

At first she was having her friends drive her to therapy three times a week, but one day when she was deciding who to call, she thought, *Why bother somebody? My van is equipped with hand controls. How hard can it be? I'll just drive myself!* And she did, all the way to Oceanside on the freeway. Ironically, Jim said to her later that day, "We're going to have to get you out in that van and teach you to drive so you can drive your-self down here."

She laughed. "Too late. I drove today!"

"You did? Well, good for you! That's great! How did it go?"

"It's not hard. I just have to think about what I'm doing. For sure I can't be drinking a soda or talking on a cell phone! Both of my hands are busy!" That's Michelle. She'll tackle anything.

In the midst of all this, three separate lawyers contacted Michelle and Doug and urged them to sue Honda, the man-ufacturer of the ATV Michelle was riding when she crashed. Each lawyer had the same plan; the company would settle out of court to get rid of them and to avoid publicity, and Michelle and Doug could expect to receive as much as two million dollars in the settlement. While the thought of col-lecting a quick-and-easy fortune was of course very tempt-ing, especially knowing the strain Michelle's paralysis would add to their finances, they never seriously considered it. Michelle knew that the accident was not the manufacturer's fault; she herself had made an error in judgment in trying to cut back across the avalanche of sand. The vehicle was not at fault. They felt strongly that it would be wrong to accept money they didn't deserve, so they declined to sue. Michelle and Doug's character wasn't for sale.

One night late that summer, Mike was working with our finances when he came in with a recommendation. "The account that covers your attendant care is slowly but surely dwindling. You need to do another album." Although sales on *Inner Voice* far surpassed all expectations, they had now leveled off. I was getting calls to do concerts, but with a new baby and Michelle's injury, I wasn't going to start back until the beginning of the next year. Because everybody I knew who wanted an album had already bought one and because I had no new concerts from which to sell, revenue was way down.

"Yeah, right. Who'd buy a second album of mine? Plus, it seems wrong to be in the studio with Michelle going through what she's going through right now. I want to be able to help her." After a short pause, I added, "As if there's something I could do." I sat and sorted out the realities of the situation, and then I continued to think and pray about it for a couple of weeks. I really couldn't think of any reason not to work on an album, except that it just seemed strange. *How can I be working on an album with Michelle adjusting to paralysis? On the other hand, maybe if I go ahead with this, it'll give her something to enjoy since she and Denise would be singing with me again. She'll get to see all of our great musician friends and spend a couple of days in the studio. She'll be productive again. Maybe it might actually be a good thing for Michelle.*

I began to think about having another kick-off concert when the album was released. Michelle and Denise would be on stage with me, which would be fun as well as healing for everyone. It was so awkward to balance being sensitive to Michelle's loss and needs with the necessity of getting on with life. Regardless of how awkward it was, both of us needed attendant care, so we decided to go forward with the project.

I started putting together the music for this album, arranging some of the numbers to give them a different slant or a funky rhythm. The next step was to get the band together for rehearsals, so they came to the house about once a week, and Michelle and Denise came down and were a part of that too. It was much the same crew as from *Inner Voice*—Jerry and Dave Klein and Rob Williams. Joining us were Lars Andersen, Roger Whitten, and Darren Klein, Jerry and Dave's brother. We were all friends, we enjoyed being together, and we especially enjoyed making music together. We laughed a lot!

Once in the studio, recording *Strength for the Journey* was exhausting—two weeks of concentrated hard work. Daniel was five months old, and we passed him from person to person around the studio with Janet, my attendant, being a wonderful caregiver when we were all busy. Because Jim May was knee-deep in a show of his own in New York and because his mother's health was failing, I didn't dump a lot of the album on him, but he did come out to play on a couple of the songs.

In some ways, this album was easier; I knew what I was doing, I had a better understanding of studio work, and my voice was stronger. Whereas *Inner Voice* featured songs of hope, the purpose of *Strength for the Journey* was to encourage people to move forward, to keep going. Both mirrored where I was in my faith walk at the time they were recorded. When I recorded *Inner Voice*, I needed courage and hope for each day. When we did *Strength for the Journey*, I was in it for the long haul and looking to the Lord.

Ironically, one night during the two weeks that I was in the studio, I watched an interview with Christopher Reeve taped not long after his injury. The next day, we recorded "Shoot for the Moon." It's a song about how a husband and wife can shoot for the moon and, together, make their dreams come true. As I was singing, all I could think about was Dana, Christopher Reeve's wife; Doug; and Mike—the supportive spouses of three paralysis victims. Of course, I didn't know Mr. Reeve personally, but I knew how important his wife was to his recovery.

We planned an outdoor concert in a plaza in San Juan Capistrano in the beginning of December, which is risky even in southern California. The youth group at church helped us set up the stage and sound equipment, and the proceeds went to Michelle and to me for our attendant care.

I did the first part of the concert, and toward the end Denise pushed Michelle onto the stage in her wheelchair. The crowd grew still; there was a silence as the crowd struggled to adjust to two sisters in wheelchairs. Denise stood there for a few seconds, then reached for a stool and quipped, "Well, I guess I'd better get a chair, too!" Everyone laughed, and the rapport with the audience was instantaneous.

Together we sang "Why Walk When You Can Fly?" and "I Will Be Here" from the album—each power-packed with meaning for us. Then we did several country numbers, which had been our bread and butter for several years—three-part-harmony, hand-clapping, foot-stomping songs like "Down at the Twist and Shout" and "Bing, Bang, Boom." Then we closed with "Mr. Sandman," which had become an audience favorite at my last benefits.

As we sat on the stage together, singing, smiling, enjoying the moment, I looked at my sisters. I remembered the three of us riding horses as kids, the three of us backpacking through Europe, our weddings, the two of them caring for me in the hospital, Michelle squealing and landing in my lap, and Denise standing with her arms raised in praise at the news of my pregnancy. Two of us were now in wheelchairs, and one was left standing. I thought of the year we'd just been through, of Daniel's birth and Michelle's accident. I thought about how fragile life is and how one moment can forever alter everything.

As we sang, I saw Michelle smiling and knew the depth of the pit she had endured. I looked at Denise's radiant face and loved her all the more for her faithfulness, her servant's heart, and the way she always seemed to know what to do and how to get it done, for how she was always willing to do what needed to be done with no regard for her own needs or schedule. I've never known anyone quite as giving as Denise. It was a freeze-frame moment.

Once again, we had battled the monster and won. He had given us his best shot, and by the power of God and with the love of each other and the rest of our family, we had emerged victorious. The year that topped all years for us—1995—was drawing to a close, and we were heading into a new year, always symbolic of a new beginning. We were all confident that collectively and individually we had strength for our journey. Together, we were making beautiful music again.

15

Back on
My Feet Again

As we entered 1996, life once again took off. During the preceding year when I wasn't working, I had numerous calls to do public appearances. We set an arbitrary date of January 1 for me to hit the road again, so when the year started, I had an eight-month-old son and a full concert schedule awaiting me.

Knowing what was coming, Mike and I took a leap of faith and hired an administrative assistant to run the business office. I needed help. I could answer the phone with the speakerphone, but I couldn't write down information quickly enough. We needed someone to schedule bookings, handle orders for CDs and cassettes, and answer the phone. This was a big step; not only would we be paying for full-time attendant care, but now we were adding another salary for office help. We knew it was necessary, but it was scary! As always, God was way ahead of us.

Once we decided to hire an assistant, I told Mike, "More than someone with great secretarial skills, I need someone who knows me personally—someone who understands my physical care and medical needs when I get to the location of a concert. I need someone who has traveled with me so that she can communicate from firsthand experience with the event coordinators."

Mike, always the businessman, replied, "Yes, but we really need someone who knows how to run an office efficiently and keep accurate records, and remember that this person will also be generating marketing materials and checklists and updating the web site. We need a secretary who has very good organizational skills."

"I know, but I think it'll be a whole lot easier to teach an attendant the business side rather than teaching a business person the attendant side. I need someone who can troubleshoot and lay the groundwork so that everything is in order when I go out to do concerts so that everything runs smoothly. I need to leave the logistics and details to someone I can trust so that I can be free to focus on ministry."

Then an idea popped into my mind—my weekend attendant! Deborah Benitez had come to work for me after answering my ad in the Penny Saver: "Female attendant needed for active female quadriplegic." On the phone she sounded pleasant and like a good egg, and she lived only a mile away, so I invited her over for an interview the next morning. Right away I liked her straightforward and warm manner, and I hired her on the spot. Soon I came to appreciate her dependability and ingenuity as well as her gentle and unflappable nature. When I got to know a little about her, she told me that she had been raised in a strong atheist home, but she had a friend and neighbor who had prayed for her for seven years. Seven years! Finally, at a ladies' retreat, Deborah accepted the Lord, and three months later she came to work for us. At the time we began looking for office help, she had been working for me for about a year and a half. "What about Deborah?" I asked Mike.

"I think she could handle it, but I thought she only wanted to work part time."

"Let's ask her and see what she says. If she doesn't want it, we can keep looking, but I really think this might work."

The next Saturday when Deborah came, I talked to her about the job, and her eyes lit up. Because of changing events in her life, she was feeling the need to increase her salary and was reluctantly considering seeking a full-time job elsewhere. We talked about her new responsibilities, mapped out a job description, and it was settled. She was an answer to my prayers, and I was an answer to hers. Like I said, God was way ahead of us.

I was busy in 1996. I was averaging seven events a month, speaking at Catholic churches and Protestant churches of all varieties—from Presbyterian to Lutheran to Baptist to Calvary Chapels to Assemblies of God. I was invited to do concerts and to speak at schools and universities, ladies retreats, and philanthropic events, and I continued appearing on the *Hour of Power* at the Crystal Cathedral.

One of my first concerts to a really large audience was the Youth Day for the Religious Education Congress at the Anaheim Convention Center that spring. I'll never forget that special event. As I rolled onto the stage to the beginning of the song "Dream High," I remember looking up, smiling broadly to God, and saying, "Lord, it is amazing how you have turned this whole thing around and worked it for good."

More and more every day I was seeing what God meant in the hospital when he whispered the words to "Be Not Afraid" and when he told me I'd rise up on eagle's wings. I was discovering what Romans 8:28 means: "And we know that all things work together for good to them that love God, to them who are the called according to his purpose." My appearance on stage that day turned out to be a wonderful memory. While I sang "Dream High," about one hundred youth dancers from inner-city L.A. danced throughout the convention hall, using beautifully choreographed movements. It was—pardon the pun—very moving! I was absolutely thrilled with their expression of praise.

After sharing a capsule testimony, I closed with "Firm Foundation." The dancers were dancing, and ten thousand teens in the arena were on their feet, clapping, and echoing the lyrics. The place was rockin'! What I saw was like an impressionistic painting—a sea of faces without features. I could see the crowd, but the Lord saw each individual and knew each heart. Ten thousand teenagers praising God sounded like ten thousand angels to me, and I suspect that the praise offering was a sweet fragrance to God. What a blessing for me to be a part of such a praise rally!

When I came off the stage, Jim Burns, who is one of my favorite speakers on the youth circuit and president of the National Institute of Youth Ministry, came to me and got right in my face. "When you were speaking, you could have heard a pin drop. I have been at these youth-day openings for the last ten years, and I have *never* heard this hall as quiet as I heard it today. You had them right in the palm of your hand. Praise God! Renée, I think you have the beginnings of an incredible ministry. Sorry, gotta go! I've got a workshop to conduct."

Before I could reply, off he went! I was so flabbergasted that I nearly fell out of my chair. As I look back, Jim's words were in some ways prophetic. Since that conference, God has expanded my ministry beyond my wildest dreams.

One day in the spring when I got home from a luncheon engagement, Deborah said, "You got a call from someone in the Christopher Reeve organization. You're supposed to call him back right away."

"Christopher Reeve? Called me? What did he want?"

"I don't know. He didn't say. I left his number by your phone. See you tomorrow."

Christopher Reeve? I thought. *Wow! Why would they be calling me?* I couldn't wait to find out, so I went straight into the office to return the call. With my wrist brace on, I reached over to pull the piece of paper with the number on it closer, and just as I pulled it toward me, I had a spasm in my hand, common for quadriplegia, which flipped the paper all the way off my desk. It fluttered through the air and landed face down on the floor. I just sat there and glared at the piece of paper as if to will it to turn over. I couldn't bend over to get it, and even if I could have, my fingers don't work, so I couldn't have picked it up. I spent about ten minutes raging. "What's the deal? All I want is this stupid piece of paper!"

It was one of those moments when my paralysis just frustrates me beyond my endurance. Why couldn't I just reach over and pick up the piece of paper like anyone else? I was at the end of my rope. I was mad! The truth is I'm not always able to take this whole paralysis thing in stride and be cheerful about it. But after a few minutes of venting and letting off steam, I settled down, accepting that all the yelling and railing in the world wasn't going to change a thing, and decided that I obviously wasn't meant to make the call right then.

About twenty minutes later, the front doorbell rang. I went to the door and called, "Come in!" There, standing in the doorway, was this darling little Girl Scout from down the street delivering cookies. *Oh, great! A Girl Scout! This is perfect!*

"Could you come in and help me for a second?" I asked. She followed me back to the office, got my little piece of paper, and laid it on my desk, face up beside the phone. I had my cookies; I had the phone number. I was all set. Do I think that little Girl Scout appeared at my door by accident? No, I believe her visit was right on time. She was God's little messenger coming to take care of my needs and to remind me that all of my ranting and raving served no useful purpose. God is a very practical God!

When I talked to Christopher Reeve's manager, he invited me to sing the national anthem at Madison Square Garden at the end of October. I couldn't imagine how he got my name, but at that moment it wasn't important. I was only too happy to accept the invitation.

Six weeks later Deborah and I were off to New York City to sing at the East Coast Reeve-Irvine Benefit. (Just for the record, this event was prior to the foundation's endorsement for using fetal tissue for stem cell research.) Singing at Madison Square Garden was a really big deal for me. I was nervous for several reasons. Deborah had never been to New York, and it was the first time I had traveled without the security blanket of Mike. Deborah would have sole responsibility for me—for taking care of everything at the airport, renting a van and getting us to the hotel, getting us to Madison Square Garden and in the right place on time, and for being responsible for me and my care with no one else around to fall back on. This trip was intimidating for both of us.

Upon landing at JFK about 8:00 P.M., Deborah transferred me from the seat in the airplane to the aisle chair and wheeled me out while airline personnel brought my power chair up. Deborah began reassembling my chair—connecting the power box, attaching the leg rests, inserting the cushion, and hanging the backpack over the back. She was struggling to get the tray under the cushion to lie flat, and at first I thought maybe it was because she wasn't used to completely reassembling my chair. But the more I watched, the more I moved toward the inevitable conclusion that something wasn't right.

"You know, guys," I finally said, "I hate to say this, but the frame of my wheelchair is bent! Deborah, look. The bars that crisscross underneath the seat are tweaked!"

Deborah and the airport personnel walked around my wheelchair and inspected it. "Yep. You're right," they concluded. "It's definitely bent!" On further examination they discovered that the power worked only sporadically. We were then told that a baggage handler had inadvertently dropped the chair from the luggage compartment onto the tarmac below. This was not good news. I was there to sing, and I did not think I could sing in a chair that was sitting on a slant. Even under the best conditions, it was difficult to push out enough air to hit those high notes on "The Star-Spangled Banner." There was no way I could project while sitting crooked in my broken power chair.

The airport personnel came back to me with what they thought was a solution. "We'll loan you a manual chair and have this one repaired."

"No, that's not going to do it. I'm really not trying to be difficult here, but I need for you to understand. I have to sing sitting in this chair in the morning, and your manual chair won't fit the bill. A manual chair has a sling bottom and a sling back, which cause me to slouch forward a bit, not allowing for a straight air passage for maximum lung power. I have so little muscle control that I can't sit straight if the chair doesn't help me out. Sorry, but this chair has to be fixed— right away."

Finally, we agreed that Deborah would get me to the hotel in the quasi-power chair, and the airlines would send a repairman from Philadelphia to the hotel to fix the chair during the night. Wasn't there a qualified wheelchair repairman in New York City?

Poor Deborah! Here we were in New York City at night, with luggage, and with me in a broken chair. When the power would cut out, she'd have to push, and a power chair is heavy even when it's empty. With me in it, well, let's just say Deborah was exhausted when we finally got to our hotel room about 11:00 P.M. She got me into bed and then lay down to rest while waiting for the mechanic.

About 2:00 A.M. the phone rang; the repairman was downstairs. Now what? Were we supposed to let a total stranger into our hotel room in the middle of the night? And if we did, I wouldn't be able to sleep with him clanging away on the chair. It wasn't a good idea no matter how you looked at it. So Deborah took the chair downstairs, wrote down the man's identification, and returned to the room. He said he fixed the electrical problem, but there was nothing he could do about the bent frame.

Being inexperienced, I didn't know we could have asked for a driver to pick us up and take us right to Madison Square Garden, so in our ignorance we went in our rented van for people with disabilities. Taxis were everywhere, driving just like all the worst stories you've heard about New York City drivers. We got yelled at and flipped off several times. We watched in amazement as a truck driver right in front of us abandoned his truck and stomped over to a cabbie. The two of them went toe-to-toe, yelling and shaking their fists at each other. We felt like we were in a Manhattan movie! We had no business being there whatsoever!

We got lost, and when we finally found the Garden, we couldn't find a place to park. Deborah couldn't simply let me out because (guess what?) our wonderful Philadelphia repairman had not fixed the electrical problem. The power was still off and on.

When finally we got everything figured out, the van safely parked, and we were inside, the power on the chair wouldn't work at all, so poor Deborah had to push me up the ramps. (I'm sure she was thinking, "How much am I getting paid for this?") And all of this was for ninety seconds on stage. But, praise God, it went really well, tweaked chair and all. Never in my wildest dreams had I imagined singing alone in Madison Square Garden. To me, it was worth it—hassle, tweaked chair, and all.

With the power in my chair still working only sporadically, we left New York City and Madison Square Garden the next day to fly to Grand Forks, North Dakota, where I was scheduled to perform concerts at two different churches. If the difference between New York City and Grand Forks wasn't contrast enough, we traded the Marriott in NYC for accommodations in a convalescent home! It didn't look like a positive trade, but as always God had a plan. When we arrived, I asked the lady at the desk if there was anyone who could fix the electrical unit in my wheelchair.

She said she'd check into it, and I went down to the convalescent home beauty shop to get my hair shampooed. While I was getting blow dried, in walked a little old man with a tool belt who was in charge of facilities at the home. He squatted down beside me, muttered something like, "Oh, this is no big deal; I'll have you rolling in no time," and went to work with his tools. Fifteen minutes later the power was on, and it stayed on.

Now think about this. We couldn't find anyone in all of New York City or Philadelphia to fix my chair, but in a convalescent home in Grand Forks, we found the man. God is too, too funny!

An important event in my life took place when Kay Warren, the wife of the pastor at Saddleback Community Church, called and asked if I would meet with her and the director of women's ministry from her church. They were looking for someone to be the keynote speaker at their women's retreat, so I invited them over to my home for the meeting, which was basically an interview. We spent an hour together chitchatting as they felt their way through what I do to see if it fit with what they had in mind for the retreat.

At the end Kay said, "We just have one more question for you. Where do you fellowship?" What seemed like a harmless question sent me into a state of anxiety. Having traveled around the country, doing concerts in all kinds of churches, I had become aware that many churchgoers, both Protestant and Catholic, have drawn a line that separates Catholics from Christians. A few times after concerts, I've had someone approach me with the comment, "I'm surprised you're Catholic; you sound so evangelical." Also, when some Catholics are asked, "Are you Christian?" they respond, "I'm Catholic." Sadly, I think there is confusion on both sides, whether it be from misinformation, lack of awareness of each other's beliefs, or just plain prejudice.

The truth is simply that both Catholicism and Protestantism are under the umbrella of Christianity because both believe and teach that salvation is through Jesus and him alone. Any person, whether Catholic or Protestant, who has accepted the death and resurrection of Jesus Christ for his sins is Christian. However, being all too aware of this ever-present confusion and knowing that my Catholicism is often an issue for Protestants, I cringed when Kay asked the question.

I'm embarrassed to admit it, but for a split second the "Peter Syndrome" crept in. I was tempted to deny or downplay my Catholic affiliation, but just as quickly I knew I couldn't. I knew I could never succumb to someone's stereotypes and deny the church that had brought me to a saving faith in Jesus Christ. "Lord, please honor what I am about to say."

I took a deep breath, smiled, and said, "The Mission San Juan Capistrano, the Catholic church right here in town." They audibly breathed a sigh of relief.

"Oh, great!"

"Really?" I was stunned. "I'm curious. Why did you ask me the question?"

"Because many speakers with a schedule like yours are so weary when they return home that they don't join themselves to an active body of believers. They don't feel that they need to be fed, and they're not in fellowship with other Christians in a church setting. They are not being ministered to, and we feel that that's very important."

I wholeheartedly agreed with them. "In my traveling, I've been exposed to all kinds of churches, and it's really wonderful to hear the different types of preaching and teaching and to be a part of different services. But the Mission is my home church."

By the end of the afternoon, Kay and I were completely comfortable with each other, and we began to make plans for my role at the retreat. Several months later on a Saturday evening, I did a ninety-minute set for over seven hundred Saddleback Valley women. Since the ladies had already been at the retreat for a day and a half, they were ready to hear what God can do in a person's life. We laughed, we cried, we sang, and we danced. It went so well that we released the recording of my presentation as *Back on My Feet Again!*

Another unforgettable event was the first time I appeared at a Joni and Friends benefit with Joni Eareckson Tada. The benefit was designed to provide funds and promote Joni and Friends, her powerful ministry that provides Christian outreach to people with disabilities. The event was held in Oakland, California; she was the speaker and I was the vocalist. On the day of the event, Deborah and I sat with Joni, her mom, and her assistant. Looking at Joni was almost like looking into a mirror. Joni has been quadriplegic since a 1967 diving accident; her degree of function is almost parallel to mine. She is a phenomenal lady and an incredible Bible teacher. I could never imagine knowing as much Scripture as she does, and she shares it beautifully and freely. I was so impressed and felt so inadequate that again I wondered what I was doing there. I wasn't interested in talking about my accident but just wanted to hear about her ministry. On the program, I sang three songs and gave a brief testimony. When I was wrapping up, I was surprised to see Joni rolling onto the stage.

"Renée, would you join me in singing a hymn?" she asked, smiling broadly.

"Sure!"

"Which hymn would you like to sing?"

"Well . . . uh . . . uh . . . uh . . ." It wasn't that hard of a question, but give me a break! I was on stage with Joni Eareckson Tada! My mind went blank. Finally it came to me.

"Let's do 'How Great Thou Art.'"

"You start."

I started singing, "Oh, Lord my God, when I in awesome wonder consider all the worlds thy hands have made." Joni joined in with a beautiful harmony line. She has great pitch, a wonderful ear for harmony, and a rich, warm tone. What a thrill for me to sing God's praises with his incredible servant, Joni Eareckson Tada.

Since then Joni has graciously invited me to participate in more of her events. I've watched how she walks closely with the Lord and how she has managed her years of sitting in a wheelchair. She has not only survived, but she has done it with poise and beauty. She is an amazing artist, holding a paint brush between her teeth, and she has written over twenty books. She is also the president of Joni and Friends

Ministries and has provided untold numbers of wheelchairs to people with disabilities in underprivileged countries. She and I laugh now because I consider her to be "Queen Quad!" Joni's example completely erases all my excuses not to live a useful, productive life and increases my courage to keep going.

It took me several years to recognize the value of spending time with other disabled people. Looking at others with disabilities was like looking into a mirror; it was painful. I'm embarrassed to admit that I resisted being associated with other people in wheelchairs; I wanted to be "normal." Without realizing it, Joni showed me how unbelievably helpful it is to walk with a veteran of the war you're fighting. When I broke my neck, Joni had been sitting in her chair for twenty-one years. When I met her, her adjustment seemed complete, and seeing her contentment gave me inspiration and courage. I could see that it would be foolish not to glean from her experience.

When we're drowning, God sends a lifeboat. When we're without direction, he sends a compass. Almost always our lifeboat and compass will come in the form of a person—someone who has been where we are and has made it safely to shore. This person knows the way, so God sends him or her to take us by the hand to guide us to solid ground. The journey seems shorter, the burden seems lighter, and the path seems straighter when we share it with a friend who has navigated these waters before.

16

Dream
High

One of the drawbacks or perks, depending on the situation, to this kind of ministry is the travel. One night Mike and I were lying in bed talking, and I asked him, "If you had your choice of anywhere in the world to go, where would you choose?"

Without missing a beat, he said, "Alaska."

"Really? Why?"

"I hear it's so beautiful, and it's raw and untouched and intact, just like God created it." Mike and his brother Steve are avid backpackers. Every summer they escape to the Sierra Nevada Mountains to enjoy the solitude and beauty. Alaska was his dream. While our next trip wasn't to his dream spot, it certainly was to mine. When I was invited to be a keynote speaker for Hawaiian Island Ministries' Heart Full of Hope Women's Conference in Honolulu, it was definitely a perk! Due to my injury, we had missed our Hawaiian honeymoon, and here was our chance to make it up.

On Thursday night when Mike, Daniel, Deborah, and I got off the plane in Honolulu, we were, like most Hawaiian tourists, absolutely thrilled to be there. We knew we were in Hawaii when someone placed the traditional leis around our necks. Because it was late, we gathered our luggage and headed straight to our hotel and went to bed, anticipating a little free time to ourselves the next day, before my sound check, to explore our surroundings and to see the beauty we'd heard so much about.

After Deborah came in the next morning and got me up into my wheelchair, I rolled over to the window to enjoy the view of the pool. With a brilliant blue sky as the backdrop, palm trees swayed in the breeze and flowers of brilliant, vibrant hues lined the walkways. Sun lovers in swimsuits and beach attire were lying in lawn chairs and lounging on beach towels on the grass. Already, many were in the water— splashing with their families or floating lazily on rafts. The scene looked like a picture postcard or, more to the point, like the picture I'd had in my head of the way our honeymoon would be. Suddenly, emotion welled up in my chest, and I started weeping.

To avoid bringing the others down, I tried to conceal my tears by sitting with my back to the room, but Mike realized something was up. He walked over and looked at me. "Are you okay?"

"I can't even lie by the pool with you or walk on the beach and hold your hand or feel the sand squish between my toes," I choked out. "We're finally in romantic Hawaii, where we were supposed to spend our honeymoon, and you're stuck with me and this stupid body of mine." I didn't throw a big tantrum or create a scene; I was just very, very sad. Mike leaned down and pulled my head over onto his shoulder, and I cried and cried, and I continued to cry pretty much the whole trip.

When I was away from the beach and inside the arena, it was easier to stuff the whole Hawaii thing and focus on giving the people my best. I spent a lot of time in prayer. "Lord, please take this sadness away. I need to get it together. These people need to see you and hear you—in my words and in my music. Enable me to push my emotions aside long enough to minister to them. Please anoint me now, Lord. Amen."

I opened with "Be Not Afraid," accompanied by Hawaiian dancers in full regalia. It was absolutely gorgeous! Watching their worship in dance lifted my spirits. The conference itself was wonderful.

As I usually do, I had a booth at the conference where I could meet the people and make CDs and tapes available to them. While I was there shaking hands and signing autographs, a lady ran up, cut in line, got right in my face, and said, "I just had a vision. I am a travel agent. For years I have been toying around with the idea of putting together a Christian cruise to Alaska. Is there any way—any way at all—you would ever consider being a speaker on a Christian cruise to Alaska?"

Remembering Mike's dream vacation, I laughed and replied, "Oh, I don't know. Let me ask my husband what he thinks.

"Mike!" I yelled at him across the way. "Mike, what would you think about me speaking on a Christian cruise to Alaska?"

He literally jumped over the table and ran up to us, "Where do we sign?" he asked. Ten months later Mike and I were sitting on the deck of a massive cruise ship, face to face with glaciers and marveling at bald eagles as they circled above us. Mike made it to his dream spot.

On Sunday morning I was invited to do a forty-five-minute set at each of the two morning services at the First Presbyterian Church of Honolulu. It just so happened that on that particular morning, their soloist was saying farewell. He was moving to New York, and this was his last morning with this congregation. While I waited to go on, he addressed the audience and said, "I'm not very good at speaking, so let me express my gratitude to you this way," and he began singing "Thank You," a Ray Boltz standard. I was deeply moved by the lyrics that painted a portrait of a man whose life had greatly influenced others for the Lord.

It put me in a frame of mind to ask myself who in my life was most responsible for bringing me to Christ and who had been the biggest spiritual influence in my faith walk. There was Herbie who showed me by example that we could get to know God better by reading his Word. There was Julie who taught me that God really does talk to us. My parents cared enough to take us kids to church every Sunday and to provide a parochial education. All of these influences were very powerful, and they all played a vital role.

Then it hit me. Father Martin! More than anyone else, Father Martin has been a consistent reminder that I should be a servant to God's will. More than anyone else, Father Martin has been God's hands, mouth, and presence in my life. He was there when I was a child; he was my boss and mentor; he was there when I broke my neck; he was at the hospital every Wednesday night when I was in rehab; he was the one who met Mike and me at the altar of matrimony; he was the first one besides us to hold our newborn son; and in all of that he always modeled Jesus Christ. This was an important moment for me; it made me realize how valuable it is for us to identify those people who have pointed us to Christ. It's equally important to tell them so.

I was still pretty much a mess when they called for me on stage, so when I rolled out, I started with, "You'll have to excuse my tears, but that song just touched me so deeply. It's just so right that he's thanking you for being a people who touched his life. We all should remember to thank those who have impacted our lives in a positive way."

Our flight home was on Tuesday, so we had a few days to see the island. Sunday afternoon we went up to Waimea Falls, a gorgeous area. To get up to the falls, we had to take a wheelchair-accessible tram up the mountain. There was beautiful scenery to look at on the ride up, but the mechanical lift that allowed me to roll onto the tram folded up beside me, creating a cage effect that obstructed my view. I felt lonely and isolated sitting in the back, alone in my cage. When we reached our destination, the operator started to get me off the tram, but the lift was jammed and wouldn't lower, so I was stuck there, feeling like a caged animal.

It was getting late; every moment was valuable at this point. I didn't want Mike, Daniel, and Deborah to miss a treat just because I couldn't go, and the falls were soon to close, so I put on my best cheerful mask and told them to go on up to see the falls and that I'd follow when and if they got me out. I smiled cheerily and urged them on, so off they went. From inside my cage, I watched the three of them start up the path together, with Mike holding Daniel's hand. They looked like a family. The picture broke my heart. I saw Mike walking away with a healthy woman. *Mike and Deborah together,* I thought to myself. *What if he were to have an affair with Deborah? She can walk, she can run. He deserves a healthy, active woman!*

I knew that Mike would never cross that line, and neither would Deborah. Actually, it wasn't Deborah per se that I was envisioning with Mike; she merely represented any woman whom Mike might choose over me. But the picture of them together brought into focus the reality that Mike deserved better because he was being gypped by being married to me. Fear and sadness engulfed me. I was held hostage in a caged cubicle, and at that moment I was a captive of my racing imagination. Panic rose inside me—panic at being locked in a cage and panic at being locked in my dead body. Hot tears of frustration rolled down my cheeks.

After a ten-minute wait that seemed like an hour, help came and brought me freedom. Just as I was released from my cage and was hurriedly rolling down the ramp, I could see Deborah coming back down the path to check on me. She pointed the way to Mike and Daniel, and I found them sitting on a rock enjoying the breathtaking beauty of the falls. I joined my family, and together we considered the creative genius of God who could design such splendor.

It's always refreshing to get my eyes off myself and onto God. That night I apologized to Mike and Deborah. "You guys, I'm trying really hard here not to rain on the parade. I really want you to know that."

Mike offered his take on the situation. "Before we left home, I realized we were coming to the place where we should have had our honeymoon, and I prepared myself. But I got so busy with the preparations and with wrapping up loose ends at work that I didn't think to check in with you to see if coming here would be a problem for you. Maybe if I had, we could have circumvented the problem."

"You're right. I didn't think about it before we left at all. I was just excited to come to Hawaii and was thinking about my message at the conference. It didn't occur to me that it would be painful because this is the place where our wedding trip was supposed to be.

"We were robbed of our Hawaiian honeymoon, and coming here just reopened the wound. I had no idea I'd feel this way. I was totally blindsided. Just when I think I'm on top of this thing, something happens to remind me of how much I've lost—how much I miss my body and being able to do the things that other people do. I'm sorry I've been such a wet blanket. Being here just triggered something inside me that threw me into a state of grief all over again. I wonder if I'll ever get to a place where this doesn't happen."

"Don't worry about being a wet blanket. We all understand," Mike said. "Dealing with this paralysis is an ongoing thing. Because you live with it every second of your life, it's not something you can simply cry over and be done with. It's never ending. Don't feel that you need to apologize; you handle sitting in that chair far better than I would!" That's Mike, always finding ways to make me feel better.

We departed the beautiful island on Tuesday afternoon. Once we were up in the air, Daniel got out a book for me to read to him, and we were settling in for the five-hour flight back to L.A. Suddenly, the captain was standing in the aisle beside my seat. "Well, hello!" I said, acknowledging his presence.

"Hi."

"Aren't you supposed to be up there? Who's driving this thing?" I teased.

Looking somewhat sheepish, he said, "Well, I drew the short end of the straw, which means that I have the unpleasant task of telling you that we left your wheelchair on the ground back at the airport."

"Oh, grrrrreeeeeeat," I said.

"They're going to put it on the very next plane, and it'll be in L.A. about two hours after you arrive. I am so sorry for the inconvenience. We'll work with you any way we can to help you work things out."

There was no use screaming or yelling. They already felt badly enough about it, so Mike and I just thought through possible scenarios. Even though we wouldn't land until 9:00 P.M., we decided to wait for the chair at the airport before heading home. Traveling with a wheelchair is always an adventure!

Still another memorable event was being asked to be a keynote speaker at a convention for the Association of Christian Schools International (ACSI) at the Anaheim Convention Center. While my schedule was always full, most of my concerts were for churches, ladies' luncheons, and schools. I have to confess that the thought of speaking to ten thousand Christian teachers was quite attractive!

When the call came from the director, Jerry Haddock, we went through all the typical ice-breaking comments and then moved into the logistical aspects of the event. We talked for a long time—maybe an hour—and it seemed like it was a done deal. But then he slowly said, "I've got to ask you one more question."

"Sure. Go ahead."

"I understand you're Catholic." There it was again, the Catholic thing. I knew all too well that a candid answer could be a deal breaker, and I certainly wanted to speak at this convention. Again for a split second I contracted the "Peter Syndrome." I wanted to deny or downplay my Catholic affiliation but quickly decided I couldn't.

As before, I shot up a quick prayer *(Lord, please honor this)* and slowly responded, "Yes, I'm Catholic." Silence. I waited for him to reply, but he said nothing.

"Is that a problem?"

"Quite frankly, it could be an issue with some," he answered. Again, there was a long silence.

Finally I said, "Please allow me to share my heart. Is Jesus Christ my Lord and Savior? Absolutely, yes. Did he die on that cross opening the gates of heaven just for me? Absolutely, yes. Have I invited him into my heart? Absolutely, yes. Do I put Mary anywhere near or equal to Jesus Christ? Absolutely not. She's honored, not worshipped."

He breathed an audible sigh of relief. "Oh, I am so thankful to hear you say that!"

"You know what, though?" I continued. "Are there people in our pews, in my Catholic church, who do not have a personal relationship with Christ and who go to church strictly out of obligation? Absolutely, yes."

He responded, "Are there people in my Protestant church who go to church every Sunday morning but do not have a personal relationship with Christ and attend solely out of obligation? Absolutely, yes."

Reflecting back on the conversation, I realized that Jerry was right to ask the question. Because he was responsible for the message that would go out to the convention, he would have been remiss not to make sure that I, or any other potential speaker for that matter, was clear on the issue of salvation. He obviously knew before he called that I am Catholic; yet he called, and in doing so he invited an open exchange that led to a mutually beneficial arrangement. I'm grateful to him for being open enough to keep the doors of possibility open so that we could dialogue. It's so important that we be willing to move past our stereotypes to listen, really listen to each other, with an attitude of discovering agreement rather than uncovering differences.

Unfortunately, the tendency to find fault shows up not only across denominational barriers but can be found within denominations as well. On occasion, for example, I have been criticized by other Catholics for not being Catholic enough, and I have received a few letters accusing me of hiding my Catholic faith because I don't come out on stage and announce, "Good evening. I'm Renée, and I'm Catholic!" I love to speak on God's faithfulness and if I start talking about my Catholicism from the stage, I am pointing the audience toward a denomination when what I really want to do is point them to Christ.

Recently I saw a cartoon that made a relevant point. There was a fence with Christians on one side and non-Christians on the other. The non-Christians were hurling rocks at the Christians, and the Christians were picking them up and throwing them at each other! Not only do we needlessly hurt each other, we send a negative message to the world, which may be even worse.

The convention was fun. I was the keynote speaker in the first morning session, doing a sixty-minute set. It was especially fun because I was speaking not only to Christians but to Christian teachers. I have such a passion for what teachers do; I know how great their impact on youth is and in turn on society. I opened with "Be Not Afraid," and from the first moment I could feel the audience was with me. We had a common bond. As a speaker, you can tell when you've got your audience and when you're losing them. What a wonderful time we had! As in Hawaii, I had a booth and stayed around for two days, greeting teachers, answering questions, and signing autographs. It was a great event, which I appreciated even more because of the honesty and candor of the conversation that brought me into the contract.

I've been blessed not only with the privilege of ministering all over the country, but also with receiving awards for doing what I love. One day in the fall of 1996, Deborah came in with the news that Barbara Todd from the Crystal Cathedral had called and that I had been named by Robert H. Schuller as the recipient of his Turning Your Scars into Stars Award. As I later learned, this award is not bestowed annually, but when the committee recognizes someone who has persevered through adversity and emerged victorious. Once the recipient has been named, there is a huge ceremony in the recipient's honor and the award is presented. At the time, the only other recipients had been Art Linkletter, Della Reese, and Coretta Scott King.

I confess that when the Schuller people called, I had never heard of the award and didn't realize what a big deal it was. They explained the ceremony and told me they especially wanted me to invite my family and friends. How do you go about inviting people to something like this? "Hi there, I'm receiving an award. Want to come see me get it?"

The award ceremony was inside the Crystal Cathedral. Mike's and my family were there. I sat on the stage for the entire ceremony, and when Reverend Schuller came to present the award, he said some lovely things. He talked about my perseverance, my voice, my ministry. I was deeply moved but felt totally unworthy of such high praise.

Embarrassed as I was to invite people to come watch me receive an award, it did have a positive outcome. As Mike and I were driving home, we talked about how amazing it was to be included in such a prestigious line of recipients. I flashed back to the early years of my injury and how insecure I was, wondering how I could ever be productive without the use of my arms and legs. I remembered my sense of unworthiness and my lack of confidence. *Wow, God. How far you have brought me.* The evening helped Mike and me recognize once again that God was using our pain for good and affirmed the value of the ministry the Lord had given us.

It's funny how God makes things come full circle. A few years later, Deborah took a phone call and told me that I had been named to receive the Walter Knott Service Award for Overcoming Disabilities, sponsored by Goodwill Industries.

The award was established to honor its first recipient, Walter Knott (best known for his Knott's Berry Farm amusement park), honoring him for devoting much of his life to giving back to his community and recognizing his exemplary service to others.

I thought little about it, knowing only that there would be an award luncheon. Deborah and Mike weren't saying much because they wanted to keep it a surprise that the award was a big deal. Deborah was coordinating with the Goodwill Industries Awards Committee, trying to give them what they needed without revealing the details to me. "They're sending us tickets for people to sit at two tables. Who do you want to invite?"

"Deborah! I told you already; it'll just be you and me and maybe Mike if he can come over on his lunch hour. I'm not going to invite my friends and expect them to sit through this thing. They've all been to plenty of banquets and eaten their share of chicken, rice, and vegetable medley!"

Finally she blurted out, "All right! I'm trying to do something good for you here, and you're really making it difficult. This is a big deal, and people are coming. I just need to know who you want to see there. Can you just cooperate with me a little bit here?"

"Oh, sorry. I didn't realize. Tell me what you need, and I'll try not to ask too many questions."

When Deborah, Daniel, and I arrived at the Hyatt Regency, Mike met us outside, and we went in together. As we walked down the hallway approaching the ballroom, Mike stopped and looked at me. "Can you believe this, Renée?"

"Wow," I said thoughtfully. "This is it, isn't it?" We were approaching the exact same ballroom where we chaperoned the prom the night before my accident. "The name of the hotel has changed, but this is definitely the room. Wow. How ironic and how bizarre that this is where I'm returning now to accept an award for overcoming disabilities."

Before we had time to reflect, we were escorted to our table. Mom, Denise, Michelle, Jim, and Sandra were there. The table adjacent to ours was filled with friends, neighbors, and old students. Of course, other recipients had their friends and family with them also. Since the *Orange County Register* was one of the sponsors, members of their staff were there as well as many other Orange County philanthropists who were happy to pay for the one-hundred-dollar ticket because they counted it as a donation to an excellent cause. Tables with black tablecloths and lovely centerpieces filled the room. I was struck with the elegance, especially unmistakable because it was a luncheon.

The emcee was Ed Arnold, noted L.A. sportscaster whom I knew from other philanthropic events in southern California. He opened the award ceremony: "Today, we honor four significant individuals for exemplifying Walter Knott's humanitarian spirit of generosity. All have helped to improve the quality of life for others who are challenged by disabilities. Please join me in expressing our heartfelt appreciation and admiration for their courage and dedication in overcoming challenges and achieving independence."

Then Ed Arnold said into the microphone, "Renée Bondi, will you please come up." Mike went with me to help me onto the stage. Once I was situated, the lights dimmed and suddenly I saw my face on the huge screen; they were showing an excerpt from my testimony video. After that, the video continued with a parade of family and friends, each speaking a message of encouragement and congratulation to me. As each precious person appeared on the screen, I squealed with delight and cried with affection. The last clip pushed the finger out of the dyke; it was Daniel waving and saying, "Good job, Mom!"

As the lights came back on, mascara was running down my face. I was presented the award from Virginia Knott Bender, one of Walter Knott's daughters. It was an oil painting done by a person with disabilities, and it had an inscription on the back.

"Thank you so very, very much," I said to the presenters and to the audience. "If there's anything I've learned from traveling throughout the country speaking to audiences, it is that everyone, disabled or not, has a cross to bear. Thank you for helping me carry mine." I felt humbled to be singled out for recognition. It was one of those occasions when I try to follow Corrie ten Boom's advice. She says that when you are praised or receive a special compliment, hold it in your heart like a flower. When you gather enough flowers to make a bouquet, offer it up to God, because he's the one who really deserves it.

I turned to the audience and said, "Before I sing, I want to tell you something. It was in this very room that Mike and I danced our last dance almost eleven years ago. I was a teacher at San Clemente High School, and we were here to chaperone the prom. Mike had just given me my engagement ring at dinner, and we came here and danced the night away. Thirty-six hours later, I fell out of bed and broke my neck. How ironic that it is in this room I have received this wonderful award." The music began, and I sang, more passionately than ever before, "Dream High."

As I sang, I couldn't help but look around the room. Ghosts from that night eleven years ago seemed to dance around me. I could see myself in my sequined top and black velvet skirt, high-heeled black sandals, my hair done in a French twist for the special occasion. I saw myself walking around the room hand in hand with Mike, being besieged by giddy high school girls eager to admire the engagement ring he had placed on my finger earlier that evening. He was my Prince Charming, and I was his Cinderella, dancing in his arms at the ball.

I could almost feel Mike whirling me around the dance floor as we laughed and giggled, dreaming of our lives together. We never imagined that this would be our last dance—that in thirty-six hours, life as I had known it would come to an abrupt halt, forever changed. Like a tornado ripping through a village, my world was turned upside down. I was stripped of nearly everything I had valued—my movement, my voice, my teaching, my independence, my privacy. How fragile the status quo is; how quickly *everything* can change!

I thought about how different my life was now from what I had dreamed it would be eleven years before at the prom. My life was not anything like I had imagined or planned. It took a turn I didn't design and would not have chosen.

I remembered in the hospital when I had heard God's voice in the night. "Be not afraid, Renée. I go before you, Renée. Come, follow me, and I will give you rest." God kept his promise. Through it all, he has been completely and fully faithful.

Disabled? Severely. Discouraged? Sometimes. Defeated? Never. Victorious? Absolutely! Why? Because my God is an incredible God who knew just how to make beautiful music of my broken life.

17

Ask Me Anything

Sometimes at my concerts, at the end of the program, there is time set aside for a question-and-answer session. This is generally one of my favorite times of the evening because the lights come up, and the atmosphere switches to that of my living room. The audience and I chitchat back and forth, so they can get a little more insight. It's a chance for members of the audience to ask any questions they've had on their minds for the last hour and a half. So, if you don't mind, I'd like to pause this concert and have a little intermission. Let's have a Q&A session. Following are some of the most frequently asked questions with my typical responses.

What losses does a paralysis victim suffer that might be less obvious?
Body language. You don't realize how important body language is to communication until you've lost it. When someone is hurting, the normal thing for me to do would be to stand up, walk over to her, give her a tight hug, and then sit

down beside her with my arm around her shoulder or my hand on her leg.

When words just won't cut it, body language is often more effective. If I need to discuss something serious or uncomfortable with someone, like my attendant, there's a body language that would help soften the words. Rather than sitting straight and academic in a chair, I would love to cross my legs, lean forward, touch her on the shoulder. Or, there's the body language when it's time for someone to leave; you stand up or if you want to leave, you get your keys out of your purse. You just don't realize how much you communicate with your body until you lose the privilege.

Another loss is my ability to release emotion physically. Psychologists tell us that there is a definite link between mental and emotional health on the one hand and physical activity on the other. Physical exertion is great therapy! When we were kids, we knew when Mom was mad by the way she put the silverware away. Crash! Wham! Clink! Clank! Smack! I can't slam a door, throw a pillow across the room, pound out a march on the piano, or stomp out of the house. I can't run down the beach or swim or get on a horse and ride like the wind. I only have my voice and my tears. I'm now a very emotional person; I cry easily, and I think it's because tears are my only outlet for pent-up emotion.

Following your accident, how long was it until you had movement in your arms? How long was it before you could speak above a whisper?

These questions are difficult to answer with any accuracy because progress was so slow. I started getting a little function in my biceps about a year after my accident, but I worked five more years with Jim D'Agostino to get where I am now. Currently, my biceps work; my triceps do not. I can wave my arms and hug my son, but my wrists, fingers, and legs have no function whatsoever. I wear a wrist brace that provides me with a few additional skills. When a fork is inserted, I can feed myself. Most of the day, I have a pencil clasped in the brace with the eraser end down. With this tool, I can turn pages, dial the phone, and perform simple tasks on the computer.

It was about a year after the accident that my voice began to come back. It was high and very soft, far too soft to sing. When I started directing the youth choirs at church, however, and had to project and use my teacher voice again, my lungs got still stronger; it was great voice therapy.

What is hardest for you mentally about being paralyzed?

Being dependent. When my son was three years old, one of his most adamant demands was, "I'll do it allbymyself!" That wasn't something Daniel learned; it was something he was born with—that need to be independent, that feeling of accomplishment, that desire to be self-sufficient.

Sometimes I want to shout, like Daniel, "I want to do it allbymyself!" But the reality is, I can't. There is almost nothing I can do all by myself. I've had to give up the luxury of aloneness. It begins before I even get up each morning. I am awakened by my attendant who has come to get me up, and I'm seldom alone for the remainder of the day. Even if I'm in a different room, I'm constantly aware of someone else's presence in our house.

Along with this lack of independence is my loss of privacy. Not to be able to shower myself, tend to my own personal hygiene, go to the bathroom alone. I can't hop in the car and run errands for the day by myself; I have to be driven and accompanied. I can't just be at home alone all day to work in the garden or clean out a cupboard or write letters to friends. I can't sit at the piano and lose myself in music. I can't even talk to someone privately on the phone because I have to use a speaker phone, and everybody in the house can hear both sides of the conversation. It is an intrusion to have someone with me at moments that should be private.

The reality is I need the help. I have no choice, and I know that. But the choice I do have is my attitude about it. I would like to tell you that I'm just naturally good-natured, adaptable, and joyful about the whole thing, but the truth is that it's very difficult and a daily discipline.

Look at the support you've had from your family and friends. A lot of other paralysis victims don't have the support network you've had. Your fiancé married and stayed with you, so it's easy for you to smile and be happy.
You're right. Nobody but nobody could do more than my family and friends have done for me, and the gratitude and appreciation I feel for them cannot be measured. To reduce my thankfulness to words would minimize the intensity of my emotions.

That being said, I must add that I work really hard—I mean, reeeeeeeeeally hard—at being the kind of person others won't mind being around. If I were always a bitter whiner, no one would want to be near me! Sometimes I'm successful, and sometimes I'm not. The old cliché about not biting the hand that feeds me seems particularly applicable here.

What you see on stage—the smiles and the joy—that's the easy part. At the moment, I'm thoroughly enjoying what I'm doing. The challenge is in living life joyfully day in and day out.

What things do you do in your marriage to survive the added strain of your paralysis?
The first time Mike and I see each other when we've been apart, whether for the day when Mike's been at work or whether I've been on a road trip, the first thing we do is kiss each other. Mike will come straight to me and kiss me on the lips. What that does is give us a quick second to look straight into each other's eyes and regroup. It is a physical way of saying, "I missed you, and I'm glad we're together again."

This affectionate welcome is a three-generation tradition. Sandra's parents modeled this loving ritual before their children, and Sandra made it a custom in the Bondi home.

We communicate, and nothing is more important than that. When I catch myself being whiny, grumpy, and irritable, I try to remember to stop and say, "Mike, I'm sorry. I know I'm being grouchy with you; you're not the problem. You know I love you with all my heart. It's just that living like this just gets to me sometimes."

Then, if it's a good time (and timing is everything!), I'll use the opportunity to invite more dialogue. "So, how are you doing with this *really*?" It gives Mike the opportunity to vent his frustrations while reminding me that this is a two-way street; someone else is in this trash can with me.

Open dialogue is mandatory in any marriage, but because of the added strain of my paralysis on ours, it seems even more vital. Generally, Mike is frank with his answers, which is equally important to asking questions. He's not afraid to admit, "I'm tired. This is getting old." At that point, I know that we need to step back, reevaluate, and try some different ways of doing things.

Something we've started the last few years is studying the Bible together. Because of my schedule and the demands of parenthood, we just can't get to a couples' Bible study, so we do it alone. We keep our Bibles and study books by our bed, and a couple of times a week when we go to bed, we spend time in the Word. We love it. It opens conversation and the exchange of ideas. Before we go to sleep, we pray together, sometimes one of us, sometimes both, and we fall asleep with God on our minds. It's an essential part of our marriage.

Even though I don't have legs and arms and hands to do the household duties, I still make sure they're done. I'm still responsible for making sure there's food in the refrigerator, that the house is clean, and that the meals are on the table—whether Mom or my attendant prepares it or we have leftovers or we order out.

We try to practice the things that other couples do or should do—not taking ourselves too seriously, not getting sucked into the materialism trap, lifting each other up in public instead of cutting each other down, surrounding ourselves with others who share our values. Although we sometimes get sidetracked and out of alignment, our stated priorities are God first, then each other, then Daniel. It works.

Would Mike have stayed with you if he had not had God in his life?

Mike would say yes. He has a lot of integrity and character. It has to be understood, however, that his character and integrity are direct results of his Christian home—his Christian foundation. Therefore, you really can't pull the Christian aspect out of the equation.

What mistakes do people commonly make around you?

Sometimes I like to give homemade things to friends or people who have blessed or helped me in some way. One of my favorite things to give is baked goods. It is disappointing when I offer a gift, and the recipient inquires, "Who made it?" I did! I had the idea, planned the gift, purchased the ingredients, used my recipe, and dictated how it would be packaged. Obviously, someone else had to be my hands, but the gift wasn't about who sifted the flour and poured the milk in the bowl; it was about who gave of herself. When someone asks, "Who made it?" it doesn't seem like she understands that I was the one who wanted to give.

Another common mistake is from strangers. Many times, strangers assume that if a person's body doesn't work, his mind and ears don't work either. Often, strangers talk right in front of me about me rather than talking to me. It's very annoying—insulting, actually.

For example, Deborah and I were on a road trip, waiting at the airport for our flight. We had been sitting near the check-in counter talking for maybe half an hour. I had come straight from a speaking engagement, so I was dressed professionally and, I assume, looked relatively intact. The ticket agent approached, ignored me, looked straight at Deborah, and asked, "How would she like to get on the plane?"

I wanted to shout at her, "Talk to me! I'm sitting right here! I am capable of speaking for myself and of making my own decisions! This wheelchair does not cut off circulation to my brain!" But instead, I just answered for myself and said, "Deborah will transfer me to the aisle chair . . . ," hoping she'd get the hint. No one intends to be unkind; I know that, but it would be helpful if people would work under the assumption that the person in the wheelchair is mentally competent until they learn otherwise.

I must share one funny story that relates to this topic. Another time Deborah and I were traveling and were in the terminal at the Dallas/Ft. Worth airport. We were sitting right in front of the check-in counter when the ticket agent picked up the microphone and, with her voice blaring, announced, "May I have your attention? Flight 234 to Orange County Airport has been delayed due to a minor mechanical problem. If you'll just take a seat in the ticket area, we'll update you on our status as we receive information."

Deborah turned to me and repeated, "Flight 234 has been delayed due to a minor mechanical problem. Let's just sit here in the ticket area, and they'll update us on our status as they receive more information."

I looked at her in utter disbelief and replied, "I'm paralyzed, not deaf!" Some travelers sitting close by heard the whole thing, and they howled with laughter. I got tickled, and Deborah started laughing at herself. We all just lost it.

How is Michelle doing?

Michelle is doing very well, considering all she's been through. About a year after her accident, Dad and Mom approached her and Doug in much the same way they had approached Mike and me, offering to help them build a house so that Michelle's life would be easier.

They built it up on the hill near Mom and Dad, and Doug, Mr. Handyman, designed it so that it was completely wheelchair accessible, down to lowering the washing machine so that Michelle could get the clothes out and put them in the dryer. It took about a year from the time they started planning it until they moved in. It is a beautiful home, perfect for them in every way, and Michelle's disability, while still very limiting, is minimized by the conveniences in her new home. While the house was under construction, Michelle returned to her job as a dental hygienist part-time in the same office where she had worked for nineteen years. Michelle's done a great job of getting "back on her feet again." She's now helping at her sons' school, running carpools, working part-time, managing her own household, and singing in the praise team at church.

As you might imagine, it's been very hard on Michelle and Doug, adjusting to her limitations. But they've worked to pull in the same direction rather than in opposite ways, working together to make the best of a tragic situation. Their faith in God and their love for each other are strong, and those are the keys that have carried them through.

How do you manage to be a mom to Daniel from a wheelchair?

It's difficult, but not as difficult as I thought it would be. Until Daniel was about four years old, I was never completely alone with him. I like the cliché "Necessity is the mother of invention." We've just had to figure out creative ways to do things.

When Daniel got too big for the original sling when he was eight or nine months old, resourceful Denise figured out a new way for me to hold him. She cut holes in the sling so that Daniel's legs went through them, and he could sit safely and snugly in my lap. Like this, we could very safely go for "walks," look at the birds, look for airplanes, admire the pretty flowers. It was "mommy and me" time when we explored together.

When he was still in his crib, I taught him to crawl out onto my lap. "Daniel," I'd say. "Grab Mommy around the neck and crawl over the top and into my lap. Hang on *really* tight, because Mommy's arms and hands don't work, so I can't catch you." Daniel would carefully follow my every instruction, and soon he was in my lap, snuggling against me as he shook off the sleepiness from his nap.

One of my big worries about being a mom was not being able to do those nurturing mom things, like running to him and scooping him up when he was injured and kissing his hurts away. Then one day when he was just a toddler, he scraped his knee. I quickly rolled over to him, did a quick evaluation to make sure there was no broken leg, then said, "Come on, honey. Crawl up into my lap so I can make it feel better." He climbed right up and snuggled up against me. "Let me kiss your poor little knee and blow some love on it," I offered. He produced his knee and held it up for me to kiss. Then I kissed his tears away and reassured him with my voice. After a few minutes of attention and appropriate sympathy, he hopped down and went about his playing. Now that's just normal at our house; Daniel knows Mom's lap is always waiting!

When Daniel was two years old, we enrolled in Deborah's Mommy and Me class. There were lots of fun things for the kids to enjoy—balls to play with, equipment to climb on, gym-type activities to do. Some of the moms got on the mats and played with their sons and daughters, and of course I couldn't, so it was hard on me emotionally because I wanted to get down and play too! Sometimes I got a little misty with regret, but I knew that it was great for him, being able to play with the other kids.

One activity utilized plastic milk crates that were nailed to skateboard-type things, and the kids loved to sit in them and ride. So one day I got an idea. "Deborah, tie the milk crate to my chair with a jump rope." When I was all hooked up, Daniel jumped on, and I towed him all around the room. He loved it, and soon all the other kids were lined up waiting for their turns. The moms were laughing and the kids were having a ball as I made what seemed like dozens of trips around the room. For once, I wasn't the handicapped mom; I was the cool mom! It felt good.

I yearn to be able to roll around on the floor with Daniel, play catch with him, teach him how to ride a horse, give him hands-on help with his piano lessons, but of course I can't. So I do what I can. We play cards and board games together, and I read him books, give him and his buddies rides on the back of my wheelchair, teach music to his class and help with the reading and computer programs at his school, and go along when we take him to school or pick him up. I make sure he knows by my actions that he and Mike are the most important people in my life, and nothing takes priority over them.

Although there is much I can't do for him and with him, I am his mom in the most important sense: the depth of my love.

How have your parents coped with your paralysis and Michelle's?

It's been very hard on them, but overall Mom and Dad have handled the reality of two of their daughters being in wheelchairs as well as anyone possibly could have.

When I reflect on Mom's childhood and teenage years—experiencing the war, enduring the German occupation of her home—I can see God's hand equipping her with the strength she'd need later. Mom is not an analytical person; she doesn't second-guess or spin her wheels asking "what if" questions. She doesn't waste her energy crying, "Why me?" She has a wonderful ability to accept things at face value and to proceed in figuring out how best to play the cards she's been dealt. She is always moving forward. I do not wish to imply that this has been easy for her. Not at all. When I was in the hospital and rehab, Mom came every single day. She simply couldn't stay away. Once I was home, she continued to come every day, and she busied herself by doing practical things—like washing and folding clothes, dusting, vacuuming, warming the meals that Rally 'Round Renée had provided.

Now that our house is just two minutes from her backdoor, Mom comes down almost every afternoon to help with dinner. Being useful to both Michelle and me has helped her to cope. Away from us, she has found an outlet for her frustrations in gardening. Working in the soil, planting, and witnessing the beauty that her labor produces has been wonderful therapy for her.

I love and respect my mother. More than words can express, I appreciate her willingness and perseverance in helping me. I have needed her, and she has risen to the occasion. She's been a real trooper, a true example of unconditional love.

I think it may have been even more difficult for Dad. By nature, men want to fix things, and he was powerless to fix my broken body or Michelle's. Because he is not used to doing domestic tasks, he has had few ways to be of daily help. Unless there's a reason for him to come, he stays away—not because of any lack of love, but because, if he's not helping, he doesn't want to be underfoot. However, he pinch-hits many times by running emergency errands for us and is Mr. Fix-it around our home. He's been a wonderful, stabilizing pillar of strength.

What problems have you encountered with always having caregivers in your home?

One of the hardest things about dealing with caregivers is the reality that I have to ask for things dozens, even hundreds, of times a day. I have to be very careful how I ask. I can't just say, "Hand me that!" As often as I have to ask, if I'm not especially diplomatic, I'd come off as barking orders and being demanding and bossy. I have to remember to ask as politely and courteously as I can. "Could you please hand me that?" Or, "Would you just grab the vacuum and run it over the living room? Are you sure you don't mind? Great. Thanks." Here again, it sounds like such a little thing, but when I have to control my requests that many times an hour—even when I'm having a bad day—well, it's just one more thing to be a drain and a discipline.

Each attendant becomes an intimate part of our home. Because they work so closely with me, friendships naturally evolve, and then the line between employer and employee becomes blurred. When I ask an employee to do a task, I feel more like I'm asking a friend, and the caregiver, also feeling more like a friend than an employee, may start to feel like the friendship is being abused. It gets so sticky! Therefore, I have to phrase my every request perfectly so that the attendant doesn't feel belittled.

Someone might respond, "She's your employee, so she's supposed to do what you say. If she's offended, tough!" On the surface, that sounds reasonable, but I can't be insensitive to my employees' feelings, and, truthfully, I wouldn't keep them very long if I had that attitude. Finding a quality caregiver is very difficult, and when I get a good one, I don't want to run her off!

What would you like people to know about how to work with you?

Let your yes be yes and your no be no. I have at times found out after the fact that people—especially friends—have said yes to things to which they needed to say no. When I learn of these situations, I can only conclude that I've been a burden, and nobody, paralyzed or not, wants to feel that way. When someone agrees to do something that she doesn't want to do or doesn't have time to do, then resentment creeps in, resulting in strained relationships. I need for people to say no to me like they would say no to anyone else.

Just the other day, I called a friend to ask a favor. "I need to go to the mall next week. Would you have any time at all to drive me?"

"You know what, Renée? Next week is really busy, and we're having company from out of town. I'm afraid I can't help you out this time, but call me again."

"Great!"

"Great?"

"Yes, great that you told me! I so appreciate your honest answer. Now that you've turned me down, the next time I ask you, if you say yes, I'll know you mean it, and I won't have to worry that I'm imposing."

The second thing I want people to know is not to ask how I got in my chair. Let me explain why.

Picture Carl. Remember Carl? He was my friend in rehab who became quadriplegic and lost his wife to gunshot wounds over a stupid car. His wounds went far deeper than the bullet holes. Imagine that he is finally having one of his first good days in a long, long time. He is out having lunch with a friend and for a brief moment has forgotten his loss. Some absolute stranger walks by and asks, "So, how'd you get in that chair?" All the memories flood back, and mental images of his wife's pool of blood shoot to the front of his mind. Alas, his brief reprieve is wiped out, all because some stranger wanted to satisfy his curiosity.

As for me, when someone asks how I got in my chair, what do I have to say? "I fell out of bed." The stranger looks at me weird, wanting four more hours of explanation, when all I want to do is run in, grab my loaf of bread, and be out of there. For sure, some people don't mind being asked, if you catch them on a good day. However, allow me to recommend that you don't ask such personal questions. More often than not, it's a bad idea.

How do you buy clothes? How does sitting in a wheelchair alter the type of clothes you select?

This is a real hassle. When I go to buy, I seldom try anything on in the store because it's just too big a pain. Remember, when I put on pants, I have to lie down. How can I do that in a dressing room? Therefore, if I need a pantsuit or a dress, I usually buy about four and take them home. Then, on a morning when I'm not pressed for time, I'll have my caregiver try them on me. I'll roll to the mirror, so I can see what it looks like when I'm sitting down, take a look, and decide yes, no, or maybe. Then she'll transfer me back down to the bed, take that outfit off, put another one on, and transfer me back up to the wheelchair. I'll once again look into the mirror to inspect and pass judgment. Then it's back down to the bed, take that outfit off, and dress for the day, then back to the wheelchair. Trying on clothes is not fun; it's an ordeal. I never ask my attendant to do more than two in a day because it's just too exhausting for her. If I've brought four home, then we'll do the other two another day.

If you're sitting in a wheelchair, nothing looks cute. Dresses are hard to manage. First, it takes two people to get me in the wheelchair if I have on a dress—one to transfer and the other to smooth my dress under my bottom so it's not wadded up under me or sticking out on one side. Sometimes my knees inadvertently spread apart—well, you get the picture; it doesn't look very feminine!

Also, a pretty dress calls for pretty shoes, but that doesn't work out either. Due to poor circulation, my feet swell so badly that they bulge out over the sides and tops of open shoes, and then my legs swell and look like tree trunks sticking out from my skirt. It's just not attractive. With all the problems associated with wearing a dress and the reality that it doesn't usually look good anyway, I usually wear pantsuits and high top shoes. I never feel dressed up.

This past Easter and again on Mother's Day, I got really sad and weepy before we went to church. I wanted so badly to put on a pretty spring dress and wear open sandals, accentuating my neatly pedicured toenails with rose-colored polish, and look all feminine like the other wives and mothers, but there I sat in my practical pantsuit and functional shoes instead. Maybe that sounds superficial, and I guess on the grand scale of things it is relatively unimportant. Nevertheless, I grieve not getting to wear pretty dresses and shoes.

Another downer is my inability to change clothes during the day. What I put on in the morning, I wear all day long. Seldom do I change clothes, because it's just too much trouble. So, if we're going to church and then over to someone's house for a cookout, I can't dress up for church and run home and slip into something different. What I wear to church stays on through the cookout. Cool mornings and warm afternoons? Too bad. The same outfit stays on.

Did you ever consider suicide?

Once. I don't remember exactly what day it was, but I know it was when I was living in the condo about a year after my injury. It was after several months of making what I thought to be a valiant effort to cope with life without my arms, hands, and legs. I was so frustrated that the thought of living the rest of my life this way was unbearable. Suicide crossed my mind as an escape, but as quickly as the thought came, I knew I had to dismiss it. I knew it to be wrong, so I couldn't do it. Suicide was not the answer.

What would you do if your body worked normally for just one day?

Everything would be in the stand-up position. I would not sit down for even one second—except to go to the bathroom with the door shut "allbymyself"! I would run and run and run and run and run, which is funny since I was certainly no athlete before this.

But oh, to feel my legs and lower back strrrreeeeeeetccc-ccccch. I'd hang from a monkey bar or a tree and feel my back cracking. I'd swim a couple of laps in a pool. I would hug every person who matters to me—a real hug with pressure and closeness and warmth. I'd give people a double high five with force and power so that the impact makes a clapping sound. I would roll around on the floor with Daniel and tickle him until he wet his pants. I'd get in the car alone and tell Mike, "Bring Daniel and meet me at the beach in five minutes!"

Then I'd drive there "allbymyself," so I could have a few moments of aloneness. At the beach I'd build sand castles with my son, walk at sunset hand in hand with Mike, feeling the warm, moist sand between my toes. I'd not speak one negative word. That night, I'd put on music and jitterbug with Mike and then with Daniel, and later I'd make love to my husband.

This question is very painful for me to answer. You have no idea how desperately I'd love to do these things and how much I feel the loss of being unable to participate in the "normal" activities of life. But you know what? One day I'm going to leave this wheelchair behind and do all those things. God has promised that when we get to heaven, we'll have a glorious new body, and I can hardly wait to get mine. I'm going to bow down at the feet of the one who died so that I could be there. I'm going to run and spin like Maria von Trapp on that mountain and turn somersaults and maybe even fly! I'm going to hug those I love until it's a good thing they're dead already. And undoubtedly, I'll approach the throne of grace and respectfully inquire, "What . . . was that all about down there?"

Knowing what you do now about the Lord and his faithfulness, would you go back and undo the accident if you could?

Absolutely, yes. I would love to undo the accident and learn everything that I've learned in some other way! However, if the price was to be ignorant of God's faithfulness, then no. I knew the Lord before my accident; I had a relationship with him, but I was not good at recognizing him in my daily life. I have learned so much about God by being in this wheelchair.

There was a story circulating on e-mail recently about a man speeding down a residential street in his brand new red Porsche—his pride and joy. Suddenly a brick hit his car, shattering the windshield, before rolling onto the hood and denting it. Infuriated, the man jumped out of the car and grabbed the assumed culprit, a little boy standing near the car.

"What were you thinking!" he yelled. "You just shattered the windshield of my new car! Look at that! What were you trying to do?"

With tears of fear rolling down his cheeks, the small boy replied. "I was trying to get you to stop. My little brother fell out of his wheelchair, and I couldn't get him back in. Nobody would stop and help, so I threw the brick to get your attention." Suddenly the smashed windshield didn't seem all that important. The man gently released his grip on the small boy's arm and then went to the little brother and lifted him back into his wheelchair. After making sure the boys were safely on their way, he returned to his car a wiser man.

Maybe my wheelchair is my brick. It slows me down so "that I may know him, and the power of his resurrection, and the fellowship of his sufferings" (Phil. 3:10).

I have to be careful here, because in no way do I believe that God put me in this chair. It was just a bizarre accident. But the Lord has used this chair in a mighty way. Again, I must go back to Romans 8:28: "And we know that all things work together for good to them that love God, to them who are the called according to his purpose." God can use even a tragic injury to bring his children closer to himself.

In Luke 22:31 Jesus tells Peter, "Satan hath desired to have you, that he may sift you as wheat." Jesus was saying to Peter, and to us today, that Satan desires to bring us to ruin. Yes, I feel like I have been sifted as wheat; Satan has tried to destroy Mike and me. However, he failed, for all of our testing has only served to bring us closer to Jesus Christ.

So, what's your brick? What will it take to slow you down—to get your attention? What needs to change in your life so that you may be able to comprehend "with all the saints, to grasp how wide and long and high and deep is the love of Christ, and to know this love that surpasses knowledge—that you may be filled to the measure of all the fulness of God" (Eph. 3:18–19)?

God's love is complete. It is wide—covering all our experiences and reaching out to the whole world. It is long—continuing the length of our lives. It is high—rising to the heights of our joy and celebration. It is deep—reaching to the depths of our despair and hopelessness. When you feel cut off or alone, remember that you can never be outside of God's love.

18

What I Want You to Know

(So You Don't Have to Break Your Neck to Find Out!)

The reason I'm writing this book is to tell you, or remind you, that God is real and God is faithful. Looking back over the events of my life, it is clear to me that God—the God who designed and created the world; the God of Abraham, Isaac, and Moses; the God who instructed Noah to build the ark; the God of David and Solomon; the God who gave miracle sons to Sarah, Hannah, and Elizabeth; the God who brought fire down on Mount Carmel when Elijah called on him; the God who sent his Son through the virgin Mary to be himself in the world and to die for us—this same God knelt down and called me by name and gently gathered me and my broken body into his arms of love. He gently whispered, "Be not afraid, Renée. I am taking care of you. I will not waste your pain."

In God's world, there are no coincidences. Nothing that has happened to me has happened without a purpose. What the world might call fate or luck or coincidence was none of those; it was my Heavenly Father taking care of his child. My life is filled not with coincidences, but with God-incidences.

God-incidence #1: Dorothy. It was no coincidence that Dorothy, my roommate, discovered me on the floor in the wee hours of morning when I broke my neck. From her bedroom upstairs, there's no way she could have heard my whispered cry for help in her sleep and through my closed bedroom door. Dorothy and I strongly believe that the Holy Spirit woke her up and led her down the stairs and into my room. There's no other explanation for it.

God-incidence #2: my family. I'm amazed when I consider how equipped my family was to take care of me. Denise is a nurse, Danny is a mechanic and a volunteer fireman, and Michelle is a dental hygienist. All three of them were already in careers that had trained them to help with my every need, from identifying a medical problem to repairing my wheelchair to flossing my teeth. I could have looked the world over and not found three siblings more qualified, or more willing I might add, to help me in practical ways.

In addition, when I had the accident, Dad and his sisters had just sold the family ranch. By the time I was released from rehab, my parents had the financial resources sufficient to buy my condo and later to help Mike and me purchase our house, which brings me to God-incidence number three.

God-incidence #3: our home. Just as we were in a position to buy, the houses on the Lacouague Ranch were ready for sale. The only floor plan that would work for us was conveniently located on one of two lots that backed up to the hill where Mom and Dad live. I don't know for sure, but I strongly suspect that we paid less for our house at the auction than anyone else—exactly three thousand dollars under our limit. The cherry on the sundae was winning the Jetta so that we could landscape the backyard. Everything came together so perfectly that if someone had written a fiction novel with these same elements, these kinds of events would have been too convenient to be believable. Only God could have orchestrated this perfect symphony of circumstances.

God-incidence #4: my training. Although I certainly didn't recognize it at the time, I can now look back and see how God used my Young Americans experience to help me cope with my paralysis. I learned from YA not to quit, not to accept defeat, and not to be stopped by obstacles. I learned to avoid taking myself too seriously. Hundreds of times in the hospital, in rehab, and since then, I've remembered and drawn on the YA motto, "Make it work."

The musical training I gleaned from YA equipped me for a life of ministry as a recording artist and speaker. It's where I learned not just to hit the notes but how to communicate a song. When you're sitting in a wheelchair, you don't have a lot of body language or stage presence! Young Americans taught me how to utilize every bit of available resources—in this case, my voice, my eyes, and my facial expressions.

Through all of my YA experiences, I thought I was just having fun, hanging out, and seeing the world. Now I see that the whole experience was key to my future.

God-incidence #5: Mike. There's not a doubt in my mind that before the foundations of the world, God picked Mike for me. I dated other good guys, but I can see now how God protected me from marrying someone who would not have been as perfect for me in my situation as Mike. There's not another man in ten thousand who would have stayed with me. We were not married, so Mike very easily could have walked away and no one would have blamed him. Even my family gave him permission to go, but God put us together, giving us a bond and a commitment that even paralysis couldn't tear apart.

Furthermore, the Lord orchestrated circumstances to help us make it work. Remember how Mike's company created a job for him and transferred him to their one facility in Long Beach? With L.A. traffic, even Irvine wouldn't have been good enough, or Brea, or Anaheim, or Placentia, or any place else. The only place that would have given Mike the ability to drop by the hospital on his way to work or during his lunch hour, or to see me after work without being stuck in traffic for hours was Long Beach!

God had all the pieces to the puzzle ready even before my accident, and then one by one they fell perfectly into place, according to God's design. He knew we had to be together through this ordeal so that we could express our fears, look into each other's eyes, laugh, pray, and work as a team. He provided a way for us to be together day by day.

God-incidence #6, 7, 8, 9, 10, 11 . . . I became pregnant with Daniel the first month after we became open to the possibility that God might give us a child. God restored my teaching career and reminded me that he was the one in control of my circumstances when I counted 150 students on the roll in the church choir.

When Jim May tested me to see if my voice was strong enough to record, he chose "Be Not Afraid," not knowing it was the song God used the most to reassure me. I thought we'd be giving copies of *Inner Voice* as Christmas presents for the next thirty years. Instead, God used it as a means for us to pay for my attendant care—a *huge* financial strain lifted from our shoulders.

I met the pope, through a series of circumstances that could only be described as miraculous. The Girl Scout came to the door just as I needed help.

The "coincidences" in my life are just too numerous to recount, but they all point to one thing—God's blessings for us.

I know that some who read this book will struggle to believe that God is personal, that he is intricately concerned about the details of our daily lives. Perhaps this is a new concept for you. Maybe you've always believed that God is only in a beautiful sunset, or in a picturesque mountain scene, or up there on an altar, or somewhere else far away. But I'm here to remind you that he is *right here*. He is present in the middle of your everyday life.

The same God who has sustained me is just as available to you. I'm no super saint. I don't have an inside track. God isn't playing favorites with me. He's not making resources available to Renée Bondi and keeping them a secret from the rest of the world. I'm just a simple woman who's learned from experience that I can trust the promises of God and that I can rely on him to be faithful. I'm not qualified as an apologist, and no one would ever accuse me of being a biblical authority. But I've learned a few things sitting in this chair, and I'd like to share some of these with you so you don't have to break your neck to find out.

By now, you should know where the strength for my journey comes from; it is from the knowledge that God's hand carries us through our darkest hours and brightest joys.

Walking with the Lord begins with recognizing who Jesus Christ is. From cover to cover, the Bible proclaims that Jesus Christ is the Son of God—God in flesh. He said of himself, "I and my Father are one" (John 10:30), and Paul wrote about Jesus, "For in him dwelleth all the fulness of the Godhead bodily" (Col. 2:9). Jesus was indeed God in a body.

While here on earth, Jesus clearly told us how to know God: "I am the way, the truth, and the life: no man cometh unto the Father, but by me" (John 14:6).

When Jesus died on the cross at Calvary, he switched places with you and me. He took our sins and paid for them—all of them! Put yourself in a hypothetical position for a moment. You have been tried and convicted of breaking the law thousands of times and have justifiably been given the death sentence as your punishment. While you're standing there awaiting your execution, knowing that your own guilt has brought you to this disastrous result, the judge's son approaches you and says, "I'm going to the death chamber for you. You are free to go. Furthermore, my dad, the judge, wants to adopt you as his son."

That's what Jesus did for you! He traded places with you. He took your sin, and he gave you his righteousness, his holiness. In doing so, he bought you the opportunity to be adopted into God's family. It is truly the most astounding transaction that's ever taken place since the world began. All you have to do is believe that Jesus is Lord, to understand what he did on the cross for you, to ask for forgiveness for your sins, and to tell Jesus that you want to accept his death and that you want to live your life in appreciation for what he did.

If you understand anything at all of God's holiness, then right now you're undoubtedly realizing that you don't deserve God's love and forgiveness. Perhaps you're focused on your failures and shortcomings and sinful acts and desires. You're feeling unworthy to be a child of God in the same way I felt unworthy to be Mike's wife. You're wondering, "How could God love someone like me?" But God's love and forgiveness are big enough to cover even the vilest acts and the most sinful thoughts. Our ability to come to the Lord is not dependent on our worthiness, because no one is worthy. Our invitation to come to the Lord is based solely on God's all-encompassing love and forgiveness, and everyone is invited! That means you, no matter what you have done.

When you come humbly to God and ask for his forgiveness, something incredible is going to happen. Jesus Christ is going to move right into your heart, and he's going to change you. You will be a new creature. Having been forgiven of every sin you've ever committed or will ever commit, you will now spend your eternity in heaven rather than in hell. Not a bad swap! Jesus suffered the most excruciatingly painful death that's ever been devised so that he could give you a gift—abundant life now and heaven later.

If you've never personally accepted the salvation that God offers through Jesus Christ, now would be a perfect time. Will you give all of yourself that you can, to all of God that you understand? If you will, then bow your head right now and tell him so. You don't have to recite a formal prayer out of a book. Just talk to God from your heart. He's listening. He's waiting. He understands. And when you offer him your life, he will hear you, forgive you, and welcome you into his family!

No matter where you are in your walk with the Lord—whether you accepted him just this minute, whether you've been walking closely with him for years, or whether you're somewhere in between—it is my desire that you recognize as never before that God can do good things with your life. No matter who you are, no matter what your circumstances, God can do amazing things with your life!

Some of you are dealing with tragedies more devastating than mine. Do you feel trapped in an unhappy marriage? Are you facing the reality that your spouse prefers someone else? Are your kids on drugs or making other destructive choices? Are you dealing with unemployment or struggling with your finances? Are you or is someone you love dealing with a devastating illness? Some of you have been misunderstood, misrepresented, unappreciated, even lied about; you certainly did not deserve to be treated so shabbily. What circumstance are you struggling with right now? How are you dealing with your pain? Are you angry? Are you hissing at or hiding from the world?

Ask yourself these questions. Have you been so busy protesting your circumstance that you've overlooked the possibilities? Are your eyes so focused on your problem that you're not aware of your provision?

Are you ready to surrender to God?

Look at it this way. There might be something positive to be gained from your pain. Your struggle just might be an opportunity for God to demonstrate his loving care and provision for you, and even to those around you. God never promised to make life easy. He did promise, however, to turn our sorrow into joy. The most secure place we can be is right in the palm of his hand.

Although misfortune may come to us, God promises that he will use our struggle for our good and for his glory. In the midst of our difficulties and challenges, there are blessings all around us, and we can choose whether to see them or not.

Sometimes we overlook God's blessings because we're expecting or wanting them to take another form. Maybe you're thinking, "Okay, I'll turn my circumstances over to God, but I expect him to fix them—to heal my marriage, to get my kid off drugs, to provide a more lucrative job, to heal me of my illness. If God will do that, then I'd learn to trust him." That's not the way it works. God promises to bless us in our problems, but he never promised to fix them exactly the way we want. I wanted God to get me out of my wheelchair and allow me to walk again, but he hasn't chosen to do that. However, he has blessed me "exceeding abundantly" (Eph. 3:20) above all that I asked or thought, and he did it in ways that were far more rich, far more meaningful, and far more rewarding than I ever could have designed myself. God really does know best.

When you say yes to God, when you surrender your life completely to him, you have to give up your preconceived notions about exactly how you believe God is supposed to express his love to you. Trust that God has a way of blessing that is far better than your way!

I believe the key to living the abundant Christian life is surrender. I learned about surrender when I sought God's will on whether or not to have a child. I think that was the first time I'd really emptied myself completely before the Lord, seeking his face, desiring only his will. And he gave us a precious son.

Another time I learned surrender was after Michelle's accident when I relinquished my anger to God and asked him to replace it with his peace. He answered and took away all my anger and replaced it with more peace than I had ever known. Both of these times I wanted and needed God's will for my life more than I wanted anything else.

Perhaps you're hesitating and thinking, "But what if I surrender and he breaks *my* neck?" First, I feel pretty safe in assuring you that God is not going to break your neck. However, if you fall and break your own neck like I did, or if some other calamity overtakes you, I can promise you that God is going to be right there, helping you to rise up on eagle's wings!

Why do these things happen? Why do people break their necks? Why do marriages fall apart? Why are some people addicted to drugs or alcohol? Why do people contract terrible diseases? Why do people drive drunk and kill others? I believe that most bad things happen for one of two reasons. The first is that God gave us free will and, therefore, people sometimes make poor choices. The second is that sin and disease came into the world in the Garden of Eden and corrupted the earth. Why trouble seems to follow some people around while others continuously enjoy good fortune, I cannot answer. But I believe the *why* isn't nearly as important as the *how*. *How* will you react when misfortune strikes you? Will you turn to God or flee from him?

I recently heard a true story about a teenage boy who stole a car and took it for a joyride. Frantic, the owner of the car called the police and told them what had happened. "We've got to find my car ASAP!" he said. "There's an open box of animal crackers on the front seat that I had bought to feed to the rats in my barn. The crackers are laced with poison." The police put out an APB and quickly located the stolen vehicle. When the teenager saw that he was being pursued, he fled, assuming that the police were out to punish him for his crime when in reality they were trying desperately to save his life!

We're like that teenage boy. God pursues us and we run, for some reason assuming that he's trying to imprison us when really he's trying to free us and bless us and love us. The safest place on earth for us to be is wrapped in God's arms of love.

In order to experience the closeness of the Lord I've just talked about, you have to trust God with your whole life— with your eternal salvation, your health, your finances, with your family, your career, with your deepest dreams and desires. It's a complete leap of faith. It's like a child running and leaping into his father's outstretched arms, squealing "Daddy! Daddy!" because the child has absolute confidence that Daddy is *not* going to drop him!

We, like children, have to leap into the arms of our heavenly Father knowing, trusting, that he will never let us down. My prayer for you is this: "That Christ may dwell in your hearts through faith. And I pray that you, being rooted and established in love, may have power, together with all the saints, to grasp how wide and long and high and deep is the love of Christ, and to know this love that surpasses knowledge—that you may be filled to the measure of all the fullness of God" (Eph. 3:17–19 NIV).

I pray that you'll recognize his truth in the pages of this book, or that you'll believe your neighbor down the street or your pastor or a relative or the Bible, so that you'll come to know God more intimately and experience his amazing love for you more fully than ever before. God is knocking at your door, and the doorknob is only on your side.

For me, there was a last dance, but it certainly was not the last song. I urge you to invite the King of Kings into your life. Will you open your heart and sing with me?

> I surrender to your will.
> I surrender to your plan.
> I will choose to believe you
> though I may not understand.
> I will trade these things of earth
> for a treasure up above.
> I surrender to your love.

Music Available

Let It Rain
2002

A deeply personal signature collection of original songs reflecting the growth, ministry, and personal triumph of Renée Bondi.

Ten songs including: "Jesus Christ Is Lord," "The Last Dance but Not the Last Song," "Let It Rain," "Run Another Day," "Make Me Your Instrument," "I Can Do All Things"

All recordings are available on CD or cassette.

Available in your local Christian bookstore or call 1-800-795-5757

or order on line at **www.reneebondi.com**

Surrender to Your Love
1999

Renée invites us to jump with full abandon into the abundant life God has planned for each of us.

Twelve songs including: "Surrender," "Shout to the Lord," "Thank You," "God Is in Control," "You Are Mine," "Holy Is Your Name"

Strength for the Journey
1995

This recording inspires listeners to move past their pain and seek Christ's peace.

Twelve songs including: "Firm Foundation," "Strength for the Journey," "Dream High," "He Who Began a Good Work in You," "Only in God," "Somebody's Prayin'," "Children Need Heroes"

Inner Voice
1992

Renée's first recording gives stregth and hope to those experiencing difficult times. 1992

Eleven songs including: "Be Not Afraid," "On Eagle's Wings," "Here I Am Lord," "You Are Near," "Mansion Builder," "All I Ever Have to Be"

Back on My Feet Again!
1998

On this ninety-minute video Renée shares her unforgettable story and sings the powerful music that drives the message home. *(Also available CD/Cassette)*

For more information on Renée's music and ministry, view

www.reneebondi.com